MACMILLAN
DICTIONARY
OF

RETAILING

Major contributors

J. S. Baron
D. J. Bennison
B. J. Davies
K. J. Harris
G. Lea-Greenwood
D. J. Muskett
J. Pal
R. S. Schmidt
D. G. Swindley

Other contributors

D. G. Couch
G. J. Davies
P. Jones
A. Pulford
J. L. Stephen
M. B. Whitehead

MACMILLAN DICTIONARY OF
RETAILING

STEVE BARON
BARRY DAVIES
DAVID SWINDLEY

**MACMILLAN
REFERENCE
BOOKS**

First edition published 1991 by
THE MACMILLAN PRESS LTD
London and Basingstoke

Associated companies in Auckland, Delhi, Dublin,
Gaborone, Hamburg, Harare, Hong Kong, Johannesburg,
Kuala Lumpur, Lagos, Manzini, Melbourne, Mexico City,
Nairobi, New York, Singapore, Tokyo.

British Library Cataloguing in Publication Data

Macmillan dictionary of retailing. – (Macmillan dictionary series)
  I. Baron, Steve   II. Davies, Barry   III. Swindley, David   IV. Series
  381.03

  ISBN 0-333-53758-0
  ISBN 0-333-56449-9 pbk

Typeset and printed in Great Britain

Dedication

To Shelagh, Krystyna and Pam, who helped;
and Peter Jones, who didn't.

Contents

How to use the dictionary

Alphabetization of headings is on a word-by-word basis. Where a heading consists of two or more words, they are grouped together by the common first word. Thus, **market test** appears before **marketing**. Hyphenated compound words are alphabetized as if they were separate words. Thus, **odd-even pricing** precedes **odd pricing**.

Cross-references to other articles are shown in small capitals, e.g. BARCODE.

Preface

This Dictionary has been created in response to the growing interest in commercial distribution (particularly retailing) as a field of study. Retailing is an integral part of the way we live – buying goods and services as needs arise. Until recently it had received little attention as an independent subject, being treated as a topic within several disciplines, notably geography and marketing. As pioneers in the education field in the UK, we are happy to note the increased spread and availability of provision of retail education, particularly at higher levels.

Those people who are involved in the systematic study of retailing may find this volume useful, as may those involved in management. We have attempted to provide a comprehensive treatment of the core area, with some of the more relevant and important terms from physical distribution, marketing and operations management being included.

To this end we must record our thanks for their support and encouragement, to the retail organizations represented on the Professional Advisory Committee for the BA (Hons) Retail Marketing course at Manchester Polytechnic – in particular Asda, BHS, Co-operative Wholesale Society, Gateway Foodmarkets, Greenall's Retail Management, GUS Home Shopping, Halfords, Ind Coope, Makro, Littlewoods, Marks & Spencer, MFI, J. Sainsbury, J. D. Williams.

The upsurge of interest in retailing is an international phenomenon – as recent events in eastern Europe demonstrate. We have tried to reflect this international spread by including references to the largest retailers in Europe and North America, and by including terms in English that are particularly used in a number of countries, especially the USA.

While we would wish to tax our contributors with errors of omission and commission, this is unfortunately not possible. The responsibility remains ours, and we would be grateful if readers would provide us with corrections and suggestions for later editions.

We hope that the dictionary is of value to users: if it is, then no small measure of credit must go to Chris Morley, who produced the initial headword list, and to those who provided the typing and administrative support – Jenny Davis, Linda Scanlan and, especially, Brenda Oldfield, to whom many thanks.

Steve Baron, Barry Davies
Manchester, 1991

David Swindley
Bournemouth, 1991

A

above the line A PROMOTION expenditure in the form of media advertising which is aimed directly at the consumer. Any other form of promotion expenditure is known as BELOW THE LINE.

absenteeism Irregular work attendance. Voluntary absenteeism covers those occasions when employees are away from work without authorization and for non-medical reasons (e.g. staying home to look after the children at half-term). Involuntary absenteeism is related to ill health and can be supported by medical evidence.

absorption costing A method of apportioning charges, developed in a manufacturing context which is based on the idea that, in order to facilitate effective decision-making and COST CONTROL, all charges should be related to products.

Certain costs, such as direct materials and labour, can be identified directly with individual products. Other costs, such as supervisor's wages etc., can be related to products through allocation to cost and profit centres such as departments or divisions.

Overhead costs, which are not directly identifiable with profit centres, such as head office costs, are apportioned between profit centres and thereby related to products.

The idea behind absorption costing is similar to the principles underlying the DIRECT PRODUCT PROFITABILITY system of costing.

Access (UK) A CREDIT CARD system provided by the National Westminster, Lloyds and Midland Bank groups and the Royal Bank of Scotland.

Retailers pay about 2 per cent of the value of each Access sale as a service charge and an initial fee. Access cards are accepted at over 300,000 outlets in the UK and at over 7 million outlets world-wide, through the MASTERCARD NETWORK.

accessibility The ease with which retail outlets may be reached by potential customers. Accessibility is generally measured in terms of travel time (usually drive time) rather than in physical distance. The growth of out-of-town retailing clearly reflects the changing accessibility of suburban locations afforded by new major highway developments and the increasing incidence of motor car ownership. Increasing traffic congestion within and around central business districts has reduced the accessibility of these traditional central retail areas.

1

accident prevention The examination of the potential hazards associated with working practices, the environment and infrastructure where employees and customers have access, the products and services which are sold, and the equipment that is used. To minimize dangers arising out of hazards at work requires constant monitoring; particular attention should be paid to the training and appraisal of staff in safe working practices, including emergency evacuation procedures and medical aid.

In the UK, companies' conduct is governed by the HEALTH AND SAFETY AT WORK ACT 1974. Retailing is not inherently a 'safe industry'; some 15 UK deaths were recorded in 1988 with over 30,000 reported accidents.

account 1. Business relationship between a retailer and supplier of specialist goods/services.

2. Client of a specialist agency service provider.

3. Record of transactions with an individual customer.

4. Balance of monies due at the end of an ACCOUNTING PERIOD.

account executive One who works for an advertising, marketing research or public relations agency managing the customer/agency interaction. This role does not usually include responsibility for the creative or technical functions of the agency. *See* ADVERTISING AGENCY.

accounting In a narrow sense, the process or art of keeping and verifying documentary records of monetary transactions; in a wider sense, it is an information system designed to further the achievement of organizational objectives. It is concerned with being responsible and answerable for money held in trust on behalf of the retail organization's shareholders and lenders, and with producing information for internal and external STAKEHOLDERS.

The accounting system has two main functions: (i) *financial accounting*, which is concerned with record-keeping and the preparation of financial statements; (ii) *management accounting* (often referred to as COST ACCOUNTING), which is concerned with the internal use of cost information for purposes of analysis, planning, decision-making and control.

accounting period A discrete length of time, chosen to suit the operations of a retail company, for which an ACCOUNT is prepared. An accounting period may be, for example, a lunar or calendar month. In addition, most legal jurisdictions require that all companies prepare accounts on an annual basis.

ACORN A geodemographic classification system. An acronym for A Classification Of Residential Neighbourhoods, ACORN is a MARKET SEGMENTATION system developed by CACI for the UK and USA. The UK system classifies census enumeration districts into 38 different types of neighbourhood. The ACORN types are themselves aggregated into 11 ACORN groups. An example of an ACORN type would be 'Cosmopolitan owner-occupied terraces/ row houses', which is a member of the ACORN group 'mixed inner-metropolitan areas'.

ACORN profiles can be produced, for example, for catchment areas for existing or proposed retailer store locations.

acquisition The change of ownership of a business by means of purchase. Where the business is privately owned, the agreement of the owner is essential. With a public corporation whose shares are traded, a change of ownership is possible without the consent of those managing the business in some jurisdictions, including the UK and USA. Shares can be purchased on stock exchanges for a publicly quoted company, subject to certain rules; where such shares confer the ownership and control of the company an offer to buy can lead to acquisition. Hostile takeovers tend to be the norm in the UK and USA, and retailing in those countries has seen its share.

With the large takeovers that were a feature of the 1980s, an important motive was to profit by selling off parts of the acquired business for more than the purchase price of the whole company. In some circumstances the buyers of the parts would be the managers themselves, often using the device of a leveraged BUY-OUT. *See also* MERGER.

added value The extra worth in the output of an organization above the worth of input (bought-in materials and components) produced by an organization's processes of production or transformation.

additive Substance not naturally occurring in particular products (especially foodstuffs) but supplemental to (i) imbue particular properties (e.g. colours); (ii) facilitate processing (e.g. emulsifiers); (iii) enhance product features (e.g. preservatives, flavour enhancers or other qualities deemed desirable by the manufacturer or required by law).

add-on sales Incremental purchases arising from an initial purchase, usually of complementary or facilitating goods or services (e.g. shoe polish with shoes).

advertisement Paid-for insertion in mass MEDIA under clear sponsorship. In broadcast media, an advertisement is often referred to as a COMMERCIAL.

advertising Any form of paid-for, non-personal message conveyed via mass media and initiated by a clearly identified sponsor.

Advertising is the most visible part of the extensive promotion and communication mix open to marketers. It is often called 'ABOVE THE LINE expenditure' in marketing jargon, although views of where the line is vary considerably. *See also* DIRECT MAIL, PUBLIC RELATIONS, SALES PROMOTION.

advertising agency An independent (or quasi-independent) organization which specializes in the creation and implementation of promotional or informational campaigns on behalf of its clients. A full service agency is one which provides creative, media planning and purchase, production (and possibly) research services to clients.

advertising effectiveness A measurement of the extent to which a promotional campaign utilizing paid-for insertions under clear sponsorship in mass MEDIA achieves the objectives set for it prior to execution.

Advertising expenditure by retailers has risen substantially, but there is little hard evidence to show that advertising is an effective use of promotional expenditure overall, particularly if compared to direct promotion in store windows or inside the retail outlet.

Retailer advertising probably has a different role from that normally associated with consumer product advertising. While product advertising is acknowledged as an effective way of creating a favourable image, retailer advertising has a more informative role. Indeed, it has been argued that attempts to create a retail image through advertising can be counter-productive if the store itself fails to live up to the image painted by the advertisement.

advertising response model A mathematical analysis which isolates and measures the outcomes, in terms of increases of sales or awareness, to a given amount of exposure to paid-for insertions under clear sponsorship in mass MEDIA. Such models usually assume a parity of value for each unit of input or exposure, regardless of the timing or creative worth of such inputs.

advice note A document accompanying a shipment or consignment of goods, usually intended to be used to check the consignment at the point of delivery against the accompanying paperwork. Advice notes are often issued in sets which relate to, for example, invoices, statements, etc.

affiliated chain Retail outlet associated with a specific organization (e.g. SPAR grocery outlets in Europe).

affiliated retailer Store associated with a specific supplying organization such as a wholesaler or national/international supplier.

affiliated store A retail outlet which is associated with a specific supplying organization or wholesaler.

after-sales service Post-purchase activities designed to provide customers with additional ongoing benefits, for the repair, updating, or modification of items bought, in order to ensure continuing customer satisfaction (e.g. one year parts and labour warranty, automobile servicing, software updates).

agent One acting on behalf of a principal in contractual matters, with delegated authority to bind to principal. More loosely, one acting on behalf of another in commercial matters, especially as advertising agent, estate agent (USA: realtor), sales agent.

air-bubble packing A wrapping material consisting of two layers of thin plastic with pockets of air trapped between welds joining the two layers. The air pockets cushion the packaged good against shock or damage during transportation. Air-bubble packing is widely used by MAIL ORDER companies to prevent damage to, for example, breakable or electrical goods.

allowance 1. Reduction in the supplier price to a retailer or wholesaler contingent upon some special arrangement, especially in merchandising and promotion (e.g. an allowance for displaying merchandise on a GONDOLA END).
2. *See* RETURNS.

ambience The total atmosphere created by a retail outlet specifically to attract a particular target group of customers. The creation of ambience is normally through the use of retail design in terms of lighting, space, interior design, store layout and graphic design (and perhaps through the use of appropriate in-store music) which is sympathetic to the company's product offering and CORPORATE IMAGE. In the UK, for example, Burton's have created an atmosphere which appeals to the teenage clothes market through its use of plastics and chrome in its store design, whereas Next have used more natural materials such as wooden floors, simple gondolas, and a narrow range of merchandise on display to appeal to an older, more sophisticated group.

anchor store An outlet, usually belonging to a major MULTIPLE RETAILER, to be found in a shopping mall whose presence is assumed to attract other retailers to locate in the mall. Anchor stores have considerable power in negotiating with developers in terms of store size, parking spaces, ease of access and prime choice of location, as they are frequently the largest tenant and at the end of the mall.

annual report A financial summary produced by public companies at the end of the financial year. The report outlines details of the company's trading policy, its current financial performance as represented by an INCOME STATEMENT and a BALANCE SHEET and an overview of the company's future plans. This report is distributed to both shareholders (as of right, in some jurisdictions) and non-shareholders who request it.

Ansoff's matrix An early (1965) conceptual framework identifying four components of strategy which describe a firm's business. (i) *Product-market scope*, which specifies the particular industries to which the firm confines its product-market position

(i.e. the products and services it supplies and the markets it serves).

(ii) The *growth vector*, which indicates the direction in which the firm is moving with respect to its current product-market posture. To illustrate the growth vector, Ansoff suggested a four-cell matrix:

Product mission	Existing	New
Existing	Market penetration (increased market share for existing product markets	Product development (creating new products to replace or enhance current range)
New	Market development (new missions for existing products)	Diversification (both products and missions new to the firm)

The growth vector matrix has become known as 'Ansoff's matrix'.

(iii) COMPETITIVE ADVANTAGE, which comprises the particular properties of individual product markets, within the scope of the growth vector, which will give the firm a strong competitive position.

(iv) SYNERGY, which is a measure of the firm's ability to succeed with a new product-market entry.

The four components of strategy should be held together by a common thread, which Ansoff defined as the relationship between present and future product-markets that would enable outsiders to perceive where the firm is heading and provide management with guidance.

area manager That level of administration which is the interface between, usually, head office and retail BRANCHES within a defined geographical location. Area management can include the responsibility for retail operations; for merchandising and display; for personnel and training; for security and maintenance and for distribution. Area managers would normally require performance in branches to conform to standards set by head office and to ensure that managerial staff in stores are applying company policy realistically and consistently.

arrears Any running account which is behind in its payment, especially charge and credit accounts.

article numbering An internationally understood means of identifying all the goods traded throughout the distribution chain for the purposes of ordering, invoicing, stock control and distribution. This system is used in Europe and many other parts of the world outside North America and is based on the fact that each and every product available for sale can be allocated a unique identifying 13-digit number. This means that every product and every variation of that product in terms of size, colour and packaging configuration carries its own number. This article number is a reference number only; it does not itself contain any information about the product such as its price, flavour, colour, or country of origin. For administrative purposes the 13 digits are split in various ways in the UK; for example, the first two digits show the number bank which issued the number (though not necessarily the country of origin of the product), the next five digits are allocated to the

company manufacturing or marketing the product, the following five digits are allocated to the particular size or variation of that product and the last digit is a computer check digit.

assay mark A series of signs stamped on a gold, silver or platinum article which provides information on the metal quality, applied after independent testing.

assessment methods Any set of procedures for the evaluation of outputs, or predicted outputs, against selected criteria especially (i) in respect of performance at work of employees, (ii) in consideration of the suitability of a potential location for a given retail format, (iii) consideration of the effectiveness of managerial decision (e.g. of advertising).

asset A property or right owned by an individual or business organization. Assets are classed as either FIXED ASSETS or as CURRENT ASSETS.

asset turnover The FINANCIAL RATIO of sales to net total assets.

$$Asset\ turnover\ =\ \frac{Sales}{Net\ total\ assets}$$

where

$Net\ total\ assets\ =\ Fixed\ assets\ +\ Current\ assets\ -\ Current\ liabilities$

The ratio measures the utilization the firm is obtaining from its overall investment in its asset base. If the ratio is low by comparison to historical data, or that for other firms in the industry, it may indicate that management are not making good use of the resources available. However, asset turnover can also be temporarily low where a retailer is in the process of undertaking a major investment programme which may result in increased sales in the future.

assortment The range of merchandise offered to customers. The two predominant characteristics of assortment are *width* and *depth*. Width is the number of merchandise categories included; depth is the number of varieties within a given category (e.g. sizes, colours, types, prices).

atmosphere The psychological climate of a store or other shopping location and the way that climate impacts upon the individual visitor. At the simplest level, some locations may be described as having 'low atmosphere'. Where the location owners or managers have determined to offer a particular type of atmosphere then this response can be considerably extended. *See also* ATMOSPHERICS, AMBIENCE.

atmospherics The management of the various stimuli (visual, auditory, tactile, olfactory) to engender desired responses from store visitors.

atrium In planned shopping centres, a central courtyard area which is usually covered.

attitude A learned predisposition to respond in a consistently favourable or unfavourable manner with respect to a given object. Such attitudes are a result of the experiences, awareness and wants and needs of individuals. Since an understanding of attitudes helps to understand behaviour, retailers need to be acquainted with the subject in order to make informed assumptions about future CONSUMER BEHAVIOUR.

attitude   segmentation   *See* PSYCHOGRAPHICS.

attitude survey An exercise of information collection designed to improve understanding of predispositions of respondents.

auction A method of publicly selling goods, such as antiques, houses or cars, where prospective buyers compete with each other and the goods are sold to the person making the highest BID. Auctions are usually well publicized in advance, the sales take place according to definite rules, and if the bidding does not reach a reserved price agreed by the seller, the AUCTIONEER may withdraw the goods from sale.

auction house A specialist retailer selling goods by LOT to members of the public, dealers etc. by means of an AUCTION. Many such houses have, on their staff, experts in the categories of good commonly sold by this method (art, antiques etc.). The house derives its income from levying a commission on the sales price of items sold and (sometimes) charging a premium to buyers relating to the price they are paying. Leading auction houses include Sotheby's and Christie's.

auctioneer A person who conducts a public sale of LOTS by BID, usually acting on behalf of the seller, normally receiving a commission from the seller on the goods sold, and sometimes a premium from the buyer also.

audio-visual display A POINT OF SALE presentation, especially of merchandise in use, with sight and sound communication, typically on a television. Such a display is used particularly to demonstrate household appliances, especially in department and hardware stores.

audit A quantitative research technique which provides systematic statistical information on sales, expenditure etc. (by analogy to an accounting audit) often on a continuous basis so that changes can be monitored over time.

authorized dealer The appointee of a manufacturer, supplier etc. who sells by retail or wholesale his or her products, especially when this right is not generally available. (E.g. authorized dealer for IBM personal computers.) *See also* EXCLUSIVE DEALER.

automatic merchandising The business of providing goods for sale through vending machines. The classes of goods sold in this way can be wide, extending from fresh flowers through to complete meals.

automatic teller machine (ATM) An electronic device for dispensing cash, and providing other services (such as information on current account balance) which is activated by inserting a plastic CARD and keying in a personal identification number. Such machines contain a visual display unit, at eye level, and a small keypad, are located at financial institutions or key retail locations, and will only accept a limited range of cash cards or CREDIT CARDS.

average The typical or normal standard or amount. More formally, there are several statistical measures

of average including the (arithmetic) *mean*, the *median* and the *mode*. The mean is the sum of the observations on a variable divided by the number of observations. The median is the middle value of a set of observations when they are arranged in ascending order. The mode is the observation which occurs most frequently. Suppose that the ages of the last 15 purchasers of items from a record store are:

15, 13, 15, 16, 89, 17, 15, 21, 18, 16, 13, 18, 15, 20, 14

There are 15 observations on the age variable. The mean is $315/15 = 21$ years old. The ages in ascending order are:

13, 13, 14, 15, 15, 15, 15, 16, 16, 17, 18, 18, 20, 21, 89

The median is 16 years old. As there are more 15-year-olds than any other age, the mode is 15 years old.

In practice, the mean is the most commonly used measure of average, but it has the disadvantage, as above, that an extreme observation (the 89-year-old) can make it unrepresentative of the full set of observations.

average markup The sum of the percentage differences between the cost and retail price for all the different lines of merchandise on offer, divided by the number of lines.

average profit The sum of the gross margin percentages the retailer makes on all the different lines of merchandise, divided by the number of lines.

B

baby-boomers The group born after the Second World War when population growth particularly in the USA and Europe, was at its highest. This 'bulge' of population covers in particular those born between 1950 and 1970, after which there was a downturn in births. This group's numeric supremacy will ensure that it will remain a target for retailers and marketers as it ages and its tastes change.

back door A common term for the receiving bay or other access to a store or warehouse into which goods are delivered.

back-of-house Those essential activities to the carrying out of a retailing function which are not observed by the customer. (The phrase is derived from theatre usage.)

back order A part of a consignment that has not been delivered on time and that is to be fulfilled as soon as the goods become available.

backdating Assigning an earlier day to a written document, such as a CHEQUE, rather than the actual day of writing.

backer card An eye-catching poster-board placed above, or at the rear, of a POINT OF SALE display

background music Songs, orchestral pieces etc. broadcast over a public address or other such system, designed to be heard by customers in the trading environment. It is a component of store ATMOSPHERICS.

backlog An unplanned accumulation of, for example, unfulfilled orders.

backward integration *See* VERTICAL INTEGRATION.

bad debt A monetary amount owing to the retailer which is believed not to be recoverable. It is written off to a bad debt ACCOUNT and treated as an expense in the INCOME STATEMENT of the ACCOUNTING PERIOD in which it becomes clear that the debtor has defaulted.

baker A person whose main business or employment is to produce and/or retail bread, flour confectionery etc.

balance The difference between the two sides of an ACCOUNT (i.e. the debit and the credit side). An excess of debit over credit entries to the account results in an overall debit balance. Where credit entries exceed debit entries, an overall credit balance results.

balance sheet An accounting statement showing the financial position of a business at a particular time. It draws on the records kept by the business and communicates information concerning those aspects of the business which can be given an objective monetary value.

The balance sheet is based on the equation *Assets = Liabilities*. Management may be held accountable for all monies that have been invested in the business, and must disclose what the business has, for the investment, in terms of assets. The information needed to draw up a balance sheet is derived from the DOUBLE-ENTRY BOOKKEEPING system.

balanced inventory The ASSORTMENT that will best satisfy customer requirements in terms of characteristics such as size, colour and style etc.

balanced stock *See* BALANCED INVENTORY.

bank 1. A financial institution for the custody of money belonging to CUSTOMERS, offering services such as payment of sums from such monies against various orders and instruments (cheques, direct debits etc.), interest on sums held on customers' behalf, the lending of money to customers at interest and a range of other related services. The conduct of such operations is usually controlled in various ways within different jurisdictions.
2. The building where such services are offered.

bank credit card *See* CREDIT CARD.

Barclaycard (UK) A CREDIT CARD issued by Barclays Bank. Part of the VISA network.

barcode The ARTICLE NUMBERING represented in a form which can be read by machines. It consists of a series of stripes and spaces of varying widths to a predetermined structure and standard. These stripes can be read using a light pen, laser gun or low intensity laser scanner linked to a computer. Barcodes are a reliable and inexpensive means of automatic identification and can be produced by any normal printing process. A barcode can be read while the product is in motion and can be read any way round. Within a shop the LASER SCANNER reads the barcode and instantly transmits the article number to an electronic price file which relays the product's price and description back to the register. This information is shown on a display panel and is simultaneously printed on the receipt, which describes each item purchased with its price.

bargain 1. A GOOD purchased at a price perceived by the customer to be less than the full, normal or expected price.
2. A process by which buyer and seller negotiate a mid-price acceptable to both sides. *See also* BARTER.

barter One of the simplest forms of retailing, where goods are exchanged for one another directly without the use of money. Barter is often seen as a precursor to monetary exchange systems. More elaborate forms of barter have evolved for trading on a large scale involving the exchange of large volumes of merchandise, often across international boundaries. Such forms of sophisticated barter are sometimes called 'counter-trade'.

basement 1. A section of a store

devoted to low-price lines, sometimes referred to as the 'bargain basement', but not necessarily located on a floor below ground level. It could, for example, feature special job lot purchases, clearance lines, GRUDGE PURCHASES or frequent sale goods.

2. The lowest trading floor in a store. In order to avoid confusion with 'bargain basement' this area is sometimes dignified with a name such as 'lower ground floor' by retailers.

basic assortment The lowest point to which the stock in a merchandise category should be permitted to fall without seriously interfering with sales opportunities. It must provide an adequate depth of styles, colours and sizes etc.

batch/continuous process In a batch process, groups of items are produced until a finite end point; changes in production process or items may then be introduced and further batches manufactured (e.g. in motor manufacturing). In continuous process, which is typical in the chemical industry, no planned stops are made to production. Examples would include oil-refining and cement-making.

More recently these concepts were applied to the 'production', processing and handling of computer data. In early computers, batch processing of finite groups of data (e.g. wages or accounts processing) was the most appropriate usage of computer power because, at the time, on-line (where the end user is connected directly to the central processing unit) real-time (where processing occurs during connection) interactions were expensive, using mainframe computers and SOFTWARE that had not been specifically designed for that purpose.

In store retailing, these distinctions are seen in the structure of EPOS systems: batch processing tends to be used for the overnight assessment of the daily sales pattern throughout a large store or chain; continuous processing is employed within the same system on PRICE LOOK-UP activities etc.

Bayesian statistics A formal set of techniques (named after Reverend Thomas Bayes) for revising probabilities (i.e. estimates of risks), associated with making decisions under uncertainty, in the light of additional information when it becomes available. The initial estimates of probabilities are often subjective, and the revisions are made through combining them with additional information obtained from sources such as sample results, observations and research.

The retail buyer, for example, may estimate the probabilities of success of a new product development in chilled foods, based entirely on 'hunch'. The decision as to whether to purchase the product, and in what quantities, may be delayed until additional information becomes available. Through the application of Bayesian techniques, it is possible to provide revised probabilities of success (in which, it is presumed, there may be greater faith), and to provide, if desired, greater objectivity to the buying decision.

behaviour The observable, characteristic activities of an organism, especially an individual. By extension, used analogously to describe the characteristic actions of parts or subsystems within an organism, or of social and other such systems, such as business firms.

below the line Promotional expenditure other than that on advertising and personal selling. Such expenditure pays for trade and consumer purchase incentives through, for example, exhibitions, point-of-sale displays, sales promotion offers etc. *Compare* ABOVE THE LINE.

benefit segmentation *See* MARKET SEGMENTATION.

bespoke Of clothing particularly, and merchandise generally, made to a customer's specific order, size etc.

best-before date The day marked on the packaging of a perishable product prior to which consumption or use should take place.

bid The offering, by a potential customer, of a price at which he/she is prepared to trade, to an AUCTIONEER or person conducting a tender offer.

bill of lading A document which is the basis of the contract between the shipper and carrier and also acts as the carrier's receipt for the goods (and in some cases evidence of title to them).

black box A simple schematic used in treating buyer behaviour, where the buyer's internal processes are treated as opaque (and not modelled), and are shown simply as an opaque container between inputs and outputs.

black market The surreptitious (possibly illegal) purchase or sale of goods which are rationed or are subject to official regulations or control.

blister pack A method of merchandising usually small GOODS (e.g.

stationery items such as pencil sharpeners, erasers, small children's toys) where the good is mounted on a card and encased under a plastic bubble. It allows items to be displayed easily by hanging the backing cards on horizontal pegs, and reduces the likelihood of theft of all, or part, of the item.

blue chip Used expressively of the best, or most highly regarded etc., in a particular field or area, especially of organizations. Thus a 'blue chip company' is one regarded as having high levels of management expertise and affording high-grade investment opportunities.

bonus A premium beyond the established payment, normally associated with the achievement of standards and/or turnover or profit in excess of the agreed norm.

bonus pack A pack to which additional contents have been added by the supplier or manufacturer, without a corresponding increase in the retail price to the consumer.

book club An organization that sells printed volumes at lower than recommended retail prices to members (who usually agree on a minimum purchase requirement), often on a MAIL ORDER basis.

book-in The recording of goods by number or price, or both, on arrival at a warehouse or retail outlet.

book inventory A perpetual system for recording the units and value (at cost) of inventory on hand at a given time. It is implemented by adding purchases (at cost) and subtracting sales (at cost), to previous inventory figures.

book token A document of a stated value which can be exchanged for printed volumes or stationery. Often purchased as a gift.

book value The worth of goods or assets recorded in a company's accounts, as distinguished from their market worth.

booking 1. The taking of an order by a manufacturer for delivery at a later date.
2. Securing in advance, as in 'booking a holiday' or 'booking a seat on an aeroplane'.

bootleg 1. The illegal manufacture or sale of alcoholic liquor.
2. The counterfeiting of manufactured (especially branded) articles for retail sale (e.g. Rolex watches or music cassettes).

Boston Box *See* BOSTON CONSULTING GROUP SHARE/GROWTH MATRIX.

Boston Consulting Group Share/ Growth Matrix One of the best known techniques of portfolio analysis, whereby products or business units are plotted on a matrix showing market share and market growth rate on the axes, and are thus defined as 'stars', 'question marks' (or 'problem children') 'cash cows' and 'dogs', as shown below.
The position of an individual unit or product on the matrix will suggest a role and give strategic guidelines for it in the organization's portfolio.
Stars. High market shares in growing markets. The company must spend heavily to gain share but costs

		Market Share	
		High	*Low*
Market growth			
High		Stars	Question marks or Problem children
Low		Cash cows	Dogs

may be declining even faster, producing a self-financing product (or business unit).
Cash cows. High market shares in low-growth or mature markets. The need for large-scale investment is low and since costs can be kept low the product can generate cash.
Question marks. Low market shares in growing markets. The company has the option to invest in growth but is unlikely to yield a positive cash flow until economies of scale can be achieved.
Dogs. Low market shares in static or declining markets. They are unlikely to generate positive cash flows.
The Boston Consulting Group has continued to develop the approach beyond this initial version.

bottom line 1. The final entry on an INCOME STATEMENT showing the computed profit or loss.
2. Sometimes used metaphorically to indicate a high degree of importance, or direct relationship to profit.

boutique 1. A shop or CONCESSION where merchandise is specifically targeted at the young (usually) female, high-fashion market segment. The term was used more in the 1960s and 1970s, when this market was first addressed.

2. More loosely, any small store serving a particular market niche.

branch Individual revenue-earning outlet of a MULTIPLE RETAILER.

branch accounting The preparation of records of revenues, expenditure etc. for individual OUTLETS of a retail organization. It is done as part of the BUDGETARY CONTROL process, and enables senior and branch management to evaluate and compare the performance of individual branches and to determine responsibility for the results. The type of accounts required varies with the structure of the organization and the resulting degree of autonomy of the branches. This ranges from a completely non-autonomous branch, where the focus is exclusively on SALES and all calculations are carried out using selling prices, to the completely autonomous branch, where the emphasis is on profits and a full set of annual accounts is prepared for each branch.

branch manager The individual charged with responsibility for the oversight of daily operations of an individual outlet within a chain or group.

brand 1. The distinctive identifying marks, livery, name etc. attached to a particular good or service in order to distinguish it from other similar products.
2. A product where the presentation of its identifying marks, livery, name etc. to consumers evokes a clear and identifiable response that the manufacturer or provider seeks to associate with the product. Used in this sense, the term distinguishes 'branded' products from those that are merely 'labelled' or named.

brand loyalty The commitment of the consumer to a particular manufactured item, TRADEMARK etc. such that the consumer purchases the product repeatedly, irrespective of competitors' products. This loyalty increases the consumer's resistance to special price offers or PROMOTIONS from competitor's products. Brand loyalty may be the consumer's commitment not only to a branded product but also to a HOUSE BRAND.

brand positioning *See* POSITIONING.

branded good A PRODUCT whose identity is supported and maintained by manufacturers' or providers' efforts through the exercise of marketing mix decisions. This contrasts with retailer 'brands', either OWN BRAND or OWN LABEL products, whose identity derives mainly from the retailer's CONSUMER FRANCHISE and image.

branded product *See* BRANDED GOOD.

bread-and-butter lines The items of stock which customers expect to find in a particular retail outlet and which reflect the core business of the retailer (e.g. sweets, cigarettes and newspapers in a CTN retail outlet).

breadth *See* WIDTH.

break bulk The separation of large loads into smaller, individual quantities for delivery to the next channel intermediary. Traditionally this was one of the major functions of the wholesaler but nowadays it is often undertaken by, or on behalf of, the retailer in dedicated warehousing.

break-even analysis The study of

the total revenue and total costs associated with the production, and subsequent sale, of varying volumes of a particular product with a view to establishing the levels of profit or loss associated with each potential volume. A break-even point exists where total sales revenue for the product exactly equals the total costs (FIXED COST plus VARIABLE COSTS) of production.

For sales volumes higher than the break-even point, a profit is made, otherwise a loss. Break-even analysis relies on several restricting assumptions (e.g. all items produced are subsequently sold, selling price is fixed etc.) and, although useful as an initial guide to decisions on production levels, it must be used with caution.

The expression 'break-even' is also used in connection with one-off events where charges for participants in the event are put at a level which, when aggregated, will cover the total costs of running the event.

break-even point The combination of sales volume, selling price and costs for which total costs equal total revenue. *See* BREAK-EVEN ANALYSIS.

British Code of Advertising Practice (BCAP) A body of rules designed to regulate the majority of paid-for insertions under clear sponsorship in mass MEDIA produced by British business. The code is under the general supervision of the Advertising Standards Authority (*see* Appendix 2) and prepared and amended by the Code of Advertising Practice Committee. The only substantial group of advertisements not covered by the code are television and radio COMMERCIALS. The self-regulating code is based on the principle that all adver-

tisements should be 'legal, decent, honest and truthful', prepared with a sense of responsibility both to the consumer and to society and conform to the principles of fair competition generally accepted in business.

British Code of Sales Promotion Practice A body of rules published under the general supervision of the Advertising Standards Authority (ASA) (*see* Appendix 2). Retailers involved in any form of sales promotion are affected by the code. It covers specifically premium offers, reduced price and free offers, voucher and sales coupon distribution, personality promotions as well as more general sales promotions. The ASA monitors promotions in all parts of the country and investigates complaints received from members of the general public. Although the code does not have the force of law, results of investigations are published by the ASA and frequently appear in the trade and general press.

brown goods Electrical equipment for entertainment in the home (e.g. televisions, VCRs, hi-fi). *Compare* WHITE GOOD.

budget A detailed short-term plan concerning the allocation of resources, usually expressed in monetary terms.

budget account A form of revolving consumer credit. Budget accounts are operated by most banks to facilitate the prompt payment of bills and the spreading of household running costs over the year. In addition many retailers offer a budget account facility as an alternative to CHARGE ACCOUNTS. A budget-account-holding customer decides on a suitable level of regular monthly payments which will be affordable. The spending limit for the account is a multiple of the monthly payment. As long as the spending limit is not exceeded and the customer keeps up the regular monthly payments, further purchases can be made in conjunction with the budget card which allows the customer to draw on the account. Once the credit facility is used, interest is payable by the customer.

budget card *See* BUDGET ACCOUNT.

budgetary control A management technique employing statements of anticipated and actual income and expenditure. It consists principally of using VARIANCE ANALYSIS etc. as a tool to compare a detailed resource plan for a time period with the actual figures achieved for that time period. Where there are discrepancies between the plan and actuality, management will examine whether the cost items in question could have been controlled. Certain costs are deemed controllable (e.g. wastage on food items) whereas others are uncontrollable (e.g. the increase in the price of oil, premises etc.) A system of 'responsibility accounting' is used to identify line managers within the cost centres who have the task of controlling individual cost items. This encourages careful planning and aims to motivate employees to achieve targets.

budgeting The process of drawing up a detailed, short-term plan concerning the allocation of resources. Starting with a sales forecast, the budgeting process produces a set of expected sales and cost figures, usually based on historic information, and, where possible, combined with information from other sources (e.g. market analyses). In the budgeting process, management often use a top-down approach, imposing sales and cost targets from above. Such an approach has the advantage that the analysis of historic cost and sales data can be centralized, the best use can be made of additional external sources of information, and uniformity across the various parts of the organization can be achieved. This, in turn, makes it easier to compare performance of different branches. However, this may lead to staff feeling that they are not involved. Alternatively, a bottom-up planning approach can be used, where line managers are involved in setting targets based on knowledge of their branches. This is felt to lead to a higher degree of staff motivation.

bulk A large quantity of undifferentiated goods.

bulk buying 1. The purchase of large amounts of stock. It has certain major advantages for the large retail business which is able to afford it, but it also produces problems.

The advantages are: (i) suppliers often offer minimum quantity discounts, thus increasing the size of order; (ii) there is a reduction in the possibility of out-of-stocks occurring; (iii) the cost of ordering, per unit, is reduced.

The disadvantages are: (i) cash resources are committed – larger INVENTORIES need additional financing; (ii) higher sales are needed if STOCK TURNOVER targets are to be met; (iii) storage space in depots and STOCKROOMS is tied up; (iv) the opportunity for stock deterioration and PILFERAGE increases; (v) the probability of price MARKDOWNS on stock approaching its SELL-BY DATE, or becoming obsolete, increases.

2. Consumer buying of larger than normal amounts at a lower unit price, especially when offered as a means of promotion by a supplier or as a condition of membership of discount clubs etc.

bulk discount *See* BULK BUYING.

business logistics *See* LOGISTICS.

butcher A specialist retailer of meats, especially red meats. Butchers may be involved in the slaughter of animals, the dressing and preparation of carcasses for retail sale, or simply the onward selling of pre-prepared meats.

buy To acquire goods or services in exchange for money.

buy-back An agreement by a supplier to repurchase unsold goods from a retailer at some future (usually specified) date.

buyer Generally, one who purchases. In retailing, the individual responsible for the purchase of particular lines of merchandise from suppliers for future retail sale to consumers.

buyer behaviour The activities that purchasers engage in when selecting, evaluating and actually purchasing goods and services. Used especially of (i) consumers to delineate the careful study and analysis of their behaviour when engaged in the buying process (which varies from impulse to extended considered actions over a long period), and (ii) the activities of individuals and groups in DECISION-MAKING UNITS buying on behalf of organizations. *See also* CONSUMER BEHAVIOUR.

buyer's market A market in which conditions are such that purchasers are able to exert control over most aspects of a transaction, for example in situations where supply exceeds demand.

buyer's risk The jeopardy associated with the purchase of goods or services without a guarantee.

buyer's role The part played by the purchasing officer in realizing the company's aims and objectives. The buyer's role varies from retailer to retailer, but normally includes product and supplier selection, negotiating with suppliers, pricing and evaluating purchasing decisions and activities. It may also include a wide range of responsibilities such as market monitoring, inventory management and replenishment, sales forecasting, new product development, advertising and sales promotion, depending on the organizational structure and size of the company. Larger retailers are likely to have specialist departments fulfilling or assisting with some of these functions.

Some retailers (for example large retailers offering OWN LABEL goods) include many responsibilities in the buyer's job, whereas others see some of the responsibilities as purely the domain of the manufacturer or another department (e.g. marketing or distribution) within their organization.

buyer's surplus The excess margin

generated when merchandise is acquired for retail sale at a discount such that normal margins are (greatly) exceeded.

buying The process by which merchandise is obtained by the retailer for reselling to the customer. It involves selecting merchandise and suppliers and negotiating the terms of trade (including cost prices, discounts and other incentives). In smaller retailers, buying is likely to be undertaken by the owner or manager of the business, but in large retailers buying is a specialist function and large teams of buyers may be employed. *See also* BUYER'S ROLE.

buying centre The group of departments or individuals typically involved in purchasing decisions. For example, buying, merchandising, marketing and quality control departments are frequently involved in buying decisions. The buying centre need not meet formally in order to exist; often it functions informally. *See also* DECISION-MAKING UNIT.

buying committee A group of individuals, sometimes from a number of functional areas, who meet on a regular basis to make purchasing decisions. *See also* NEW LINES COMMITTEE.

buying error The results of a failure to purchase the right goods in the right quantities from the right suppliers and offer them for sale at the right price. Buying errors lead to excess stocks of unsaleable goods or STOCKOUTS, excess MARKDOWNS or inappropriate quality. Above all, buying errors result in OPPORTUNITY COSTS and diminished profit margins.

buying habits Tendencies to perform certain actions or behave in certain ways on the part of a purchasing officer or consumer; routinized responses to buying situations.

buying-led A shorthand description for those retail organizations where the purchasing function is the dominant political force.

buying period The amount of time over which the purchasing officer plans and reviews purchasing activity, often a lunar or calendar month or, for fast moving items, a week or day.

buying plan A scheme for accomplishing a purchasing officer's objectives prepared in advance of a particular period. It will specify what, when and where to buy and the quantities required.

Before the buying plan can be developed, financial plans must be made, based on the company's sales plan for the coming period and including stock investment, planned markups and MARKDOWNS. Once the forecast and budget has been agreed, the buyer must translate the financial projections into physical amounts, that is, the MODEL STOCK.

buying power 1. A subjective evaluation of the ability of any purchaser to control the terms of trade with sellers, based on a view of that purchaser's resources and influence.

2. A measure of relative purchases in a market analogous to market share in sales terms.

buying process 1. The stages through which a consumer passes while selecting, purchasing and evaluating goods and services.

2. The series of actions and events encountered during the discharge of purchasing officers' duties.

buyout A form of ACQUISITION where a business is acquired by its managers (who were not previously the owners). The terms 'management buyout' and 'leveraged buyout' became commonly used in the 1980s. A leveraged buyout implies the purchase of a company using a high proportion of borrowed money.

C

cabinet Items of furniture used to provide display and storage space for merchandise, especially when of the form of a lidded chest; used for the display of jewellery, frozen foods etc.

cabinet-maker Skilled craftsperson manufacturing carcass furniture, such as dining and occasional tables, wardrobes and other cupboards. With the increasing industrialization of their craft, there are few cabinet-makers today who both manufacture and retail the pieces that they make.

cable television A system of distributing signals via wire or optical fibre to individual receivers, in contrast to broadcast transmission, usually providing a wider range of stations than can be received via conventional broadcasting.

call-off The arrangement, or process, permitting a retailer or other purchaser to place a bulk order with a supplier, which permits the buyer to specify, at a later date, the quantities and times of CONSIGNMENTS drawn from the bulk quantity. *See also* BULK BUYING.

campaign The promotional effort supporting a particular product over a given short-term period. Most frequently the term is used to refer to ADVERTISING but can also be used of PUBLIC RELATIONS and SALES PROMOTION efforts.

capital The investment made by the owners of a business organization. *See also* EQUITY.

capital account The section of the BALANCE SHEET which shows the investment of the owners of the business, as well as the accumulated profits which have been reinvested in the business.

capital employed The owners' EQUITY plus any long-term loans made to the business by various lenders.

capital expenditure Any cash disbursement on FIXED ASSETS (i.e. assets of an expected life of more than one year) which will be used in the running of a business.

capital investment *See* CAPITAL EXPENDITURE.

capital turnover The FINANCIAL RATIO of sales to capital employed. With capital employed equal to net total assets, this is the same as ASSET TURNOVER.

captive market Consumers who, for one reason or another, are obliged to purchase goods/services from a particular outlet. There is often no alternative to purchasing products due to the specialist nature of the merchandise sold or the location of the outlet.

car boot sale Informal markets for second-hand goods by non-traders at selected locations (car parks etc.), often organized to support charitable work; more recently, formalized and trader-dominated 'markets' showing superficially similar characteristics.

car parking The provision of space for the storage of unattended motor vehicles. The direct integration of car parking facilities with new shopping developments is now commonplace. New central shopping complexes usually include multi-storey car parks. Superstores, retail warehouses, retail parks and regional shopping centres developed outside traditional town and city centres usually have their own surface-level parking space. Here the average provision is around one car parking space per 100 square feet of retail floorspace.

card 1. Relatively thin stiff heavyweight paper or paperboard used especially in retail settings for the production of price tickets, point of display materials, signs etc.
2. Small, rectangular piece of plastic, bearing customer and account identification in a magnetic strip, especially CREDIT CARDS, DEBIT CARDS and CHARGE CARDS.

cargo Freight goods carried by a ship or aircraft, or possibly road vehicle.

carnet A document used to facilitate passage of vehicles and/or transport of goods, across a frontier, especially by road.

carrier 1. A person or organization which undertakes the transportation of goods, especially where defined legally as a licensed organization.
2. Short for CARRIER BAG.

carrier bag (UK) Thin, flexible, container, normally of polythene or paper, often incorporating carrying handles, used by customers for the conveyance of purchases.

carrying charge The fee payable for transportation undertaken on behalf of a client by a THIRD PARTY.

carrying cost 1. The charges, disbursements etc. incurred during the process of transporting goods.
2. The charges associated with holding a particular level of INVENTORY.

cart 1. Wheeled, flat-bed vehicle designed for transporting goods, especially a handcart or a vehicle designed to be drawn by draft animals such as horses.
2. To transport goods from one location to another, especially by public road or railway. Because of the widespread nature of the activity this action has, in many economies, given rise to particular forms of contract and law.

cartage The charge incurred for transporting goods by land.

case study The documentation of a series of events normally written to provide the basis for a discussion of one or more principles in, for example, business. The case study approach is used in a wide range of activities from clinical research to television documentary. In a teaching or training situation the business case study has a proven worth in group activities and where there are a range of possible ways of addressing practical issues. Most business courses will use case studies at one stage or another and some rely heavily on their use. The Harvard Business School has a tradition in both writing and teaching case studies.

cash Money (seen as a store of value) represented by notes and coins in circulation. For payment purposes, CHEQUES and DEBIT CARDS have cash equivalent status. Cash is the most liquid current asset held by a business organization.

cash and carry A particular type of LIMITED FUNCTION WHOLESALER, usually frequented by small, independent retailers, from where goods can be collected and taken away in the retailer's own transport, having been paid for at the point of sale.

Such wholesalers do not generally provide credit, nor a delivery service, and are only available to other traders. The benefits for retailers are low costs, availability and convenience. The decline of the delivered wholesale trade has caused many independent retailers, who would prefer a full service wholesaler, to make more use of a cash and carry.

cash cow *See* BOSTON CONSULTING GROUP SHARE/GROWTH MATRIX.

cash discount A deduction from the amount due, given for immediate monetary payment.

cash flow The volume of money being expended and received by an organization in a particular period of time. The balance of expenses and receipts is different from profit and loss; it is possible for a company that is trading profitably to experience cash flow difficulties.

cash incentive A monetary payment used to encourage a person to act in a certain way (e.g. to work harder, to carry out a task beyond the normal scope of activities, or to purchase a certain brand).

cashing-up An end-of-day process of reconciling money takings with the TILL records, and preparing the takings for transmission/delivery to a BANK.

cash low A shortage of money due to inadequate CASH FLOW management. This is not to be confused with a loss; a business may be temporarily short of cash but operating in a profitable manner. Ideally, future cash lows can be detected during the BUDGETING process, and temporary sources of the required cash organized in advance.

cash refund A monetary payment made on the return of goods.

cash register *See* TILL.

cash sale The purchase of goods in exchange for money, CHEQUE or payment by DEBIT CARD.

cash terms A contractual condition relating to the period and manner of payment, usually the specification of a due date by which monies are to be received by the seller.

cash till *See* TILL.

cash with order A condition of the CONTRACT of sale that payment is made in full when the order is placed.

cashier 1. An employee of the retail organization who is in charge of money, especially either as one who accepts money from customers, or one who is responsible for the safe handling of money and the recording of transactions within a retail outlet.
2. A bank teller.

catalogue The list of merchandise obtainable from a retailer, especially in MAIL ORDER, where the list is likely to take the form of an extensive illustrated book.

catalogue agency The system whereby one who supplies goods from an illustrated book to friends and neighbours receives commission, typically of between 10 per cent and 15 per cent of the value of goods supplied, either in cash or kind.

catalogue buying The customer choice process conducted via an illustrated book rather than in-store. This process relies on the presentation and description of goods in the catalogue to stimulate choice. *See also* CATALOGUE MERCHANDISING.

catalogue house A retailer using illustrated lists etc. as the basis of its operations.

catalogue merchandising The process of design, layout, presentation and description of goods on offer in book form. It has to attract the attention of the 'browsing' customer, but in addition must also depict and describe merchandise accurately in order to ensure appropriate ordering and to minimize returns of unwanted goods by customers.

catalogue retailer *See* CATALOGUE HOUSE.

catalogue showroom A shop where customers choose merchandise by reference to extensively illustrated books (catalogues) showing the range on offer, rather than by examining the goods. Usually a 'no-frills', priceled, non-food, variety retailer whose formula is very low service from edge-of-town centre sites. The system is supported by the distribution of free CATALOGUES to customers who come to the store. Stores typically have restricted display areas, and customers must complete coded paper orders which are checked by staff for stock availability, using a computer system, before payment is made. The selected items are collected from an attached warehouse and delivered to the customer at a counter.
Experiments with catalogue superstores displaying virtually all merchandise at out-of-town retail parks are currently being undertaken in the UK.

catchment area The district, territory etc. from which a shopping centre and/or individual shop draws its custom. It is sometimes also known as the trade area (*see* TRADE AREA ANALYSIS) or hinterland.

categorization The process of placing products, people etc. into classes or groups which possess similar qualities (e.g. the categorization of foods into fresh, chilled, frozen, packaged, canned, ready-to-eat etc.).

catering The provision of prepared food and drink for consumption by the purchaser at or about the time of sale. Catering is also sometimes taken to include the provision of other hospitality services, such as accommodation.

caveat emptor A Latin term meaning 'Let the buyer beware', which regulated relationships between traders prior to consumer protection legislation. As a buyer had little or no real remedy of redress against a seller who sold faulty merchandise, purchasing goods and services was a high risk activity.

CBI/FT Distributive Trades Survey (UK) A monthly survey indicating the current state and future prospects of the distributive trades. Expectations of trends and investment intentions are monitored, together with employment levels, price changes and import penetration.

Ceefax (UK) Teletext services available on BBC television providing news, travel, weather and other information. *See* VIDEOTEX.

ceiling price The upper psychological limit which customers feel marks the end of a fair and just charge range for a product. The impact of this more formally produces a typically kinked demand curve with a 'fair' price range within limits where price elasticity is lower. Beyond these limits demand tends to expand and constrict more rapidly in response to price cuts or rises (greater price elasticity).

Psychological price limits are a particular problem in times of inflation and put an acute pressure on retailer margins. A commodity, price-driven

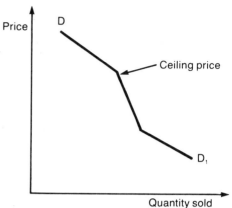

product like coffee provides a good illustration. Coffee suffers severe sales drop when retail price increases rapidly in times of crop shortage. Retailers are forced to raise prices well above consumers' ceiling price and demand suffers. The contradiction faced by retailers is that if they aim to restrain selling price increases they lose margin, whereas if they follow cost increases they lose sales.

census 1. An official count of the population carried out at regular intervals. Data gathered in a census might be about peoples' gender, age and occupation.

2. A survey of an entire statistical population, as distinct from a sample survey covering only a proportion.

Census of Distribution (UK) A former official statistical survey of distributive trades. Information collated related to the numbers, size, turnover, location and nature of merchandise sold in retail outlets.

central business district (CBD) Within a city, the core area that provides the chief concentration of retailing, service, commercial etc. facilities.

central buying A form of purchasing activity or organization in which the authority and responsibility for purchasing is vested in a single department, usually in the head office or main branch. Some buying may also take place at local level, but the extent and nature of this DE-CENTRALIZED BUYING is laid down and limited by company policy.

central market 1. The chief or most important trading site within a given area.

2. A place for the exchange of items of value (usually a particular class or type of merchandise), having a major role in the trade for that item of value. For example, the Billingsgate fish market (based in London) may be described as the central United Kingdom market for fish.

3. A trading location which is used to determine the price for a particular class of merchandise or goods item (e.g. tin, cocoa markets), this price being then used more widely in the trade.

Central Office of Information (COI) (UK) A government department which provides specialist information and publicity services for other government departments at home and abroad. It is responsible for government advertising and produces books, films etc., and mounts exhibitions.

central place A settlement providing commercial and/or non-commercial services to a surrounding population in its HINTERLAND.

Central Place Theory Conceptual framework originally developed in 1933 by Walter Christaller to explain the GEOGRAPHICAL PATTERN of distribution of towns and cities over a terrain. Such towns and cities would be evenly distributed over a region/country, and would form a regular hierarchy by size with clearly defined levels. For example, in one formulation, Christaller postulated that for each city of a particular size, there would be three of the next size lower down, and for each of these another three at the next level down, and so on. The hinterlands of cities of a given level would be of equal size, and those of the settlements below them in the hierarchy would be wholly incorporated within them.

The theory became very influential in town planning after 1945 since it was seen to form an ideal arrangement of centres. From being concerned with the distribution of settlements in general terms, the theory was applied specifically to the location of shops and other service activities. This was done not only at the inter-urban scale but also at the intra-urban. Centres at different levels were described, in descending order of size, as REGIONAL SHOPPING CENTRES, DISTRICT SHOPPING CENTRES and NEIGHBOURHOOD SHOPPING CENTRES and were thought to be characterized by particular types and sizes of shops with their own well defined hinterlands.

The belief that a well structured hierarchy was the natural and logical arrangement for shopping centres became enshrined in UK planning policy and practice. It was a major reason for the comparatively late development of free-standing hypermarkets, out-of-town schemes and retail parks, which did not fit easily with the preconceived model. It needed a combination of consumer and retailer pressures, and the demise of Structure Planning during the 1980s, for the rigidities in the retail system imposed by Central Place Theory to be relaxed.

centralized distribution A form of transportation and delivery system which locates the inventory of a company in a small number of strategically located warehouses which feed the stores. By this system, direct deliveries from manufacturers to stores are avoided and selling space at the stores is released as more frequent stock replenishment is made possible. The total inventory in the system is reduced, the number of vehicles delivering to stores reduced and retailers are able to control the frequency, size, timing and mix of deliveries.

Suppliers are required to deliver to the warehouses, rather than direct to stores, thus simplifying their transportation requirements. Retailers normally negotiate lower prices with suppliers in recognition of supplier cost savings and the increased costs borne by the retailer.

centre of shopping Any place, node or focus providing a range of retail outlets that attracts consumers from within a particular geographical area.

chain A form of retail organization where multiple branches display a relatively uniform presentation to consumers.

chain of distribution *See* CHANNEL OF DISTRIBUTION.

chain store 1. Any retail outlet belonging to a multiple unit operator that is identifiable as such.
    2. More specifically variety chain stores. Larger retail outlets (approximately 20,000 square feet plus) offering a wide (though not comprehensive) range of domestic and personal merchandise at average to low market prices (e.g. F. W. Woolworth). Such stores typically offer fewer services and trade from fewer floors than full-line DEPARTMENT STORES.

challenge A problem or opportunity with characteristics leading to higher than normal risk of failure.

change management The conscious process of seeking to plan, organize and control shifts in an organization's current position with regard to environment, markets, systems, operations etc. The term is customarily used to identify deliberate attempts to seek such shifts in an organization's stance.

channel 1. *See* CHANNEL OF DISTRIBUTION.
    2. That group of broadcast frequencies assigned by a government or other regulatory body to a television operator, giving that operator the right (within certain constraints) to transmit, originate, produce etc. programming, often including advertising, for distribution to homes etc.

channel appraisal The process used for evaluating the success or the appropriateness of performance of a chosen system of DISTRIBUTION. *See also* CHANNEL PERFORMANCE.

channel behaviour The typical activities undertaken by members of a chain of distribution collectively as part of the distribution system.

channel captaincy The ability of a

particular member of a distribution system to exercise control over the behaviour of other elements of the system, especially the behaviour of other members. For example, large supermarket operators may exercise control (to some extent) over branded goods manufacturers because of their BUYING POWER. Conversely, confectionery manufacturers are able to control CTN outlets by virtue of their greater resources, as many CTN's are individually owned.

channel conflict Disputes which arise between members of a distribution system, say, a manufacturer and a retailer or wholesaler, regarding the distribution operation overall. An example may be where a retailer refuses to handle an extra quantity sales promotion because the larger packs are less space efficient.

channel interface The point of contact between different members of a distribution system. For example, between manufacturer and wholesaler, wholesaler and small retailer. *See also* CHANNEL MEMBER.

channel intermediary *See* CHANNEL MEMBER.

channel member Any individual organizational element within a distribution system, which at some stage in the distribution process exercises control and/or ownership of the merchandise.

channel of communication Any of the various mechanisms which connect a transmitter to a receiver and provide for the transmission of data/information between the two. Such a channel usually comprises a medium

and a media vehicle (i.e. a general transmission process – the printed word – and a particular form – cardholder's magazine).

channel of distribution The physical and organizational system employed in moving goods or services from the point of their production to the point of sale to ultimate purchasers. A major component of the MARKETING MIX, such channels are sometimes referred to as 'marketing channels'.

The idea is rooted in the view of intermediary institutions (such as wholesalers and retailers) as providing a physical conduit through which merchandise moves. The actions that are seen as provided by a channel are basically those of ensuring that the correct products are made available in appropriate amounts at convenient points of sales at the required time and prices desired by target CONSUMERS.

channel performance The outcome of the discharge of its functions by a distribution system, especially when evaluated against customer requirements or the desires and targets of individual components of the system, such as channel intermediaries or regulatory bodies.

charge account A means of providing customers with credit from a particular retailer against, usually, a prearranged credit limit, by allowing purchases to be made with payment to be affected (on an agreed basis) at some later date(s).

charge card 1. A payment vehicle, issued by organizations such as American Express and Diners Club, and accepted by retailers in lieu of cash, where the user is required to pay the issuer in full, for purchases made, at the end of the (monthly) accounting period. (Issuers derive their income from levying an annual charge on users, commission from retailers and interest applied to over-due accounts.) Charge cards are also frequently issued as 'gold cards' by CREDIT CARD issuers. Such cards are also distinguished from credit cards by the absence of a preset spending limit.

2. A term often used by stores to distinguish their own card from other CREDIT CARDS. Store charge cards are usually issued on a CREDIT SCORING basis and work as a credit card. While interest charges may be high such cards are said to encourage store loyalty, and provide DIRECT MAIL potential for retailers. Customer advantages often include sale pre-views, private late night pre-season shopping, free magazine etc.

charity shop A retail outlet of a recognized organization (e.g. Oxfam, Age Concern, Cancer Relief) which usually sells SECOND-HAND goods (e.g. clothes donated to the charity), and/ or a range of handicraft, utilitarian and seasonal or specialist goods (e.g. Christmas cards, minority interest books, trade goods from developing countries). The shops are often in secondary retail locations and most of the sales assistants work on a voluntary basis. Through posters, and limited POINT OF SALE literature, the shops act as visible reminders of the aims of the charity.

Although many charity organiz-ations would not claim retail sophisti-cation for their shops, there are charities (e.g. the National Trust in the UK), which can identify a clear

customer profile and merchandise their specialist shops accordingly.

charter The lease of a vehicle (ship, aircraft etc.) to a hirer for his/her exclusive use, often with the crew etc. being provided by the lessor.

check (USA) *See* CHEQUE.

checkout A FIXTURE in a SUPER-MARKET and other SELF-SERVICE outlet which provides the point to which customers bring their goods for pay-ment before leaving the store. Checkouts consist principally of a small area of countering, which may take the form of a moving band onto which goods are placed by the cus-tomer, a TILL and a seat or standing position for the SHOP ASSISTANT or checkout operator.

checkout operator The person staff-ing the TILL in a self-service retail outlet, particularly grocery and DIY.

cheque (USA: check) A form of pay-ment of CASH equivalent status. Payment is made by drawing up a written order (usually on pre-printed forms supplied by the bank) to the bank to pay a certain amount out of the payee's current account to the other party. In the UK retailing situation, this transaction is usually supported by a cheque guarantee card issued by the bank to the 'current account' (USA: checking account) holder, guaranteeing pay-ment to the retailer.

cherry picking The process of select-ing from a wide merchandise offer only those items offering a particular benefit, such as extremely good value for money, high design desirability or other such features. More widely, the process of selecting only the best from a range.

Chicago Central Place Theory *See* CENTRAL PLACE THEORY.

chilled food Consumable products stored at temperatures of between 0° and 4° C to prevent rapid deterioration in edibility. Dairy products, such as milk, yoghurt and cheese, were amongst the first to benefit from such storage, distribution and display, though today a wide range of pre-prepared foods benefit (e.g. cooked meats, pizzas etc.). The term has come to signify cook/chill products, especially main entrées, in a ready to heat form for microwaves and other ovens.

cinema advertising Commercials shown before main features at movie theatres. It is a medium with a highly 'captive' audience, but it reaches only those who are regular cinema-goers, principally the under-34 age group. It was a shrinking medium until the late 1980s, since when, with the expansion of the number of screens, it has grown.

circular A piece of printed material, usually in the form of a leaflet or letter, containing promotional messages, distributed to individuals or households.

circulation The number of copies of a newspaper, journal or magazine which are printed and subsequently sold to readers, or sent to a prequalified readership (sometimes without charge). Circulation figures are audited by independent organizations and used by publishers to attract advertising.

city centre The traditional commercial focus of a town or large conurbation. The area is often dominated by retail and commercial activities. In terms of CENTRAL PLACE THEORY, the city centre occupies the highest level in the hierarchy of centres for its region. It is sometimes referred to as the CENTRAL BUSINESS DISTRICT, and is usually surrounded by an outer frame of industrial, wholesaling and transport activities.

Within many European city centres there has been extensive redevelopment since 1960, incorporating large planned shopping centres, and the pedestrianization of streets. Increasingly, city centre retailing has been coming under pressure from out-of-town developments; in North America the retail role of the city centre has been largely eclipsed by suburban centres, leading to what has become known as the 'doughnut effect'.

claim 1. A demand for payment with respect to an insurance policy.
2. A demand for reduction in invoice price, or additional merchandise to compensate for shortages or damaged deliveries.

class A group of people/items differentiated from other groups on the basis of one or more CLASSIFICATION VARIABLES. *See also* SOCIAL CLASS.

classic A work or item of acknowledged excellence.

classification The allocation of people/items into groups on the basis of specific criteria. *See also* CLASSIFICATION VARIABLES.

classification data Information about

the characteristics of people or items which is used to delineate them into groups.

classification variables The characteristics used to type people or items (e.g. age, income, employment).

classified advertising Small paid-for insertions under clear sponsorship, in newspapers or periodicals, which are grouped together in columns by subject (e.g. employment, housing, cars), usually consisting entirely of words (i.e. without illustration).

classify The process of allocating items into separate groups on the basis of designated CLASSIFICATION VARIABLES.

clearance 1. Means by which a CHEQUE is scrutinized for authenticity or ability to pay by being passed through the BANK or (in the UK) cheque clearing house. The process usually takes three days, but express clearance within 24 hours can be provided for a charge.
2. The act of granting permission for a consignment of goods to pass through customs.

clearance sale An end-of-season PROMOTION when the price of merchandise is reduced in order to make way for new stock or store closure.

client One who pays another to undertake work on his/her behalf, especially professional or quasi-professional work.

close The element in a sale when the order is requested by the sales person; the culmination of any selling activity. It is also a point of tension for customer and salesperson alike when a decision has to be made. Many techniques are taught to ease this process, for example the alternative close or the assumptive close. Retailing examples of these techniques would be respectively, 'Do you want to pay by cheque or credit card?', and, 'Shall I wrap this for you?' *See also* CLOSING THE SALE.

closed-back window A backdrop to a WINDOW DISPLAY, access to which is severely restricted to customers. Entry can be gained only via a locked side entrance. This makes a solid backdrop to any display, which is also secure. This arrangement is favoured by DEPARTMENT STORES.

closed circuit television (CCTV) A narrowcast system in which the showing is to a restricted audience and not broadcast (used, for example, in security work and training/demonstration purposes).

closed display *See* CLOSED-BACK WINDOW.

closed question A query or interrogative item in conversation, questionnaire etc., which permits of only a limited number of responses, either through the availability of such responses (gender: male, female) or through the categorization of all likely responses (income: below £10,000; £10,001-£100,000; or above £100,001).

closed shop An establishment in which only members of a specific trade union are employed.

closing entry The final item recorded in the REVENUE accounts and expense accounts of a retail organization in order to draw up the INCOME STATEMENT at the end of the ACCOUNTING PERIOD.

closing hours The times at which an establishment ceases to trade with the public on a daily basis.

closing inventory *See* CLOSING STOCK.

closing stock The value of an INVENTORY at the end of an ACCOUNTING PERIOD, calculated in accordance with agreed principles. The most common accounting methods of stock valuation are FIFO and LIFO. In times of changing prices the BOOK VALUE of closing stock at the end of the period depends on the method used. The closing BALANCE of the accounting entries concerning stock must also be reconciled with PHYSICAL INVENTORY to determine the value of stock at the end of the accounting period. This is necessary to allow for SHRINKAGE, MARKDOWNS and wastage.

closing the book The process of balancing off the ledger accounts prior to drawing up a trial balance at the financial year end.

closing the sale The act of asking the customer to decide to make the purchase being considered. Sales people tend to avoid what is known as a 'direct' close (e.g. 'Are you buying this item, sir?') because it might appear abrupt or even rude and put the possibly undecided customer off the very purchase being considered. A better idea is often to employ an 'implied' close (e.g. 'Will you be paying cash or account sir?'), where the statement from the sales assistant assumes the customer has decided to purchase. Other examples of implied closing statements would be: 'Would you like it delivered or would you prefer to take it with you?' or even, 'Would you like a silk tie to go with that shirt sir?', which is an example of both a closing statement and an attempt to make an associated sale.

Many sales assistants are nervous about asking the customer for the sale; others might be too pushy. In those retail areas where PERSONAL SELLING is still part of the retailer's marketing mix, training in how to close a sale is very important.

closure The element of a package which seals the product during transit and is used to gain access to the package contents (e.g. a ring pull). It also, where appropriate, enables part-consumed products to be safely stored without leakage and helps maintain product quality. Examples include household cleaners. Closure security is a major concern of retailers for reasons of health and hygiene regulations.

club 1. Form of social organization having a membership on a controlled basis, either through selection by current members, or applicants meeting specified criteria for joining.

2. In retailing, sales mechanisms available only to the prequalified or specified interest groups (e.g. BOOK CLUBS or warehouse membership clubs, such as BJ's and Price Club in the USA).

club plan selling A relatively old-fashioned system whereby customers prepay a small amount every week to save for a major expenditure event, typically Christmas. For a retailer it has the advantage of increasing sales, encouraging customer loyalty and spreading sales revenue forward, away from seasonal peaks. Wider use of CREDIT CARDS has tended to eclipse this system.

cluster A group of coherent, juxtaposed elements within a statistical population.

cluster analysis A statistical technique which analyses a number of variables for a large population, and identifies common groupings (clusters) of elements who share similar characteristics.

cluster sampling A probability sample involving a two- stage process: (i) the population is divided into mutually exclusive sets (clusters), and (ii) a random sample of sets is selected.

clustering techniques Statistical procedures for identifying groups in a set of data (e.g. cluster analysis, factor analysis etc).

code 1. A system of letters or symbols which communicate a specific message.
2. A set of rules or standards of behaviour or conduct, established with the support of a number of people (e.g. BRITISH CODE OF ADVERTISING PRACTICE). *See also* CODE OF PRACTICE.

code of practice A body of rules designed to regulate the activities of different organizations. These codes are almost entirely voluntary and have been developed by a number of professional trade associations in consultation with the OFFICE OF FAIR TRADING. Codes are designed to complement the law in a given area of business.

UK examples in retailing include the Code of Practice for Launderers and Dry Cleaners, administered by the Association of British Launderers and Cleaners and the Code of Practice for Furniture, administered by the National Association of British Furniture Retailers.

coding A method of recording data for the purpose of subsequent computer analysis. Questionnaires, for example, are often precoded, and the interviewer will be required to circle the coded digit corresponding to a particular response, rather than write down the actual response.

coefficient of correlation A measure of the strength of linear association between two variables. Possible values of the coefficient lie between -1 and $+1$. A negative value for the coefficient would indicate that, in general, high values of one variable are associated with low values of the other variable. Thus the variables 'price' and 'quantity sold' may be negatively correlated. A positive value for the coefficient would indicate that high values of one variable are associated with high values of the other. Thus, the variables 'sales' and 'number of customers' may be positively correlated. A near zero value of the coefficient would indicate a poor correlation between two variables. A number of differently calculated coefficients are available, each tailored to particular circumstances, especially the type of data (e.g. Spearman's Rank correlation coefficient).

cognitive dissonance A feeling which

may arise, for example, when a consumer has bought one brand while holding positive attitudes about another brand and experiences post-purchase doubts about the wisdom of the purchase. Cognitions are any knowledge, opinion or belief about oneself, one's behaviour or the environment; dissonance is inconsistency between any two states of being that gives rise to tension.

cold calling The action of a representative in visiting a potential customer without a prior appointment, especially where the customer is not an established one.

cold canvas *See* COLD CALLING.

cold start Opening an OUTLET in a location without a retail history.

cold storage Refrigerated chamber(s) in which goods are stored at predetermined low temperatures to ensure the maintenance of satisfactory condition.

collateral An asset given in exchange for a financial loan. If repayments of the loan are not met, the asset can be taken by the lender to satisfy the loan and repayments.

collectable An item that people buy to add to a group of similar cultural objects they already own, especially where the class of object is not one traditionally gathered (e.g. stamps, antiques).

collectible *See* COLLECTABLE.

collection 1. A season's range previewed at a fashion SHOW for the benefit of store buyers, press and potential clients; the principal collections are those shown in Milan, London, New York and Paris. A Spring Collection, for example, would be shown the previous autumn. For the fashion buyers it indicates the next season's COLOURS and STYLES.
2. Any range of merchandise manufactured or arranged to show general facets (e.g. a collection of sportswear).

collection system 1. Means by which goods are picked up after purchase particularly in retail situations where goods are delivered to customers other than at the point of ordering (e.g. at a parking area for collection by car).
2. A system by which outstanding debts are gathered. Systems often work by increasingly strongly worded letters being sent to slow payers, finally culminating in the institution of legal proceedings for the recovery of the debt.

collective bargaining The process whereby wages, hours and working conditions and practices are freely negotiated by representatives of companies and employees (often represented by trade unions) on a formal and regular basis.

collective mark An identification mark synonymous with a trade name or product group.

colour (USA: color) A stimulus used in retailing particularly in VISUAL MERCHANDISING, display, packaging and store design, to create specific moods, ATMOSPHERES and positive selling responses. Overuse of a particular colour believed to have certain positive effects (e.g. red is vibrant, exciting, warm) can result in adverse effects (e.g. red is overheated, oppressive, dangerous).

colour supplement A magazine, given (almost) free with newspapers, usually weekend editions, often carrying extensive advertising associated with the chief editorial content, especially fashion, personal care and home products.

co-makership A form of relationship between retail buyers and suppliers, through which they work together to achieve the common goal, providing quality products for the final consumer. Traditionally retail buyers and suppliers have been renowned for their adversarial relationship, constantly negotiating for short term advantages over each other (e.g. better margins). In negotiation terms this would create a win-lose situation. Co-makership is based on the principle that in the long term each party can gain more benefits by co-operation. A win-win situation would be created. Some characteristics of a co-makership relationship would be open exchange of information and detailed understanding of both the buyers' and the suppliers' situation and bargaining limits.

combination store (USA) A retail outlet which mixes a drugstore and a SUPERMARKET, or a drugstore and a DISCOUNT STORE.

commercial Advertisement appearing in broadcast media.

commission 1. Payment for selling merchandise usually based on a percentage of total sales. Its function is to provide sales staff with an incentive to sell more goods than they might otherwise do, or when goods have to be 'demonstrated' in terms of benefits or UNIQUE SELLING PROPOSITIONS.
2. A payment for AGENTS etc., based on an agreed procedure for calculation related to total sales.

commission house A business organization which takes delivery of goods, but not title over them, and then resells on behalf of principals in return for a fee related to sales value achieved. *See also* AGENT.

commitment A promise or pledge to follow a certain course of action. A retail organization might state in its MISSION statement that it is committed to providing a high standard of service for its customers.

committee buying A process where the responsibility for purchasing is divided up among various individuals within an organization. This reduces the autonomy of an individual buyer. One of the stated benefits of committee buying is the application of a wide range of expertise to the purchase decision-making process. Individuals commonly included in a buying committee are technologists and quality controllers as well as buyers and merchandisers.

commodity A physical GOOD, usually a basic agricultural or mining product (e.g. coffee, tea, oil).

commodity exchange An organized market for the buying and selling of primary products.

common carrier A for-hire transportation contractor who offers to serve the general public without discrimination.

Common Market Popular term for the European (Economic) Community.

communication The process of transferring information or data from one point to another. Communication is said to have occurred when the meaning inherent in the data (or transparent in the information) so transferred is comprehended by the receiver. *See also* COMMUNICATION MODEL.

communication channel *See* COMMUNICATION MODEL.

communication model The most basic version of a communication model consists of a *transmitter* (the point of origination of the communication), a *channel* along which the message is to pass, the message itself, and a *receiver*. The transmitter is the originating source for the message. The process of origination is seen to consist of a decision as to what to transmit, a process of encoding into a form suitable for transmission, the selection of an appropriate channel (e.g. memorandum, television or newspaper) and the transmission of the message in the direction of the intended receiver. The receiver (the point at which the message is received) is seen to go through an analogous process: that is of decoding and interpretation to discover meaning. This simple model can be considerably extended to include other factors such as selective reception, noise and interference and multiple channels. The field of communication

has in itself given rise to an area of academic activity and managerial activity in marketing.

communication skills That set of abilities possessed by individuals enabling them to engage successfully in the efficient and effective transmission and reception of messages. These skills involve a wide number of facets, but at the level of the interpersonal are seen to comprise the skills of listening, reading, writing clearly and appropriately for the intended audience, and the ability to present orally, whether in conversation or on a wider scale, in a way such that the intended message is successfully conveyed to the audience.

Community legislation Under article 189 of the Treaty of Rome, the Council and the Commission of the European Community can make regulations, issue directives, take decisions, make recommendations and deliver opinions. Regulations have general application and are directly applicable to all member states. They do not have to be confirmed by national parliaments in order to have a binding legal effect. If there is a conflict between a regulation and existing national law, the regulation prevails. Directives are binding in member states as the result to be achieved within a stated period, but leave the method of implementation to national governments. Decisions are binding in their entirety on those to whom they are addressed, whether member states, companies or individuals. Decisions imposing financial obligations are enforceable in national courts. Recommendations and opinions have no binding force but merely state the views of the institution that issues them.

community radio A broadcast station catering for a local population, usually offering a combination of music, local news and interest items.

company A continuing association of individuals formed for the purposes of carrying out defined types of business activity. The regulation and control of such business organizations has given rise to a wide number of types and forms in different legal jurisdictions.

company mission *See* MISSION.

comparative marketing The study of business transactions which attempts to contrast form, nature and conduct of such transactions in differing kinds of trading environments. The term is often taken to describe different national markets and thus to include an element of cultural comparison.

comparative pricing 1. The use of promotional labels, such as '20% price reduction' or '30% off'. Such usage of comparative pricing by retailers is subject to legislation of various forms in different markets.
  2. Sometimes a synonym for market-ruling or going-rate pricing.

comparison advertising A form of paid-for insertions under clear sponsorship in mass MEDIA in which the properties or price of an organization's products are contrasted with those of a competitor or competitors.

comparison shopping The visits, by consumers, to generic retail outlets for the express purpose of contrasting prices, style and quality of goods before purchase. The particular goods that are compared are ones that are offered in various stores with only minor variations in price, style and quality (e.g. clothing and footwear stores). *See also* BUYER BEHAVIOUR.

competence The ability to perform the activities within an occupational area to the levels of performance expected in employment.

competition 1. A fundamental economic process whereby suppliers/sellers in a market seek to secure an increased number of buyers over their rivals, through offering additional benefits or utility (e.g. lower prices, quicker delivery). Perfect competition is a theoretical situation where (broadly) all the products offered by sellers are identical, all relevant information is simultaneously available to all market participants, and there are no barriers to entry or exit from the market. In such a market, price is the only means of competition. In the imperfect markets, in fact, competition is conducted through the control of all the MARKETING MIX elements of an organization.
  2. A form of SALES PROMOTION (mounted by manufacturers, retailers etc., either singly or jointly) where consumers, through a qualifying purchase are able to exercise skill or judgement in the playing of a game, answering a quiz etc. in order to seek prizes for correct entries. The permitted form of such promotions is often controlled by various legal and other requirements.

competitive advantage The ability of a business organization to perform more effectively and/or efficiently in a given market situation than its rivals on a basis which is not readily exploitable by such rivals. It grows out of a sound understanding of the market place coupled with the exploitation of the firm's 'distinctive competences' (i.e. the skills, expertise and resources unique to that firm). In a retailing context, it may be developed by seeking specific merchandise requirements and/or customer service needs appropriate to the target customer group.

Competitive advantage may be built in a wide variety of platforms in retailing (e.g. low operating costs, trading format, customer services, merchandise range, careful customer targeting, customer communications etc.).

competitive analysis The examination of the nature of other participants within a given market or industry, based on the forces such as the bargaining power of suppliers, or the ease with which new companies can enter the market, which are believed to determine the conduct of business in that market.

competitive pricing See GOING-RATE PRICING, KNOWN-VALUE ITEM.

competitive strategy The determination of how a business is to conduct itself in rivalry with other market players.

Strategy formulation takes place at many levels within a business, including strategies for the business as a whole (or group of businesses), operating units within the business or functional areas such as marketing, personnel or finance. Whatever the level, strategy is about ends and means – the goals for which the company is striving and the policies by which it is seeking to achieve them.

What distinguishes competitive strategy from other types of strategy is its emphasis on how to compete in a given market. In order to formulate a competitive strategy, a thorough understanding of the market, CONSUMER BEHAVIOUR and attitudes, the forces driving competition, the nature of competitors and competitive responses are all required.

competitor awareness The state arising from the purposeful consideration and evaluation of the observable characteristics of rivals in a market and possible market entrants.

complementary product A good or service whose UTILITY is contingent upon, or is enhanced by, possession, use etc. of another good or service (e.g. gasoline, motor car).

completely knocked-down (CKD) An item sold to the purchaser in a form which requires the assembly of the product after purchase. This form of sale is particularly common with furniture and other bulky items and is used to keep down transportation costs, and provide for smaller packages for more convenient delivery.

computer-aided design (CAD) The process of utilizing electronic processing machines to speed up or optimize the process of planning or styling a production method or manufactured article. Such applications are particularly useful where the design structure is capable of being determined optimally (e.g. as with bridges or electronic circuit layout). The process can also be used to provide optimal design for the fixturing of a store.

computed-aided manufacture (CAM)

The use of electronic processing machines to optimize the production either of individual components or the overall organization of the flow of work in the process itself. The term is sometimes restricted to aspects of automation, and the wider-ranging usage is described then as 'computer-integrated manufacturing'.

computer mapping The visual representation of, for example, customers within a particular geographical or residential area, usually using proprietary SOFTWARE for visual representation of spatial DATA, combined with the additional data set.

computerized re-ordering The application of electronic processing machines to the automatic repurchase of merchandise, when stocks fall to a predetermined level. The technique is customarily used in conjunction with computerized stock control systems generally. The system maintains, in its memory, records of current stocks and is provided with 'floor levels', which when reached, cause orders for replacement stocks to be automatically generated.

concentrated marketing strategy The application of a firm's resources to the development of only a narrow segment from among all potential purchasers of a product.

concentration ratio A measure of the extent to which a number of firms dominate sales in a specific industry or industry sector. It is often calculated by taking the total sales of the four largest firms and expressing that figure as a percentage of the total industry (or sector) sales. The higher the ratio, the greater the degree of concentration.

concentric zone theory An explanation of patterns of land use within a city on the basis of the differing ability of uses (e.g. retailing, industry, housing) to pay rent at particular sites. Under idealized conditions, with movement equally easy in all directions, a concentric pattern of land use develops with retailing at the centre, and then office, industrial and residential uses following in zones out from the centre.

concept 1. An idea in mind that enables 'X' to be distinguished from 'not X'.
2. A word loosely used to mean 'idea', especially in marketing (e.g. a 'new concept store' may be one painted a different colour).

concession A 'shop-within-shop' retailer operating an outlet located within another retailer's store. There may or may not be a link, through ownership, between the concession and the host store. Staffing is usually undertaken by CONCESSIONAIRES but some relief overlap is necessary from the host store, particularly in the case of perfume counters. Rents for a concession are usually calculated as a percentage of turnover and relate to the position within the host store and the size of the concession. Host stores tend to be DEPARTMENT STORES.

concessionaire One who rents an area within a larger store in order to trade under a distinct identity. Typically found in the DEPARTMENT STORE, the concessionaire enhances the attractiveness of the overall store franchise and earns more returns in rental per square foot than the host store itself could earn in the short term.

conditions of contract Those specific

requirements within a legal agreement to perform some act or provide some service, which are determined by the parties at the time the agreement is struck (e.g. delivery dates, payment terms).

confectionery, tobacconist, newsagent (CTN) A type of outlet (defined by the products offered), which is particularly prevalent in the UK. Known as newsagents or CTNs, they represent a large sector for independent operators, with only two major chains. Independents have tended to develop into a form of CONVENIENCE STORE, with a limited grocery offer, while chain operators stress books, music products, toys etc.

confidence level The expression of the degree of statistical reliability in the estimate of a POPULATION characteristic. Population characteristics of interest to a retailer, such as 'the mean expenditure per superstore customer' (an example of a population mean), or 'the proportion of males, under 21, who purchase at least one suit per year' (an example of a population proportion), often have to be estimated using information derived from RANDOM SAMPLING from that population. Rather than presenting the estimate as a single figure (e.g. 'The mean expenditure per superstore customer is £23.25') it is advisable to provide an interval estimate at an acceptable confidence level (e.g. 'The mean expenditure per Superstore customer is between £21.80 and £24.70, with 99 per cent confidence'). Such a confidence interval recognizes, and allows for, the potential sampling error and level of uncertainty, which is inherent in the sampling process.

Assuming that the sample size is large, 99 per cent confidence intervals for a population mean, and for a population proportion, can be calculated using the following formulae:

Estimate of population mean

$$= \bar{x} + \frac{2.58\, s}{\sqrt{n}}$$

where n = the sample size
$\bar{x}$ = the sample mean
s = the sample standard deviation

Estimates of the proportion in the population possessing a specified attribute

$$= p \pm 2.58 \sqrt{\frac{p\,(1-p)}{n}}$$

where n = the sample size
p = proportion in the sample possessing the attribute.

For confidence levels of 90 per cent, 95 per cent or 98 per cent, the multiplying factor of 2.58, should be replaced by 1.65, 1.96 or 2.33 respectively.

conglomerate A business firm, often with many subsidiaries, that operates in a wide number of different markets, these markets having no particular thematic relationship to one another.

conglomerchant A centrally owned retail organization dealing in many product lines.

consignee The outlet or individual to whom goods, monies or documents are sent, transferred or entrusted.

consignment The item or items sent together in a single delivery to a specific outlet or individual.

consignment note The document accompanying goods, giving specific details about numbers, sizes, or other appropriate data.

consignor The individual or company responsible for the dispatch of goods.

consolidated buying The process whereby several organizations join together to purchase goods. Individuals within the group benefit from strengthened purchasing power and buying procedure 25.

consolidated delivery A system of grouping together merchandise from different suppliers as part of the same CONSIGNMENT, usually at a central warehouse etc.

consolidation The process of making stronger or more stable.

consonance The psychological state arising from the post-purchase feelings of a consumer matching prior expectations. The concept is most often used in connection with the idea of post-purchase DISSONANCE.

consumer The individual who ultimately uses and benefits from a good or service; that individual could also be called the user of the good or service. The consumer is not necessarily the BUYER of a product, as for example in the case of mothers' purchases for children. However, the consumer in this latter case retains considerable influence over the buying decision and is the direct target of marketers and retailers. Often the term is used to distinguish domestic users from industrial or commercial ones (e.g. the consumer market for cars).

consumer advertising Persuasive marketing mass communication which is directed at domestic users and purchasers, as opposed to intermediate trade or industrial customers. *See also* ADVERTISING.

consumer behaviour Often defined as the decision process and physical activity which individuals and groups (decision making units) engage in when evaluating, acquiring, using and disposing of goods and services. It may be engaged in by CONSUMERS acting on their own behalf or on behalf of others. It therefore covers the entire process of decision- making, buying and consuming, irrespective of who is involved.

There are no precise limits to consumer behaviour as an object of study, and some have argued that the three chief phases of consumption are obtaining, consuming and conserving. The study thus needs to relate all these phases of the process to the way in which 'decision-making units' conduct themselves, which may require a perspective other than the decision-oriented one. *See also* BUYER BEHAVIOUR.

consumer boom A period of rapid growth of household expenditure, resulting from a rise in real income, changes in fiscal policy, or a fall in the savings rate etc.

consumer co-operative A retail organization owned chiefly by the people who shop there.

Consumer Credit Act 1974 (UK) The main source of law governing modern credit procedures in retailing. It makes it an offence for retailers to carry on a consumer credit business without the appropriate credit licence. The law also states that even after having signed a credit agreement the consumer is allowed a 'cooling-off' period of five days to change his or her mind and cancel the arrangement.

Consumer Credit (Advertisements) Regulations 1980 (UK) Legislation governing the content and presentation of offers of household finance through mass media.

consumer debt The total amount of monies owed by households in any society, comprised of mortgages, consumer credit and other loans.

consumer durable A household good which is not consumed in, or by, a single or limited number of uses.

Consumer durables are usually 'shopping goods' bought after comparison of price, specification and availability. They usually have a low emotional attachment for the consumer, as they are bought principally for function (e.g. fridges, freezers, washing machines). This may not be the case, however, for personal consumer items like hi-fi, cameras and particularly cars, whose advertising appeal tends to be dominated by emotional content.

Consumer durables such as fridges are closely linked to demographic trends as once market saturation is reached, they require replacement demand only. Consumer durable retailers suffer greater cyclical fluctuations than food retailers as interest rates and recession force consumers to delay replacement or upgrading a particular durable.

consumer franchise The situation that arises in markets when a supplier's product has achieved a high level, both of acceptance and of loyalty, among target consumers, to the extent that, for a significant number at least, the BRAND or supplier represents the only one within the category that such consumers will consider.

consumer good A tangible product which is used by an individual or household, or from which an individual or household may benefit. The category is determined by the nature of the consumer, not the good itself. A typewriter, if bought for domestic use, is a consumer good, but when bought by a business for use within the firm, is not – it is then often categorized as an industrial good. A subset of consumer goods are FMCGs (fast-moving consumer goods), which are items such as confectionery and grocery products where the consumption cycle is short and repeat purchase frequent. Such fast-moving goods are often seen as the archetypal products for the application of MARKETING principles.

consumer legislation Civil or criminal laws which are designed to grant certain rights to both buyers and sellers of products: protecting the interests of the buyer and placing obligations upon both buyers and sellers. Civil law grants remedies to the buyer (i.e. compensation or damages); criminal law imposes sanctions upon the seller (i.e. fine or imprisonment).

In the UK the TRADE DESCRIPTIONS ACT 1972 is a major item of criminal law affecting retail organizations, whereas the SALE OF GOODS ACT 1979 is an important statute of civil law. *See also* CONSUMER PROTECTION ACT 1987.

consumer marketing The study and/ or management of the processes of mutually beneficial exchanges undertaken in an economic context between organizations and individuals buying on behalf of themselves or their households. Retailers are mostly consumer marketers, whereas branded goods manufacturers, who sell to and through retail outlets, are involved in both consumer and TRADE MARKETING.

consumer motivation The internal psychological stimulus which activates behaviour, and influences its duration and direction.

consumer panel A group of people involved in the buying process at the domestic level, who are used to monitor, for example, behaviour or attitudes over a period of time. The same sample of respondents is retained over the full period of measurement and used to obtain a continuous and complete record of the data required.

Panels are not easy to operate. Recruiting and maintaining a panel is expensive and time-consuming, but for some purposes the advantages more than outweigh the drawbacks. A larger amount of data can be obtained from a panel than from a series of one-off surveys, and the depth of analysis possible from the continuous stream of data provides a powerful method of understanding behaviour.

There are a variety of useful consumer panels in operation in the many markets. For example, the Television Consumer Audit, operated by Audits of Great Britain, monitors consumer purchases for many grocery product fields. Also in operation are panels covering toiletries and cosmetics, baby goods, motoring products, household durables and financial services.

Another well known use of the panel technique is the monitoring and reporting of television viewing, radio listening and readership of newspapers and magazines. Most panels are operated on a syndicated basis; that is, data can be purchased on subscription from the market research companies offering the service, yielding substantial cost savings compared with each client company running its own panel. However, panels are also run on a short-term basis to address particular problems faced by one company only.

The importance of consumer panels is likely to grow as technology develops. For example, with the growth of EFTPOS, consumer purchasing behaviour may be cross- referenced with media habits, lifestyle, socio-economic status and secondary data.

consumer profile A description of the type, nature and salient characteristics of a group of people who buy for themselves or a household. The detailed contents of the profile will vary, but in retailing may include information about buying habits, brand preferences, age, occupation and housing data etc.

Consumer Protection Act 1987 (UK) Legislation which makes it a criminal offence to give consumers a misleading price indication about goods, services, accommodation (including the sale of new homes) or facilities.

consumer research The systematic identification, collection, reduction and analysis of data on the behaviour of individuals, and the factors that underpin the behaviour. It forms an important input into the development of marketing strategies and tactics.

consumer sovereignty A fundamental tenet which is reflected in most definitions of marketing, where the centrality of customer needs, desires or wants in driving the whole marketing process forward is emphasized. It implies that manufacturers and retailers should satisfy customer requirements rather than offering what they see fit and is best reflected in the aphorism: 'The customer is king.' *See also* MARKETING CONCEPT, CUSTOMER ORIENTATION.

consumer survey A market research instrument which is used to collect data relating to household attitudes, interests and opinions about goods, services or issues. Such data are relevant to organizations in developing their market strategy and the mode of its implementation. The instrument may be administered in different forms: by telephone, in person or by mail. Each method has distinct advantages and disadvantages, and can be used either independently or in combination. Instruments often contain a mix of open-ended and closed (predetermined response) questions, depending on the nature of the data required.

consumer taste The positive or negative disposition of a relevant group of household purchasers towards CONSUMER GOODS and/or services.

consumerism Activities which focus society's attention on the way in which organizations match corporate capabilities to consumer demand. In countries such as the UK and USA it has taken the form of a social movement of individuals and government agencies which aims to enhance the rights of buyers vis-à-vis sellers, particularly by promoting the consumer's right to safety, to be properly informed about the choices available, to have a choice, to have their opinions taken into account, to enjoy a clean and healthy environment, and to safeguard the interests of the poor and minority groups.

consumption The end of all production. The utilization of resources by any organism or organization to sustain its continuance and/or development.

container A receptacle, especially those large rectangular, metal, refillable boxes into which are placed goods to be shipped. The goods themselves are not rehandled in shipment until they are unloaded at their destination, since the container can be transferred from one mode of transport to another. There are a range of internationally agreed standards covering the sizes, weights, disposition of doors etc. of such containers.

containerization *See* UNITIZATION.

content description The indication on the exterior PACKAGING, particularly of foodstuffs, toiletries, medicines etc. of the breakdown of the individual components of the product, including all ingredients and ADDITIVES. The precise form, nature and extent of the description may be regulated by law in various jurisdictions.

content theories Explanatory models of workplace motivation which assume that all individuals possess the same set of basic needs and which also focus upon those factors believed to make employees perform their jobs effectively and efficiently. Maslow, Alderfer, Herzberg and McClelland have produced the best known examples of such theories.

contest A method of SALES PRO-MOTION in which customers are given the opportunity to win a prize through skill or chance. In the USA contests which are judged to be lotteries may be illegal. *See also* COMPETITION.

contingent liability Possible financial consequences arising from some earlier contractual arrangement, action, or failure to take required action, associated with more general legal requirements. (E.g. a retailer may have contingent liability for injuries caused to a third party because of defects in goods sold by them to a second party.)

contraband Smuggled goods.

contract A legally enforceable agreement between two or more parties to provide goods, services, actions etc. in exchange for valued consideration. The terms of the agreement may be written or oral.

contract carrier A transport undertaking offering vehicles for hire to one shipper, or a limited number of shippers, under specific contract with those shippers, rather than with the general public.

contract distribution *See* THIRD-PARTY DISTRIBUTION.

contract purchasing A system for the

acquisition of goods and services whereby an agreement is made to purchase specified amounts of product(s) at predetermined times. Such an agreement may ensure maintained levels of supply and outputs from manufacturers, thus avoiding capacity problems associated with seasonality, and other time-dependent factors.

contractual vertical marketing system The SUPPLY CHAIN through which goods pass on their way to the CONSUMER, defined in terms of the organizations which take title to the goods. *See also* PHYSICAL VERTICAL MARKETING SYSTEM.

contribution A measure of the excess of income derived from the sale of any unit of output which is available to defray the fixed and overhead costs of the producing organization, and remain as a residual profit. It is used in the context of BREAK-EVEN ANALYSIS. The contribution made by each unit sold can be calculated by using the formula: Unit Contribution = Selling Price/Unit − VARIABLE COST/Unit. At low sales volumes the unit contribution goes towards paying the company's FIXED COST. Once the break-even point has been reached, the contribution from any additional units sold is profit.

control To determine the outcome of the interplay of situational forces. The process of exercising control confers the power to plan, direct, supervise and monitor an activity, and to have influence over the outcome. *See also* BUDGETARY CONTROL.

control account A summary of the total debit and credit entries in an organization's records of transactions.

controllable costs Those expenses of an organization which can be influenced by management action. In a system of 'responsibility accounting' individual managers take charge of these expenses within the area of their authority.

controlled circulation Newspapers, magazines etc. which are delivered direct (usually by mail) to readers who meet specified criteria, and which are not available to a wider readership (e.g. Management Consultancy).

convenience food Edible products (particularly main dishes) designed, processed and manufactured in such a way as to make meal preparation straightforward and rapid in a domestic context.

convenience good An item of consumer merchandise purchased frequently and having a short consumption cycle (e.g. grocery item). Such items are seen as a distinct class of product because purchase may become habituated, and different from the prevailing decision process view of CONSUMER BEHAVIOUR.

convenience store A small shop which looks to satisfy immediate consumer needs for groceries, foods and other items of daily use. The concept of convenience is expressed in a number of ways. Stores have long trading hours (opening for typically 16 hours per day, seven days of the week), they have a clearly laid out self-service style to allow quick shopping and they carry a wide range of CONVENIENCE GOODS. The product range will normally be geared to meeting the everyday and impulse needs of the local population and might typically include fresh food and vegetables, frozen foods, confectionery, newspapers, books and small toys, toiletries, beers, wines and spirits, cigarettes and tobacco, small everyday household goods and fast food, as well as photographic printing, dry cleaning and video hire services. Location is important in that store operators look to be close to the central or focal point of a residential area and hence be convenient for pedestrian shoppers while at the same time offering adjacent car parking to attract passing motorists.

The concept of the convenience store originated in the USA. The Southland Corporation who trade as 7-Eleven and Quick Mary claim to have opened the first convenience store in 1927. Rapid development has only occurred since the 1960s in the USA and since 1970s and 1980s in Europe, South East Asia, South America and Australasia.

co-operative advertising A form of joint paid-for insertions in mass media between, for example, a manufacturer of branded goods and a retailer. Usually both the manufacturer's and retailer's names are featured and the costs shared.

co-operative advertising and promotion A form of persuasive marketing action in which different organizations involved in a distribution channel agree to work together to achieve specific common objectives involving various aspects of the promotional mix and, in many cases, to share the costs of such work. Such joint collaboration is more extensive than that in CO-OPERATIVE ADVERTISING, and may involve the provision of special store FIXTURES, consumer CONTESTS etc.

co-operative buying Arrangement whereby various retail or manufacturing organizations act jointly in their purchasing activities. The major advantage accruing to participants in such an arrangement is the larger discounts that can be secured from suppliers for greater quantities ordered.

Co-operative Movement The modern Co-operative Movement started in 1844 with the opening of a store by the Rochdale Pioneers. Their basic principles of democratic control and the distribution of surplus profits to members have become enshrined in co-operative movements around the world. In the UK, Co-op Retail Societies account for about 5 per cent of retail turnover, and they have seen their share of trade decline over many years. The societies collectively own the Co-operative Wholesale Society (CWS) (*see* Appendix 3) which is the national trading and manufacturing organization.

Co-operatives form an important element of retail trade in some European countries, especially Switzerland (27 per cent of trade), Denmark and Finland (both 20 per cent of trade).

co-operative wholesaler A trading intermediary owned by an association of retailers or agents, who share out profits arising from the higher-level trade.

copy 1. The text of an advertisement. Copy is produced by copywriters working in co-operation with visua-

lizers to produce the final advertisement which also includes GRAPHICS.

2. A term used by journalists and other writers for material which is submitted to editors of newspapers, journals or magazines etc.

copyright Ownership or control of an original literary, musical or artistic work granted by law for a specified number of years. The law gives the owner the exclusive right to produce copies of the original work. *See also* INTELLECTUAL PROPERTY.

core activity Those elements of the operations of an organization that constitute the chief area of expertise within. In an organization having more than one basic line of business the phrase would be used to refer to the major line of business (e.g. Marks & Spencer's core activity is the retailing of textiles).

core operating system Within service providing organizations, the total technology (including 'soft' technology) used to provide the service product, particularly when such mechanisms for production are decoupled from the point of consumer contact (e.g. in a TRAVEL AGENT the airline reservation system forms part of the core operating system).

core product 1. The basic or original good or service in an extended line or family of goods and services, and from which the line has developed. It can prove difficult to drop a core product from a line, even if sales fall relative to other items, because of its symbolic value for customers. Kellogg's Cornflakes provide a good example of a core product.

2. That set of benefits seen as cen-

tral to consumer satisfaction in any particular consumption act, in distinction to secondary benefits that are also enjoyed (e.g. a fine theatrical performance, coupled with excellent customer facilities in the theatre).

corner The act, or result of, acquiring the entire stock of an item or commodity, available for sale on a market.

corner shop (UK) A local store, normally isolated from other retailers and situated in a residential area, supplying a limited range of food and basic household items.

corporate culture The pattern of typical ways of behaving or responding to recurring situations that are shared by employees or a dominant subgroup within an organization.

corporate identity Those operations, artefacts, procedures, and design elements used by an organization to distinguish itself from others in a uniform way over time.

corporate image The mental picture of an organization as perceived by its various publics. Elements which influence this are both tangible (e.g. logotype, letter heading, projected corporate designs on packaging, delivery vans and uniforms) and intangible (e.g. perceived public-spiritedness and environmental sensitivity).

corporate liability The indebtedness, responsibilities or actions required of an incorporated association by law.

corporate strategy The determining mechanism whereby an organization, or the controlling influence group within it, selects objectives, defines policies and articulates the means by which the organization is to pursue its goals. The subject of strategy has received considerable attention and yet there is no one view that has achieved pre-eminence, nor indeed agreement, on the meaning of many words associated with the subject, such as 'MISSION', 'goal', 'target', 'objective'. *See*, in particular, ANSOFF'S MATRIX, BOSTON CONSULTING GROUP SHARE/GROWTH MATRIX, POSITIONING, IMAGE, CORPORATE IDENTITY, PORTER'S GENERIC STRATEGIES, SWOT ANALYSIS.

correlation *See* COEFFICIENT OF CORRELATION.

cost The amount of resource, expressed as a monetary value, used to acquire goods and services necessary to the running of a (retail) organization. Costs are often classified as FIXED COSTS, VARIABLE COSTS and SEMI-VARIABLE COSTS, depending on the extent to which the retailer can exert CONTROL over them in the short term.

cost accounting Also known as management accounting, it is the branch of the construction and use of records of income and expenditure which studies internal systems used to relate revenue expenditure to activities, departments or products, with the aim to control expenditure and to increase profits (*see* ABSORPTION COSTING, COSTING SYSTEMS, DIRECT PRODUCT PROFITABILITY). The ability to achieve this aim depends on the degree to which the costing system enables the various internal departments and functions to co-operate, and the ability of management to determine appropriate measures of company performance.

cost/benefit analysis The attempt to quantify (usually in monetary terms) the ratio of resource usage in an action to the rewards obtained from the action. The subject has given rise to a specialist area within economics, and the analysis, because of its complexity, may often only be undertaken for major projects involving large expenditures (e.g. the studies of the third London airport).

The term is sometimes used informally to indicate the managerial consideration of expenditure and reward in an organizational context.

cost centre A unit of activity for which a number of expenditure items can be identified directly and to which other overheads can be apportioned in a logical manner in order to exert BUDGETARY CONTROL. In a retailing organization, cost centres can be departments, counters, or even product lines.

cost code A brief description of a specific expenditure heading in the form of a cypher, often using a numerical system. Examples of such headings are departments, or different types of labour. Cost codes are used to allocate COSTS to COST CENTRES.

cost control The application of the following steps within the BUDGETING process: (i) comparison of actual results to the PLAN through VARIANCE ANALYSIS; (ii) identification of the line managers responsible through a system of 'responsibility accounting'; (iii) investigation of reasons behind the variances; (iv) implementation of corrective measures where possible.

cost-effectiveness An analysis of the possibility of any particular current expenditure resulting in a future increase in income, profitability etc. or a future decrease in anticipated expenditure sufficiently great to exceed the current expenditure.

cost insurance freight (CIF) A method of pricing goods such that the price to be paid includes the expenditures incurred in transportation and associated costs to a port in the country of the purchaser.

cost measurement The accurate identification of levels of expenditure on specified goods, services etc. used in the production process. In theory, where the costs of retail operations can be assessed and related to the goods sold or services provided, this enhances the quality of decision-making. In practice, the cost of DATA CAPTURE and processing can be prohibitive, and it is often more practical for decision-making purposes to use standard costs based on historical data rather than actual costs. These standards can then be used as a yardstick to judge actual expenditure. This principle has been used in the development of DIRECT PRODUCT PROFITABILITY, where industry-wide standards are used.

cost method of inventory valuation The use of historic purchase price as the basis for valuation of stocks.

cost of goods sold (COGS) The value of opening stocks (inventory on hand at the beginning of an accounting period), plus the value of purchased goods in the period, less the value of goods on hand at the end of the period (closing stock).

cost-plus A method of pricing where

the price charged for a product is based on the total expenditure incurred in producing or purchasing the item to which a MARGIN is added.

In retailing organizations, the application of the cost-plus method of pricing means that the selling price is directly related to the purchase price by adding the MARKUP.

cost-plus pricing *See* COST-PLUS.

cost/volume/profit *See* BREAK-EVEN ANALYSIS.

costing system A process for the provision of management information as to how various types of expenditure of retail operations are related to the goods sold and services provided. The establishment of a costing system allows management to more effectively: make pricing decisions; identify profitable and fast-moving product lines and plan space allocation and promotions accordingly; identify and deal with problem areas; predict future costs and revenues, and control costs through a system of BUDGETING; involve line management in COST CONTROL through a system of responsibility accounting; use forecasts of future costs and revenues associated with a capital investment project as the basis for decision-making.

Traditionally, many retailers have tended to have very sophisticated costing systems, largely based on margin. With the advent of information technology retailers were capable of generating sufficient data to switch to 'direct product costing' (DPC). (*See* DIRECT PRODUCT PROFITABILITY.) Developed in co-operation with manufacturers, DPC is based on a similar rationale as the ABSORPTION

COSTING systems traditionally used by manufacturing organizations.

counselling A communication process seeking to identify and discuss areas of technical or emotional difficulty, diagnosing needs and enabling the respondent to assess an appropriate constructive mode of behaviour or course of action.

counter A raised table, possibly used for the display of merchandise, but mainly used as a platform for the exchange of goods for money. Counter service, with merchandise and customers segregated by the table predominated in British retailing until the 1950s, when self-service outlets began to appear and the CHECKOUT replaced the counter in its traditional role.

counter cache device An in-store retail cash collection system which protects cash at the point of sale by providing a safety deposit box for the sales assistant and at the same time allows a more convenient method of secure cash collection from the till.

counter service A system where customers indicate their requirements for merchandise, which is then selected by a sales assistant (counter clerk). The transaction is then concluded over the COUNTER. *Compare* SELF-SERVICE.

countlines One of a variety of filled bars which dominate (accounting for 50 per cent of sales) in the chocolate confectionary market. The best known brands are products such as Mars bars and Kit-Kat. They outsell solid chocolate bars approximately 4:1. The successful countline is a heavily advertised product with distribution as widespread as possible (e.g. in CTNs, garages, convenience stores, supermarkets, sandwich bars). They are low-value consumer non-durables bought individually for personal consumption with little thought or planning. Where a count-line is out of stock, the consumer will often switch brands rather than try elsewhere to obtain the out-of-stock line.

coupon 1. A paper certificate, usually of small size (up to 3 inches by 6 inches), having a notional monetary value in respect of the purchase of (particularly) fast-moving consumer goods. Coupons are used as a sales promotion device to encourage consumers to try a new product or to buy more of an existing product. They may be printed separately or may form part of a label, packaging or an advertisement. Coupons may offer money off the next purchase. They are returned to the supplier and may form an important input into customer data bases.

2. *See* REDEMPTION.

coupon clearing house An intermediary who collects and credits retailers with the value of redeemed sales promotion COUPONS. It charges fees to the originators of sales promotions for collecting small batches together and processing them.

couponing 1. A form of sales promotion whereby money-off certificates, tokens etc. are delivered directly to houses in a given area, usually defined by postal district and/or ACORN category. This is usually undertaken by specialized delivery companies. It is used to encourage trial of new

products and repeat purchase of mature products. *See also* SALES PROMOTION.

2. More generally, any form of SALES PROMOTION using COUPONS.

courtesy period A period of time, in addition to that granted by the terms of a sale, whereby a customer can still use credit for purchases without having settled the account.

coverage A measure of the relative proportion of people in the target audience within a chosen universe that will be reached by a particular media vehicle in a specific promotional campaign.

creative That part of an organization, especially an advertising agency, responsible for the origination of ideas, COPY and GRAPHICS, for promotional campaigns and individual advertisements.

creative selling Achieving a purchase by a customer in a situation where the customer wants a product, but is prevented from being able to buy by some impediment. For example, if a customer cannot buy a new product because of an existing stock of old products, a creative sell would be to arrange disposal of the unwanted stock elsewhere to enable the sale of new merchandise to go ahead. Alternatively, if finance is a barrier to an immediate sale, leasing, deferred payment or partial credit can ease customer worries and help the sale. *See also* SELL.

credit 1. The indication of a lender of its willingness to allow a borrower to purchase goods or services up to a prespecified limit while deferring payment (e.g. a credit account for £1,000 has been opened).

2. To advance a sum of money to a borrower on the basis of deferred repayment, usually with the addition of interest (e.g. 'We will credit you with a sum of £2,000 to be repaid in instalments.').

3. Non-cash transactions (e.g. 'Will this be cash or credit?').

4. An ACCOUNT entry representing a BALANCE SHEET liability or revenue in the TRADING ACCOUNTS.

credit card A means of payment using a small, standardized rectangular piece of plastic bearing identification and an account number. The card signifies to participating retailers that an individual has an instant line of purchase credit up to a preset limit agreed with the issuer. A credit card is not to be confused with CHARGE CARD (for which a monthly bill is issued for full and complete payment of debt and which stands in lieu of cash), nor with DEBIT CARD (where the card stands in lieu of a cheque and transactions debit the holder's bank account directly at the point of sale).

Two group schemes dominate the credit card scene – Visa and Mastercard. The issuers have formed a wide network with mutual recognition of cards from all issuers within the respective schemes in outlets world-wide. Issuing organizations charge relatively high interest on outstanding monthly balances but do not charge for accounts cleared at the appropriate payment date. While such cards were often issued without an annual fee, many issuers have declared an intention to change to a system which involves charging an annual fee for usage, but offering lower interest rates on outstanding balances.

Retailers who offer credit card facilities to customers are charged a negotiable percentage discount on the value of sales, by the credit card companies. In the UK the credit card issuers have been spurred to greater competition by the recent change of government policy to allow premiums to be charged by retailers for credit card sales.

credit limit The agreed maximum amount of money to be outstanding from a customer or owed to a supplier at any given point in time.

credit note 1. A document stating that the customer's account has been adjusted by the amount due, which is issued when a customer has been overcharged or is entitled to a refund on goods returned.

2. A document issued to a customer, having a monetary value, which may be exchanged for goods or services at some unspecified future date. Such documents are usually issued to customers in respect of faulty merchandise or as a gesture of goodwill after the failure of a transaction to produce satisfaction.

credit purchase The acquisition of goods or services on account, with payment expected at some future time, either at the end of an accounting period, or in a series of staged multiple payments. Where payment is deferred to a series of multiple smaller amounts, a charge for the credit advanced is often levied.

Retail customers can obtain credit from store cards, from major CREDIT CARDS or from credit sale agreements (usually financed by an outside provider of funds). Retailers favour the tied store card because of high chargeable interest and because the customers loyalty can be maintained. *See* CREDIT SALES.

credit rating A system used to evaluate applicants seeking to borrow money from a financial institution etc. Such systems often involve, for individuals, the allocation of points to particular SOCIO-ECONOMIC CLASSIFICATIONS, geodemographic characteristics etc. (*See* CREDIT SCORING.) For institutions, credit rating is usually carried out by skilled analysts working for organizations such as Dun & Bradstreet, Moody's, Standard & Poor etc., using ANNUAL REPORTS etc.

credit sale The offer of goods or services to customers with a provision for payment to be deferred. Such an offer may be considered an important element in retail customer service, particularly for expensive CONSUMER DURABLE products. Retailers in those lines of trade are thus likely to offer several different mechanisms for customers to defer payment (e.g. through the acceptance of CREDIT CARDS, the provision of store cards, credit sale agreements etc.). Credit sales also form a major proportion of the sales of organizations serving the travel and hospitality markets, especially through the acceptance of CREDIT CARDS and CHARGE CARDS.

credit scoring The means of determining whether to offer deferred payment facilities to a customer, based on awarding points for various attributes of the customer (such as owning a house, type and length of employment) and totalling the points. A customer whose points score reaches the required level will be regarded as likely to pay the INSTALMENTS and will be offered the credit facilities.

credit transfer The paper or electronic switching of amounts of money between businesses or bank ACCOUNTS without the use of cash or cheques. The transfer of credit from one account to another provides a convenient method of payment for a business TRANSACTION.

credit union A mutual organization which offers small savings and loan facilities to its contributing members. Members usually share a common social background (e.g. through working for one large employer, or living in the same housing development). The organization collects regular weekly or monthly savings subscriptions from members which are invested at interest. From the subscriptions, members are able to take loans at a lower rate of interest than they might be able to obtain elsewhere. In various jurisdictions there is often specific legislation controlling (and fostering) the function of such organizations.

crime analysis An approach to the prevention of theft, fraud etc., recommended to retailers by the UK Home Office Crime Prevention Unit. It involves basing preventative measure on a precise analysis of the type, frequency and circumstances, of an offence and the sort of person who commits it. The benefits of the approach through crime analysis are seen as twofold: (i) it helps to identify cost-effective preventative measures which will reduce theft without jeopardizing profit margins; and (ii) it can bring management and security staff together to promote a greater mutual understanding of a shop's particular crime problem. The technique has been used effectively by many retail organizations in the UK.

cross-merchandising The visual presentation of two or more distinct product classes with the objective of creating a theme and thereby encouraging linked sales. (E.g. A holiday display may contain not only swimwear but also sunglasses, suntan lotion, towels, beach bags, garden furniture and glasswear.)

CTN *See* CONFECTIONARY, TOBACCONIST, NEWSAGENT.

cube effect in merchandising A display technique which uses FIXTURES which are more than seven feet tall.

cue An independent psychological condition to which specific responses are likely to be associated, evoking distinctive response tendencies.

culture That complex whole that includes knowledge, beliefs, art, morals, law, custom and any other capabilities and habits acquired by humans through learning as members of society. Culture refers to those unique patterns of behaviour and social relations that characterize a society and distinguish it from other societies.

cumulative quantity discount A reduction in the price payable to a supplier on condition that the purchases from the supplier exceed a certain minimum value over a given period of time.

currency market The arena for the sale and purchase of individual, national monies, which provides for large traders the mechanism for exchanging one national money for others (e.g. the sale of pounds sterling for US dollars and Deutschmarks). Such trading is required to facilitate the international flows of goods and services which have increasingly characterized world trade in the post-war era. The prices at which bargains are struck in these markets is known as the exchange rate. The exchange rate of a currency is (sometimes) subject to the management of a central bank, or group of central bankers acting in concert, or a particular currency may be left free to 'float', subject only to market forces. The factors (or forces) which affect exchange rates are many and complex, and subject to the influence of market sentiment. Forces acting in determining the exchange rate between currencies include domestic inflation and interest rates, market demand for a currency and available supply, terms of trade, purchasing power, market expectations etc.

current asset An item of value appearing on a BALANCE SHEET which will be turned into CASH within the next financial year or sooner. Current assets include stock, debtors, prepayments, the bank balance and cash.

current liability Those debts presently due for discharge, or where payment will be required within a short period.

curriculum vitae (CV) (USA = resumé) A career statement, usually typed or printed and prepared by an applicant, giving structured information about his or her name, age, address, education, qualifications, industrial experience, hobbies and interests, professional activities and names of referees.

curving traffic flow Another term for the design of displays and walkways in a FREE-FLOW PATTERN. *See also* GRIDIRON PATTERN.

customer The individual making a purchase from a retail store, catalogue, vending machine or other retail outlet. The customer may not be the CONSUMER. Many purchases are made jointly, for example a CONSUMER DURABLE may be bought by a male and female who together constitute a DECISION-MAKING UNIT for the purchase. The study of customer behaviour is normally referred to as CONSUMER BEHAVIOUR. *See also* CUSTOMER CARE.

customer care A label for services offered by retailers and, in particular, the level of service provided to patrons. *See also* CUSTOMER SERVICE.

Customer care can encompass the provision of 'hard' services, such as automatic telling machines in-store, as well as 'soft' services such as training in interpersonal skills for contact personnel. A retailer will often appraise its service(s) with customers to identify key service requirements and the standards that might be appropriate. For example, customers might be concerned about the time taken to shop and the retailer might respond by setting standards for sensitive areas such as the length of a checkout queue.

In the 1980s considerable emphasis was placed on staff/customer interactions. Many major retailers produced staff training videos in customer care identifying idealized responses to specific service situations; how to deal with irate customers for example. This 'If this happens, you do this' approach to customer care training has been criticized as missing the fundamentals of MOTIVATION to improving human relationships, and the need to ensure the employee feels confident about him- or herself and valued by the employer, before any real change in behaviour can be achieved. Many retailers have therefore sought to introduce organizational changes, such as improved benefits packages, simultaneously with customer care training.

A central issue in customer care is the ratio of employees to customers – a high level of delivered service often implies high labour costs. The long-term trend in retailing towards reductions in staffing levels seems to militate against any meaningful improvement in customer care. The UK retailer Texas, a DIY chain, deliberately increased its staffing levels in 1989 as part of an attempt to improve customer care. Whether this heralds a new era where, in effect, customers will be willing to pay more, or shop more, in a higher service store remains to be seen.

customer complaint The expression of consumer dissatisfaction through oral, non-verbal and written forms. Customer complaints require a trained and effective response by retail staff who identify the cause of complaint, and attempt to build a positive, supportive relationship. Evidence suggests that where a customer's complaint has been effectively handled by a retailer's staff, such customers will evaluate the retailer even more highly than those who have not had cause for complaint.

customer conversion That aspect of selling in which new purchasers are moved from being a prospect to being an active patron for the first time. Salespeople are frequently assessed on their customer conversion rates because such conversions constitute new business and the seeds of potential future growth. *See also* SELL.

customer flow The pattern and/or volume of potential purchasers (store/mall visitors) around a retail sales. area, or past a particular measuring point within or in the vicinity of a retail outlet.

The study of customer flow is in its infancy, despite its centrality to the design of retail facilities at the level of town centres, shopping malls or individual stores or units. The need to provide a 'logical' pathway through any retail facility is widely accepted, but consideration of current provision shows that this is not often done, either through the failure to address fundamental layout questions or indeed to understand the underlying bases of customer behaviour when using the facility. Much of the current belief about customer flow does not survive empirical scrutiny.

customer orientation The practice of focusing an organization's activities closely upon the needs, wants and desires of selected groups of potential consumers of the organization's potential products. In retailing such an orientation finds limited expression in the elaboration of service and fair trading policies, because of the perceived need of organizations to operate standardized, regimented operating systems.

customer profile The analysis by a company of its list of patrons for MARKET SEGMENTATION purposes. For consumer product companies this is usually analysed by demographic, socio-economic and behavioural data. For industrial/commercial product companies it is often analysed by size of order and geographical location.

customer service 1. The reason for the existence of a retail business.

2. The provision of facilities, activities, benefits, environments etc. by a retailer as an augmentation of the fundamental exchange relationship between merchandise supplied and money taken (CORE PRODUCT).

3. The perception held by a (potential) patron of the likely provision of facilities, activities, benefits, environments etc. by a retailer in support of the exchange relationship and its continuation, or a patron's experience of this 'total purchase package'.

4. The explicit provision by a retailer of: (i) post-purchase facilities for the alteration, customization, after-care etc. of products sold; (ii) a complaints handling procedure.

customer service level The perceived measure of the functional discharge of actions relating to the maintenance of mutually beneficial exchanges between an organization and its patrons, whether in the mind of patrons or in the operational planning of the organization (e.g. in defining queuing times – operational – or subjective evaluation of an interaction against prior expectation – customer).

cut-case display Items exposed for sale which have not been removed from the outer container, but where the latter has been so cut as to permit the removal of the individual items.

cut-price Items exposed for sale at a cost lower than normal in a particular, or competitors' outlets, or below the usual price recommended (or determined) by the supplier or manufacturer.

cut-throat competition The situation where the contest to secure customers in an industry is particularly intense (i.e. many firms offering homogenous goods and services to too few customers). Companies may be seen pursuing deliberately aggressive marketing policies to obtain a competitive advantage. *See also* PREDATORY PRICING.

cyclical Occurring at the same point in a regular pattern of variation over time (e.g. a cyclical buying pattern would exist where a retailer orders prespecified amounts of merchandise at Christmas and Easter in one year and repeats the ordering process at the same periods the next year).

D

data (*singular*: datum) Basic observations (measurements or impressions), often scaled, that need to be summarized, reduced and/or analysed to provide meaningful information.

data capture The process of identifying and seeking out meaningful observations which can be turned into management information to be used for planning, decision-making and control.

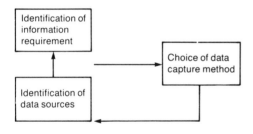

Data capture methods have increased greatly in variety and ease with the introduction of INFORMATION TECHNOLOGY, so that the emphasis can often lie on the careful processing of the data and evaluation of management information, rather than on the question of data capture.

The following are some examples of data capture methods within a retailing environment: direct observation (e.g. queue counts); market research (e.g. questionnaires, interviews, group discussions); buying-in information from a forecasting specialist; published information on industries, markets and consumers (e.g. Mintel and Keynote reports); trade press; industry averages (e.g. DIRECT PRODUCT PROFITABILITY data used in IGD model); EPOS data generated at the checkout; portable data capture units (e.g. to update stock information); TRADACOMS, EDIFACT (e.g. electronic data interchange between manufacturer and retailer via the public network); networks (i.e. electronic data interchange via a retailer- or manufacturer-owned private network).

data file A systematic, organized record, or set of records, containing basic observations on variables of interest to the record holder (e.g. personal or accounting records.) 'Data file' is the term used specifically for the electronically held versions of such sets of records on a computer-based information system.

data integrity The maintenance of computer files in such a way as to avoid corruption. Integrity can be jeopardized, for example, through such factors as human error, a lack of consistency between different files and applications, and lack of control over the output produced by personal computer users within organizations, especially where a variety of software packages is used.

data reduction A term coined by the consultant and lecturer A.S.C. Ehrenberg to describe the process of seeking patterns and relationships in numerical observations and collapsing them to summaries which can more readily be interpreted and communicated.

database A coherent set of computer files of basic observations or measurements. The structure of the data is independent of any particular application. The relationship between files can be along hierarchical, network or relational lines. Uses of databases in retailing include payroll, stock control and ordering.

database management software Specialized computer programs which have been developed to facilitate the manipulation of coherent sets of DATA FILES.

database management system (DBMS) A software program to access data stored in a computer file. In an organization, a department may only have access to that part of the of the database relevant to its work. The database management system ensures that data can be stored in such a way as to remain independent of applications.

database marketing An electronic information-based system, containing records of the basic observations and measurements relating to (potential) customers, that enables an organization to contact such individuals directly without the intervention of intermediaries. As such it is a form of DIRECT MARKETING in which the customer's name, address and demographic details are contained on a computer record. This database of customer information is then used for analysis and mailing purposes. Database marketing is growing strongly as a technique because of advances in computer technology.

date marking The process of printing, or otherwise applying the time of production or the desirable time for the use or consumption of a product in order to ensure consumer satisfaction as far as possible. Mechanisms for date marking are controlled by various pieces of legislation. *See also* SELL-BY DATE, USE-BY DATE.

dating The establishment of a time limit for when a retailer must pay for purchases.

deal 1. To buy and sell, especially by way of trade (e.g. 'She deals in antiques').
2. A special, promotional offer.
3. A BARGAIN, as in 'a good deal'.

dealer One who engages in buying and selling, especially by way of trade for a particular class of goods (e.g. car dealer).

debit card A means of payment by consumers for purchases from retailers whereby customers present a plastic, rectangular, identifying 'card' (issued by banks, building societies and finance houses), which, when used together with EFTPOS systems, transfers the amount owed by the customer to the retailer directly from the customer's current account

(USA: check account) to the retailer's account. No exchange of cash or cheques is required. However, some debit cards can also function as a cash card and as a cheque guarantee card.

debt Money owed. In retailing, debts arise in two main ways: (i) as the result of transactions by the retailer with suppliers (*trade debt*), and (ii) as a result of the retailer becoming the creditor of customers using CREDIT facilities (*consumer debt*). In most retailing organizations trade debt plays an important part in the financial structure of the business.

It is useful to differentiate between short-term and long-term debt. Short-term debt consists of any amounts payable within the next financial year. In the BALANCE SHEET these are found under the heading 'Creditors: due within one year'. Here such items as trade creditors and bank overdrafts are listed. For the smaller retailing organization there is often a tendency to rely very heavily on such short-term sources of finance. However, trade creditors, in particular, are also an important source of finance for large retailers operating in an oligopsonistic market (e.g. food retailers), who can exert a lot of buying power over their suppliers. The ability of a retailing organization to meet its short-term obligations is assessed through the use of LIQUIDITY RATIOS.

For many retailers long-term debt forms part of the long-term financing structure of the organization (*see* SOURCE OF FINANCE). The cost and availability of debt finance is related to the risk of non-repayment, which is linked to the volatility of the businesses' CASH FLOWS. The proportions

to which the company is financed through EQUITY on one hand and debt on the other is known as GEARING (*see also* LEVERAGE).

debt/income ratio The balance between an economic entity's liabilities (in money terms) to its monetary returns for a given period. In the domestic sector the ratio is used as a measure of household's ability to service/pay their debts.

decal Abbreviation for DECALCOMANIA.

decalcomania A transparent gelatinous film, containing an advertisement or product name, which can be fixed on a shop window.

decentralized buying A form of organization for the purchasing function in which the authority and responsibility for purchasing is vested in the operating units of the business, for example at store, area or regional level. This contrasts with CENTRAL BUYING, in which purchasing is controlled through a single, usually head office, department. Decentralized buying is more commonly experienced in sectors such as DEPARTMENT STORES.

decision-making unit (DMU) A group or network of departments or individuals involved in determining courses of action, either on a formal or informal basis, particularly in BUYING situations. *See also* BUYING CENTRE.

decision support system Computer-based methods which aid the management process in specific functional activities, and are designed for use by non-technical management. Examples of decision support systems in the retailing context include DIRECT PRODUCT PROFITABILITY models, SPACE ALLOCATION models and EXPERT SYSTEMS.

dedicated In PHYSICAL DISTRIBUTION, describing a facility operated by a THIRD PARTY on sole behalf of a specified client.

delegation The process of conferring a specific authority by a manager to his or her subordinate(s) in order that the subordinate(s) carry out certain tasks. This process has a dual 'responsibility', in that the subordinate is responsible for undertaking the task, while the manager is responsible for seeing that the task is completed.

delist The action of a retailer removing a particular line of merchandise from a supplier from its selection of items to be offered for sale.

delivery 1. The goods within any particular consignment of merchandise (e.g. a delivery of bedding).
2. The act of consigning goods to the consignee – the final component of a transportation process.

delivery date The day on which a consignment is due to arrive.

delivery note A piece of paper which specifies the content of a consignment and which is normally signed by the consignee to acknowledge receipt.

delivery order The actual instructions to consign or transfer goods, issued by a retailer to the party holding the goods.

delivery receipt The acknowledgement of the arrival of goods through the signature on the appropriate document by the party receiving the goods.

delivery scheduling The process of working out a programme or time-table for the transportation function, consignments etc.

delivery time The particular hour at which a consignment of goods is to be received by the consignee.

delivery window A period of time during which a buyer and seller agree that a consignment may be transferred to the buyer.

demographic Pertaining to the characteristics of a human population, or individual, including factors such as age, gender and SOCIOECONOMIC CLASSIFICATION. The term 'socio-demographic' is sometimes used when the emphasis is on attributes such as social class and lifestyles.

demographics Collectively DEMOGRAPHIC characteristics.

department 1. Any specialist sub-unit of a larger organization (e.g. marketing department).
2. Within mixed goods retailers, a coherent merchandise grouping viewed as part of the overall merchandise ASSORTMENT (e.g. a dairy department in a grocery store).
3. Any clearly identifiable subsection within a large retail outlet, especially DEPARTMENT STORES (e.g. a ladies fashion department).

department store A large retail shop operating on more than one floor that sells a wide variety of merchandise, including women's fashion, toiletries/ cosmetics, household goods etc. One of the features that often distinguishes a department store from other trading formats is the presence of CONCESSIONS.

depreciation The 'writing down' of the value of an asset after the time of the purchase to reflect the decreasing utility of the asset through usage.

The most popular method of calculating depreciation, used in a large number of business organizations is the Straight Line Method. Here the cost of the asset is spread over its life in equal parts, using the formula:

Annual depreciation =

$$\frac{Cost - Residual\ value}{No.\ of\ years\ expected\ life\ of\ the\ asset}$$

This method is easy to understand and use. It is most appropriate where the business is getting the same amount of use out of the asset in each accounting period (e.g. leasehold land).

Where the asset is most useful to the organization in the earlier years of its life, as is often the case with assets that are based on the latest technological developments and may become obsolete quickly, the Reducing Balance method is more appropriate. This method allocates a higher depreciation charge to the earlier accounting periods, using the formula:

Depreciation percentage rate =

$$\left[1 - n\sqrt{\frac{residual\ value}{cost}} \right] \times 100$$

where n = number of years expected life of the asset

depth That characteristic of ASSORT-

MENT that refers to the number of varieties of merchandise within a given category. *Compare* WIDTH.

descriptive statistic A single computed numerical value which represents some feature of a distribution of DATA. Where a limited number of statistics are computed in order to succinctly, but adequately, describe such a distribution, they would be termed 'descriptive statistics'.

For example, the age distribution of a retail group's credit card holders may be adequately described by giving some of the PERCENTILES of the distribution (e.g. median = 49 years; 10th percentile = 38 years; 90th percentile = 58 years). The example highlights the value of computing a limited number of appropriate descriptive statistics, as this allows some initial judgements to be made on key features of the group's current customer age range which may have been obscured in the raw age data.

descriptive statistics The collecting, organizing and presenting of DATA in summarized form in accordance with established principles. (The other branch of statistics – 'statistical inference' or 'inductive statistics' – is concerned with predictions or inferences about POPULATIONS based on SAMPLE data.)

The use of graphs or charts to summarize, for example, the sales of own-label wine by country of origin, or to present company annual reports, would be examples in the field of descriptive statistics, as would be the calculation of, say, a COEFFICIENT OF CORRELATION used to describe the relationship between sales of retail outlets and population density of CATCHMENT AREA.

de-skilling The substitution of mechanical, electrical etc. and procedural means in a production process to remove or reduce the necessity for the employment of individuals with particular capabilities.

desk research *See* SECONDARY DATA.

developer An organization or individual who identifies a demand for new floorspace and/or buildings, and organizes the resources – finance, land, labour, materials etc. to supply the demand. The completed 'development' may then be sold to a third party or kept and managed by the organization.

In the retail sector three main types of developer can be identified: (i) specialist companies who develop integrated, multi-tenanted shopping centres; (ii) retailers who develop their own free-standing stores, or smaller centres where their own store is the principal unit; (iii) local authorities/councils who may develop centres by themselves, or in partnership with specialist companies and/or retailers.

differentiation 1. The perception by the customer of distinctions between various goods, services, or brands competing in the same marketplace.

2. The deliberate attempt by a manufacturer, supplier, retailer etc. to induce, in the minds of potential customers, a psychological distinction of a desired kind between their product offering and those of competitors.

Differentiation is often therefore associated with image- building and is a central objective for the marketer of a branded good or service. Differentiation is also claimed by some to be the major objective of any business strategy. 'Being different because it pays to be so' became a widespread objective for retailers and product manufacturers alike. However, two issues became clear from research into the importance of differentiation. First, consumers require there to be substantial distances, based on appropriate measures, between products or retailers before they see them as different. Second, marketers often believe they have achieved a differentiated offer, only to find that the point of difference is not valued by the customer.

diffusion model A theoretical construct used to describe how a new product is adopted by society in a series of stages rather than by all at once. The best known model was first described by Everett Rogers in 1962 (*Diffusion of Innovations*, The Free Press). He proposed that a small minority of consumers (2.5 per cent) purchased a radically new product in its early days – the so called 'innovators'. However, the lifestyle of this group means that few other people get to hear of their experiences. Innovators tend, it seems, to be double-income couples without children, or young professional people with high disposable incomes but not well integrated into their local community. They like to try new things, but the fact that the innovators have adopted a new idea is no guarantee that the idea will catch on generally.

A second and larger group, the so-called 'EARLY ADOPTERS' (13.5 per cent) are similar in many ways to the innovators but are more integrated into the mainstream of society. Once they have taken the new idea on board it will probably succeed.

Early (34 per cent) late (34 per

cent) majorities then follow, showing characteristics typical of the population overall.

At the tail end of the diffusion process are the 'laggards' (16 per cent), less well-off, older and more conservative. The new idea has had to become an everyday product before they adopt it.

The relevance of the model to retailers is probably twofold, in trying to spot a new trend and in adjusting their promotion policies at different stages in the diffusion process. Taking fashion as an example, a new fashion trend might be observable first among a small group of young or well-off people who always appear to dress distinctively. The trend might not diffuse out from this group at all, but as soon as it does a mass market retailer will need to stock the line if they appeal to the more fashion conscious sector. A retailer with a more traditional or conservative clientele would need to hold back longer before its customers will be willing to adopt the new idea.

diffusion of innovation The notion that new ideas, products etc. achieve acceptance by a population in a phased or progressive manner which is seen as occurring within populations with a shared culture, and communication system. *See* DIFFUSION MODEL.

dinkie An informal term (derived from 'double income, no kids') applied to a group of consumers, especially childless couples, to indicate a certain type of lifestyle.

direct broadcasting by satellite The transmission of radio frequency signals, usually television, in which the signal is relayed directly, from a man-made device orbiting in space, to individual receiver dishes located on the ground, which feed the signal to television receivers.

direct check An audit of incoming goods against the invoice presented by a supplier for its goods, to ensure that the lines and quantities which were ordered and invoiced have been received by the retailer.

direct mail The use of the postal system to distribute letters, brochures, circulars and other promotional materials to intended recipients.

direct marketing The process of building and sustaining a mutually beneficial exchange relationship with individuals or organizations through the use of methods that do not rely on the support of any CHANNEL intermediary (e.g. MAIL ORDER retailing).

direct product profitability (DPP) The process by which retailers seek to measure the CONTRIBUTION made by the sales of an individual merchandise item. Retailers attempt to identify as many costs ('direct product costs') as possible which can be directly allocated to the item – ordering, storage, transport, price marking, shelf space occupancy, selling etc. They can then identify those items of merchandise which are generating profit, identify loss-making items and use this information to delist unprofitable lines or to approach manufacturers to renegotiate terms. A further use is in shelf space-allocation; the less profitable products may have their shelf space adjusted.

As more retailers adopt the DPP

approach, its use may well spread beyond space planning and range adjustments to analysing efficiency problems in distribution and warehousing, comparing suppliers, packaging and evaluating promotional activity. Furthermore, manufacturers can use DPP to understand and manage the true costs of their operations. *See also* SPACE ALLOCATION.

direct response advertising Paid-for insertions in mass media under clear sponsorship from which the customer replies to the sponsor without involving any other CHANNEL intermediaries.

direct selling The establishment of an immediate exchange relationship with a customer in which the usual intermediaries in the distribution chain are omitted (e.g. between a kitchen manufacturer and members of the public).

Director General of Fair Trading (UK) The government-appointed official responsible for the OFFICE OF FAIR TRADING.

discount 1. Any reduction in a stated list price etc., given to individuals or organizations either in the usual course of trade or as a promotional benefit. Certain types of discount have become institutionalized, namely bulk or *quantity discount* given on the occasion of buying greater than usual quantities; *trade discount* given to one whose occupation requires the use of goods in small quantities, where such goods are usually sold by retail (e.g. a painter may receive trade discount from a retail supplier of decorating products), or by a wholesaler selling to a retailer for sub-

sequent onward resale; discounts given for immediate payments in cash, or for prompt settlement of ACCOUNTS (*cash discount*).
2. Describing those retailers who sell at below market ruling prices. *See* DISCOUNT STORE.
3. The reverse of 'compound' (i.e. to estimate the current value of future projected CASH FLOW).

discount store A retail outlet which sells goods at low prices by accepting low gross margins and looking to sell at high volumes. Such outlets are often characterized by a limited range of popular brands, low staffing levels and a high level of self-service and basic shop fittings. This format is particularly prevalent in the USA (e.g. Walmart).

discussion group A widely used MARKET RESEARCH technique involving the meeting of a small number of respondents (usually 8 to 12) who come together to deliberate and debate a subject. A researcher (often called a moderator) guides and leads the meeting. It is a qualitative method, commonly used to develop understanding of motivation and attitudes, and sometimes acts as a preliminary to quantitative research. *See also* FOCUS GROUP.

disk A flat, circular recording mechanism which can magnetically or optically store (write) or retrieve (read) computer DATA. *See also* FLOPPY DISK, HARD DISK.

display An arrangement of merchandise in a trade or retail outlet designed especially to attract the customer's attention.

display advertising A form of paid-for

insertions in print media which uses size, colour, illustration, photographic, GRAPHICS etc. to attract the reader's attention. Advertisements for similar products are not grouped together (unlike in CLASSIFIED ADVERTISING).

display card A form of message which is printed, usually on thick paper, for information purposes at the POINT OF SALE. Such information includes prices, product benefits, brand names and special offers.

display case A form of equipment designed especially to visually merchandise a product at the POINT OF SALE; a vitrine. A display case is often produced and supplied by a manufacturer to encourage a retailer to stock a particular brand.

display loader An inducement to a dealer or retailer, to provide space for the visual merchandising of a manufacturer's product, in the form of an element of the fixturing to be retained by the dealer/retailer when the merchandising period is over.

display outer A carton or other form of packaging which has been specially designed for opening and merchandising at the *POINT OF SALE*. It is sometimes used in conjunction with special promotions.

dissonance A psychological state arising from a discrepancy between internal beliefs and actual behaviour that creates cognitive strain. Dissonance theory would hold that an individual in this state of cognitive strain would engage in behaviours that would resolve some of the conflict. For example, such a discrepancy results if

an individual is persuaded by advertising to buy a certain product that he or she is not really particularly interested in, because outside pressures demand it. The buyer of the product would in these circumstances be expected to engage in activities to find reasons for his or her behaviour, such as the notion that purchase of the product facilitates family harmony.

distance decay The concept of decreasing intensity of any activity, behaviour or pattern with increasing displacement from a the point of origin of the activity etc.

distress purchase *See* GRUDGE PURCHASE.

distribution 1. One of the basic functions of the retailing system by which place UTILITY is generated. The process involves the transportation of goods, or the making available of services, at points of convenience for potential customers. *See* CHANNEL OF DISTRIBUTION.
   2. Within a retail, wholesale or manufacturing organization, that department charged with the responsibility for the safe and timely transportation of merchandise, often using the organization's own transport. *See* PHYSICAL DISTRIBUTION, DISTRIBUTION CENTRE.
   3. That pattern of observations on a chosen variable within a given SAMPLE or population (e.g. age distribution of population).

distribution centre A facility, normally a large warehouse, where goods are received, sorted, bulk-broken where necessary, picked and then sent out to the places where they are ultimately required (e.g. in store-format retailing, shops; in MAIL ORDER, the customer or mail order agent).

distribution channel The set of intermediaries who own and/or control a commodity, good or service during the marketing process, from the first (e.g. a producer) to the last (e.g. a retailer).

Few channels involve only one organization; many are complex. Usually there is a set of interfaces between channel members – agents, wholesalers, specialist distribution companies, retailers etc. – each of which has its own policies, objectives, needs and problems and provides manufacturers with wider potential markets and specialist expertise. Retailers are good examples of such channel intermediaries.

Many different types of channel are possible, but various classifications may be helpful. A distinction may be drawn between long and short channels, the former having many intermediaries, and the latter few. Another distinction may be drawn between wide and narrow channels, according to the breadth of availability of the product or service. Most manufacturers prefer wide channels (e.g. confectionery is available in grocery stores of all types, CTNs, petrol stations, kiosks, public houses etc.), but some specialist and luxury goods producers prefer narrow channels to limit their availability and maintain their exclusiveness, image and price.

It is quite possible for a manufacturer to use several different types of distribution channel for different products all at the same time. For example, a pottery manufacturer may use long channels to export high-quality products, a short channel to sell 'seconds' in a factory shop, a wide channel to sell its products in department stores and hardware shops, and a narrow channel to sell specially produced souvenir items at a tourist attraction.

distribution check A widely used market research technique whereby teams of observers visit a sample of retail outlets and record whether a brand is in stock. The data is then grossed up using an appropriate DISTRIBUTION MEASURE to give an overall picture of the availability of the products.

distribution cost Any expenditure which is incurred as a result of the process of making available, at the point of consumption, goods and services from their point of production. Such costs include the cost of transport, order processing and related administrative activities, stockholding (both the handling and storage of stock and financing it), warehousing, packaging and management and supervision. They also include labour, depreciation on fixed assets, interest charges, fuel, maintenance, taxes and insurance.

Different retailers are likely to have different levels and structures of distribution cost depending on the type of goods and services sold, geographical dispersion, relationships with suppliers, types of customer service outlet and the efficiency of operations.

distribution measure An analysis of the availability of products/brands in particular sectors of retailing. (E.g. 'Brand X has 73 per cent distribution in grocers', or 'Brand Y has 42 per cent distribution in CTNs'.)

Distribution measures take two forms. The first, 'numerical distribution', is the proportion of relevant shops stocking the product at a given time. The second, 'monetary distribution', is calculated by weighting each shop type by the proportion of annual turnover requested by shops stocking it at a given time; this reflects the quality of distribution, since product availability in a larger store will result in more sales than in a smaller store. *See also* DISTRIBUTION CHECK.

distributive trade All those organizations, individuals etc. engaged in the creation of time, place and possession UTILITIES through moving goods and services through the CHANNEL towards final consumers.

distributor An intermediary in a CHANNEL OF DISTRIBUTION standing between the manufacturer and the final customer. Distributors may be operating at either wholesale or retail levels. Within certain distribution channels the term 'distributor' may be used to signify one appointed to that role by a manufacturer (e.g. in the case of motorcars). Such intermediaries are sometimes described as 'authorized distributors'.

distributor brand A mark, name, or combination of identifying devices used to distinguish a merchandise offering which is exclusively available from a particular CHANNEL MEMBER; a PRIVATE LABEL; a retailer/wholesaler brand.

district shopping centre A retailing facility of intermediate size within an urban area, coming, in terms of CENTRAL PLACE THEORY, between the regional (city) centre and the local neighbourhood centre. In the UK it is characterized by having at least one large supermarket or a superstore, small branches of national multiples, banks and other financial institutions, and a range of specialist independent retailers.

During the 1970s there was a rapid growth in the UK of planned district centres, built and managed as a single unit. They consist usually of a single grocery superstore with a limited number of adjacent smaller shops occupied by complementary businesses such as CTNs and dry cleaning. A 'pub' and community facilities (for example, a library or a health centre) are sometimes provided as well. Extensive car parking is an integral part of the development. Grocery companies have been the main instigators of these developments, which fit more readily into conventional planning philosophy than free-standing stores.

diversification Generally, a strategy in which a business simultaneously develops new products and new markets. A firm diversifies for many reasons, such as the identification of an opportunity outside its current sphere of operations, attempting to spread its risks over a greater number of business areas, and as a response to declining markets or profits in current trading areas.

Diversification may take place into related businesses – i.e. beyond the present products and markets but still within the broad confines of the industry in which it operates (e.g. a retailer of one product type setting up a chain of stores selling a different range of products to a new group of customers) – or into unrelated businesses where there is no clear relationship to the present product/market. The more unrelated the diversification, the greater the degree of risk.

Many writers on strategy suggest that diversification should be considered only after other generic strategies have been explored, since the company will have no experience of operating in the new market (i.e. consider consolidation and productivity improvements, product development – supplying new products to the current market – and market development – supplying existing products to new markets – before embarking on a programme of diversification). *See also* ANSOFF'S MATRIX.

division of labour A means of organizing work so that overall productivity and efficiency may be enhanced, by subdividing the total task into a number of distinct suboperations in the expectation that, by so dividing the work, operators are able to complete each suboperation more efficiently through increased experience and skill.

DIY superstore A large retail outlet specializing in non-food items which are associated mainly with the home, garden or personal transport.

dollar control An evaluation and management of store stocks and sales in terms of their value in dollars (either at retail or cost).

domestic market 1. The internal, national arena for the sale of merchandise or services available to any supplier.

2. The market consisting of households, in distinction to say institutional or industrial markets.

door-to-door selling Traditional practice of retailing goods or services directly to the consumer in the home, on the basis of COLD CALLING. Manufacturer's representatives call literally from door to door peddling their wares. The system is expensive and is becoming less popular. Also there are recruitment difficulties, as, traditionally, door-to-door salespeople were paid a high percentage commission on sales and little or no basic salary. Some organizations use this method for sales of low value items, for example Avon cosmetics and Bettaware household products. Door-to-door selling is also used for services and high-value household purchases such as insurance and double-glazing.

double-entry bookkeeping A system of recording ACCOUNTING transactions first introduced by Luca Pacioli in an Italian textbook written in 1494, based on the rule that for each financial transaction there are always two ledger entries: a credit entry and a debit entry. If a retailer sells goods to a particular value, then the procedure will be: (a) an entry of this amount on the debit side of the cash account; (b) a corresponding entry on the credit side of the sales account. The following rule can be applied:
The system ensures that the total credit entries always equal the total debit entries at any point in time. The ledger balances therefore form the basis of the BALANCE SHEET.

down-market Goods or services which are designed to appeal to those

Debit entry	Credit entry
Increase in an asset	Decrease in an asset
Decrease in a liability	Increase in a liability
Increase in an expense	Decrease in an expense
Decrease in sales/profits	Increase in sales/profits

with low incomes or to those who do not share the aesthetic or other standards thought to be socially acceptable by some others. *Compare* UP-MARKET.

downstream Literally, in the direction of flow away from a source towards the ultimate destination. Used figuratively of goods along the SUPPLY CHAIN to the final USER, and of production processes.

drive time The period (usually expressed in minutes) for which consumers are prepared to travel by road to visit a particular retailer, location etc. Points having an equal drive time from a location are joined by lines known as ISOCHRONES.

dummy An artificial figure or statue, usually of the human form, used for displaying merchandise in a retail shop. *See also* MANNEQUIN.

dummy pack An empty pack which is often used as part of a retail display.

dump display A bulk visual presentation of goods, normally located in mid-aisle or at GONDOLA ENDS, where the items have been removed from outer packaging and tumbled into the display container.

durable good *See* CONSUMER DURABLE.

dutch auction A form of open public sale at which the goods are initially offered at a higher price to an audience which is invited to bid; the price is reduced until a buyer is found.

E

E number Standardized alphanumeric code (starting with the letter 'E'), used within the European Community, for labelling a food ADDITIVE that is 'generally recognized as being safe'. All foods made after 1 January 1986 had to include on the packaging a list of those ingredients that are included in the E numbering system. Not all additives were necessarily allowed in every EC country. Flavourings were not included in the classification. Permitted colours were assigned numbers from E100 to E180, preservatives from E200 to E290, antioxidants from E300 to E321, emulsifiers and stabilizers from E322 to E494, sweeteners E420 to E421, solvents E422, mineral hydrocarbons E905 to E907, modified starches E1400 to E1442 and other miscellaneous additives E170 to E927.

The E number system does not normally cover additives already used as ingredients within foodstuffs (e.g. sulphur dioxide in sultanas), nor does it cover residual chemicals such as crop sprays.

early adopter A customer type who buys a product towards the beginning of its life-cycle. *See also* DIFFUSION MODEL.

early closing (UK) British retail tradition whereby (almost) all shops in a trading area agree to close for one afternoon per week, in midweek, to compensate staff for working a full Saturday. Sometimes known as 'half-day closing', the practice is progressively being abandoned by MULTIPLE RETAILERS who operate full shift systems, but is still retained by many independents in smaller towns.

economic batch quantity (EBQ) The specific, finite number of items made in a production run which will minimize the total of holding and production set-up costs. Sometimes used as an alternative expression for ECONOMIC ORDER QUANTITY.

economic development The process of growth in the wealth a country obtains from business and industry, which is related to changes in the structure of such business and industry. Parallel with overall economic development, changes in retail structure and organization are commonly found – in particular, the development of self-service and large stores, the concentration of activity in the hands of fewer retailers, the concomitant decline of the small independent shop, and the emergence of NICHE RETAILING.

economic order quantity (EOQ) The

theoretical product requisition size which minimizes the total product inventory costs. Total inventory costs for a product are normally considered to be the sum of order costs, holding (carrying) costs and, if appropriate, shortage costs. The economic order quantity (calculated by the formula below) may provide a satisfactory first estimate of a practical order quantity for the product. As such, and combined with a suitable re-order point for the product, it forms the basis for an INVENTORY CONTROL system. The formula, however, should be applied with care as its derivation is based on restrictive, and perhaps unrealistic, assumptions regarding the demand for the product, the supplier LEAD TIME etc.

$$EOQ = \frac{2Kd}{H}$$

where d = (constant) demand per unit of time

K = order cost (per order)

H = holding cost of keeping one item in stock for one unit of time

economy pack A large cardboard box, bag etc. of goods, which, through size economies, gives better value for money to the customer than a smaller version containing similar goods.

EDIFACT An international standard, or common language, which allows electronic data transmissions to be understood by both the sender (e.g. a retailer) and the receiver (e.g. a manufacturer). *Compare* TRADACOMS.

EFTPOS Electronic Funds Transfer at the Point of Sale. A customer payment system which requires electronic communication between the retailer's and the customer's bank (building society) account. A DEBIT CARD is used to transfer the amount owed by the customer to the retailer's account, as soon as the sale has been registered. Ideally this transfer should take place instantaneously. In the UK, however, the time involved is similar (two to three days clearing) to that for payment by CHEQUE. There are a number of EFTPOS systems in operation and retailers are required to pay a commission to the companies whose system they wish to operate.

Eighty–Twenty Rule (80:20) A principle, believed to have a general applicability in business, which states the approximate degree of concentration or importance of the major part(s) of a business operation to the whole of that operation. For example, many companies find that approximately 80 per cent of sales turnover comes from 20 per cent of the lines they sell. Other examples may be that 80 per cent of sales come from 20 per cent of the customer list, or that 80 per cent of the need for spares are met from 20 per cent of the spares stockholding. The rule is associated with the 19th-century economist Pareto.

electronic catalogue The product listing, containing descriptions, details, prices of items of merchandise available to potential consumers, given via media such as television, computer systems, or Viewdata (*see* VIDEOTEX) systems.

electronic data interchange (EDI) The standardized, systematic transmission of structured messages between computers (often using VALUE-ADDED NETWORKS) belonging to different CHANNEL MEMBERS, particularly in support of invoicing and ordering procedures.

electronic data processing (EDP) The use of computers to store records and files, and to retrieve, and sort, the information according to management needs. Early applications in retailing were for accounting, administration, inventory management and ordering. Before the advent of DATABASE MANAGEMENT SYSTEMS, much of the time of data processing departments was spent on administering data files and modifying programs, rather than in identifying management needs.

electronic mail A system for transmitting messages from one computer to another via telephone cables. The messages can be seen on a VISUAL DISPLAY UNIT and the receiver is advised, on logging in, that 'post' or 'mail' is awaiting attention in an 'electronic mailbox'. The system is increasingly being used by retail companies as an alternative to national and internal mail systems.

Email *See* ELECTRONIC MAIL.

employee discount The percentage of the authorized company price which management and staff are permitted to have deducted from purchases made of all, or specified, company goods.

employee handbook A booklet issued to staff, normally when joining a company, giving details pertaining to their employment (e.g. rules and regulations, benefits, disciplinary and grievance procedures).

employee legislation The law pertaining to the job(s) of any member of staff in an organization.

employee services Provision by retailers of staff welfare benefits (e.g. meals, pensions, transport, accommodation, health care). In addition, retail companies may provide a counselling and advisory service for staff who are experiencing personal crises, emotional or financial difficulties. The entire costs of predetermined employee services may be met by the employer.

Some retail companies encourage staff welfare committees, comprised of employee representatives to assume responsibility for advising on or administering the services provided.

employment profile The characteristics of the labour force employed by an organization or the industry as a whole. Age, gender and SOCIO-ECONOMIC CLASSIFICATIONS are the usual external characteristics. Internal characteristics include length of service, job stability factors, occupational or grade classifications, and productivity indices.

Employment Protection (Consolidation) Act 1978 (UK) Legislation on minimum standards and requirements affecting contracts of employment, pay and conditions, employee rights, grievance and disputes procedures and equal opportunities at work.

empty-nester A LIFESTYLE term for a couple whose children have grown up and left home.

end-aisle display A visual merchandising feature, placed at the extremity of a walkway, which is used in SUPERMARKETS to increase impulse purchases or to present promotional stock. It is changed frequently to maintain interest. In percentage visitation terms, end-aisle displays will be passed by many more customers in the store than each aisle itself.

Engel, Blackwell and Miniard Three American academics who have written and researched widely on CONSUMER BEHAVIOUR. Their consumer behaviour model relates the consumer decision-making process, to the various influences on that process (e.g. individual characteristics, social and situational influences), and also considers the post-purchase outcomes and their effects on future decisions. See James F. Engel, D. Roger Blackwell and Paul W. Miniard, *Consumer Behaviour*, 6th edn (Illinois: CBS College Publishing, 1990).

enumeration district (UK) Basic unit, set up under the Representation of the People Acts, for the purpose of defining the minimum size of electoral areas. It consists of a given number of dwellings and is given a unique code number. It provides a classification unit for UK geodemographic studies (*see* GEODEMOGRAPHICS).

EPOS Electronic Point of Sale. At a cash desk or CHECKOUT, a SCANNING system, linked to a computer, is used to read the product code, marked on the packaging of goods in the form of a number or BARCODE. For each good there is an electronic display of the description and price, visible to the customer, who will also be given an itemized receipt for the total payment. The system provides valuable information for management use (e.g. a line-by-line sales analysis as well as detailed information concerning the timing of sales). This makes it relatively easy to fine-tune sales forecasts and to plan staffing levels. It also allows head office to carry out a detailed comparison of branch performance. EPOS is best used as part of a fully integrated system. In this context the sales registered on the EPOS tills can be used to trigger automatic re-ordering from the regional distribution warehouse and even from suppliers, where the communication links are available. EPOS systems can also incorporate an electronic funds transfer unit to facilitate direct communication links with the banks.

Equal Pay Act 1970 (UK) Legislation which established the principle that individuals must receive the same level of pay, be placed on the same salary scales and enjoy the same working conditions and prospects for career advancement, irrespective of their gender.

equity The risk capital invested in a company by its shareholders. Shareholders are the owners of the business. Their gain from the investment in shares takes two forms: (i) dividends and (ii) capital gains. With the exception of preference shares, shareholders are not legally entitled to dividends, and the amount will vary depending on the profitability of the business. Capital gains arise as the business prospers and the market value of the shares increases. Unlike DEBT finance, shares are irredeemable. However, they are transferable and a large and active UK market exists in the form of the Stock

Exchange, the Unlisted Securities Market and the Third Tier Market.

ethnic Belonging to a human group who have certain cultural traits in common. These traits commonly relate to language and/or religious beliefs.

ethnic employment The appointment of members of a workforce with religious or cultural characteristics which may be different from those possessed by the host or indigenous population.

ethnic retailer An organization selling products to domestic users, where the owner or manager possesses religious or cultural characteristics which may be different from those possessed by the indigenous population. Different cultural beliefs of such retailers often translate into marked differences in retail practice and the range of merchandise sold.

ethos 1. The distinctive operating systems, characteristics and atmosphere provided by specific organizations.
2. The habitual manner of operating, living or behaving.

exchange The process, between consenting participants, of the mutual transfer of valued considerations.

exclusive clause A section included in a contract which exempts certain circumstances, situations from that contract.

exclusive dealer A trader granted territorial rights to sell a particular product or range of merchandise. Such a dealership may apply to highly valued goods such as cars, audio equipment or jewellery. *See also* AUTHORIZED DEALER.

exhibition An event mounted by an individual organization, or a group of organizations, during which their goods or services are shown to potential customers. Trade exhibitions are considered to be an important route to selling items on a business-to-business basis.

exhibition stand A unit of construction, often of a uniform nature, on which organizations present their goods or services at a specially arranged event.

expense *See* COST.

expense centre *See* COST CENTRE.

expense control *See* COST CONTROL.

experimentation The process of testing a product or design by the systematic observation and analysis of its impact on a group of representative consumers/shoppers. It is used when it is difficult to predict results from existing experiences.

expert system A form of computer software where the expertise of an individual, in a specific area of knowledge, is made available as advice to others faced with routine decisions which require such knowledge. In retailing, expert systems are used, for example, in 'help lines', and in the screening of job applications where clerical assistants, advised by the computer, can undertake work normally requiring more senior person-

nel. *See also* KNOWLEDGE ENGINEER-
ING.

exploratory research The process of
inquiry undertaken to discover more
about the nature of a marketing problem, and the variables that relate to
it, than is possible from SECONDARY
DATA sources alone. Exploratory research is usually flexible in approach,
with the emphasis on insight and
understanding. The techniques involved are many and varied but are
usually small scale and qualitative
(e.g. brainstorming, DISCUSSION
GROUP, semistructured interviews,
observational studies, EXPERIMEN-
TATION etc.).

exponential smoothing A method of
forecasting the value of a variable
one period in advance when data on a
variable, such as product demand, is
monitored by an organization on a
regular basis (e.g. daily, weekly or
monthly). It is, in effect, a weighted
average of the past demand data,
which attaches the greatest weight
(and hence the greatest importance)
to the most recent data and progressively less weight to data the further
back it is from the current period.

Forecasts, using exponential
smoothing, are of particular value
when linked to a stock ordering
policy where the order quantity of a
product will depend on the likely
future demand for that product.

Simple exponential smoothing is a
dynamic process which uses the formula below repeatedly, and conse-
quently has the advantage of only
requiring the storage of two items of
input data for each product at any
one time. The general formula for
simple exponential smoothing can be
represented as:

$$F_{t+1} = \alpha \, D_t + (1 - \alpha) \, F_t$$

where F_{t+1} = the forecast for the
next period

D_t = the actual demand for
the current period

F_t = the previously calculated forecast for the
current period

α = a smoothing constant,
with a value between
0 and 1, which is
chosen by the user in
order to determine
the relative weight-
ings of past data

Normally, to effect a 'smooth'
series of forecasts, low values of α,
such as 0.1 or 0.2 are chosen initially.
The simple exponential smoothing
system works on the assumption that
the mean demand remains un-
changed over time, and that periodic
fluctuations in demand occur in a random fashion. Where this is not a valid
assumption (e.g. when significant
trends or seasonal patterns are evi-
dent), low values of α may be inappropriate, and it may also be
advisable to use an adjusted exponential smoothing procedure.

export 1. To sell goods and services in
foreign markets, especially by direct
sales from the domestic business, but
also more loosely through the overseas sales of SUBSIDIARIES and affili-
ates. *Compare* IMPORT.

2. Such goods and services so sold.

export distribution The physical
movement of merchandise, and the
fulfilment of allied legal and commercial procedures, when exporting from
one market to another. Exporting
tends to be dominated by cost and
complexity, cost from the price of
transport, packaging, storage duties

and fulfilling procedures, and complexity from the large number of bodies involved in even the simplest export transaction. Free trade areas such as the European Community reduce both cost and complexity which tend to act as barriers to trade. Simplification of documentation, and the introduction of door- to-door transportation in the 1980s, helped to reduce international trade barriers, but many issues remain to discourage particularly smaller companies from exporting. Professional advice on export distribution is available from freight forwarders, banks, transport companies and government departments in exporting countries.

extended credit The offer made to customers by, for example, high street stores or mail order companies, which allows a purchase payment to be made over a finite period, rather than immediately. Such facilities are usually offered for the purchase of high-priced goods such as furniture or electrical goods. The credit terms may vary, and are sometimes offered 'interest-free' by stores as a means of PROMOTION.

extended dating *See* EXTRA DATING.

extended trading hours A retailer's availability to the shopping public which is more than the period which full-time staff normally work. Extended trading hours may be a seasonal phenomenon which occurs before Christmas, or a feature of the normal working week, such as late night trading on Thursdays and Fridays. They are often a characteristic of small independent retailers providing convenience shopping for essential items in the local community.

extra dating An agreement with a supplier whereby the retailer is allowed an extended period of time before payment of an invoice. *See also* DATING.

extrapolation Projection into the future, based on past experience. Extrapolation of the TREND in TIME SERIES ANALYSIS of, for example, sales volume is a relatively simple and useful component of medium- to long-term sales forecasting.

extrinsic Not contained or included within. Specifically, in the context of retailing the term is often used to describe rewards accruing to a participant in the exchange process that are themselves not the subject of valued consideration.

F

facing The FIXTURE that a customer encounters 'head-on' in a normal shopping flow. Generally held to be the part of the fixture that creates the most sales per linear, or square, foot.

factory shop A retail outlet selling manufactured goods such as pottery or clothing, which is often located on the same site as the manufacturing unit.

fad A short-lived fashion for a GOOD or lifestyle which, when first introduced, creates an immense amount of publicity and high profits for the retailers who are at the forefront of distribution. Usually it is not long before such a good is widely available because of the DIFFUSION OF INNOVATION effect. It will then move either into mainstream mass retailing or die due to market saturation or demand being satisfied. Examples of fads include: *1960s* paper clothing, bell bottoms, loons, trolls; *1970s* platform shoes, midis, maxis, multiple ear-piercing; *1980s* filofax, boxer shorts; *1990s* Mutant Ninja Turtles, psychedelic clothing, bum bags.

fair trade The process of market transactions carried out within a framework which is seen as being equitable to all participants. The phrase has a particular usage in the area of non-discriminatory treatment of suppliers or customers, and in the application of rules to ensure equitable treatment in exchanges between developed and less developed economies.

Fair Trading Act 1973 (UK) Legislation concerned with regulating trading practices between companies and consumers. A major feature of the Act was the appointment of a DIRECTOR GENERAL OF FAIR TRADING to monitor the effect of trading practice on consumers. Specific activities might include authorizing new codes of practice established by organizations and recommending detailed government investigations into activities which might be considered against the consumers' interest (e.g. a monopoly trading situation).

family branding The use of a distinguishing name or mark to identify a group of products originating either with one manufacturer, or from one distributor. More specifically, the phrase is sometimes used to describe such a process being applied to products sharing similar characteristics originating from a single source (e.g. all chocolate COUNT LINES from a particular manufacturer bearing a manufacturer's brand, as well as individual brand names).

family influence The indirect power exerted over an individual by his or her close relations, by non-physical means such as wisdom, wealth or strength of character.

family life-cycle Descriptive analogy for the phases in a unitary family's history: (i) nest building, (ii) full nest, (iii) empty nest 1, (iv) empty nest 2, where the descriptors relate to the presence of children and latterly a single parental survivor. Used to indicate potential demand for product types and potential LIFESTYLES.

family packaging The use of a consistent design of external covering or wrapping, through its visual elements, to present a unified or unitary face to the customer. Such packaging may be extended across all the ranges provided by an individual distributor (e.g. consistent treatment of packaging in private label for a retailer), or more narrowly within any one packaging area (e.g. similar packaging for different types of ground coffee produced by a manufacturer).

farm gate An expression for the selling of goods, especially PRODUCE, at the place of production.

fascia The area immediately above the customer doors and main windows of a retail outlet, sometimes illuminated, bearing, normally, the name of the company or store concerned.

fashion 1. What is currently popular and accepted.
　2. Styles of clothing which are currently popular in the retail market.

fashion cycle The tendency for the sales of style-related items, particularly clothing, to progress through the following stages – spreading, rising, culminating and declining – in a relatively short time period.

fast food A prepared, usually hot, meal or snack sold at a quick-service retail catering operation. While there are variations in the specific styles adopted by fast food operators, their establishments tend to have a number of characteristic features. They offer a simple and fairly restricted menu within a carefully controlled operating system. A variety of hamburgers in a bun, fried chicken, pizza, french fries and baked potatoes provide the main course; typical desserts are ice cream and fruit pies and the drinks range includes milk shakes, fizzy drinks and coffee. Customers queue up to be served at a counter, the aim being to serve a large number of people with the minimum of waiting time. Operators endeavour to serve customers within three minutes of entry into their premises. The food is sold in disposable packaging without cutlery (so-called 'finger food'). Some operators offer facilities for customers to consume their food on the premises; others tend to cater more for the takeaway trade. The major operating companies (e.g. McDonalds, Kentucky Fried Chicken and Burger King) have pursued vigorous marketing strategies, using both press and television advertising to stress quality, value for money and nutritional value.

fast-moving consumer good *See* FMCG.

fent *See* REMNANT.

field selling The process of actually

going out to seek new customers (in order to gain immediate or future orders) rather than contacting them by phone or by mail. For manufacturers or suppliers selling to retailers, field sales forces have become less important in the UK as the percentage of total retail turnover attributed to the MULTIPLE RETAILERS has increased. This is because the multiple retailers put the onus on key account negotiations from a limited number of centralized buying points.

field visits An excursion to a specific location (a region, shopping centre, factory etc.) to examine or study, *in situ*, particular issues through observation and/or communication with people living or working there.

FIFO First in first out. A method of stock valuation which assumes that the goods first purchased are the first ones to be sold.

In times of INFLATION, FIFO assigns a realistic value to stock in the BALANCE SHEET. However, this implies less accuracy in matching current sales revenues with current purchase costs in the INCOME STATEMENT, which results in a higher gross profit figure than that obtained by using LIFO.

The FIFO method is legally acceptable in the UK. It is most useful for retailers selling goods of considerable value per item.

final accounts The INCOME STATEMENT for the ACCOUNTING PERIOD considered, together with the BALANCE SHEET as at the end of that period.

financial control The management and administration of all resources within an organization as far as their value can be expressed in money terms. For line managers it will be mainly concerned with the control of WORKING CAPITAL and the achievement of budgetary targets. There are four main areas of financial control: (i) *debtor control*, which is concerned with ensuring prompt payment from debtors, monitoring trends (e.g. through the use of ageing schedules), and generally implementing the company's overall policy with regard to credit sales; (ii) *creditor control*, which includes negotiating credit terms, ensuring prompt payment to suppliers, making full use of discounts for prompt payment etc.; (iii) *stock control*, which is mainly concerned with striking the right balance between the costs of holding stock and the need to hold sufficient stock to meet demand; (iv) BUDGETARY CONTROL.

financial life-cycle The belief that, as firms go through the various stages of their lives, they will utilize different SOURCES OF FINANCE in response to booms and slumps in trading. The time series diagram puts labels on the significant cyclical stages, and the preferred sources of finance available in the UK are then listed.

financial management An area of business or organization control, which normally consists of: identification of monetary support requirements; measurement and reporting of organization performance in monetary terms; control and administration of funds; establishment of performance measures; development of monetary control systems. The focus of financial management depends on the nature of the business. In a retailing organization, day-

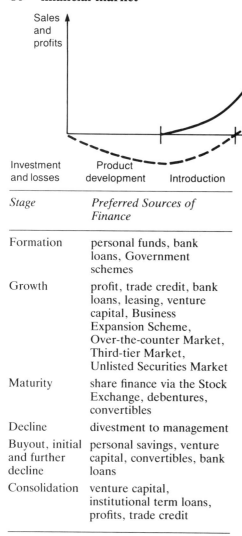

Stage	Preferred Sources of Finance
Formation	personal funds, bank loans, Government schemes
Growth	profit, trade credit, bank loans, leasing, venture capital, Business Expansion Scheme, Over-the-counter Market, Third-tier Market, Unlisted Securities Market
Maturity	share finance via the Stock Exchange, debentures, convertibles
Decline	divestment to management
Buyout, initial and further decline	personal savings, venture capital, convertibles, bank loans
Consolidation	venture capital, institutional term loans, profits, trade credit

to-day money management will concentrate on cash management, margins and stock turnover, whereas at a strategic level financial management is concerned with the long-term financing needs of the business.

financial market The place where, or mechanism by which, instruments of monetary value are traded. Financial markets serve as primary markets to enable organizations to raise new funds. In addition they function as secondary markets encouraging speculation, thus increasing the marketability of the various financial instruments. A distinction is also made between money markets (short-term trading) and capital markets (long-term trading).

financial merchandise planning The expression in monetary terms of the desired future mix of products to be sold, with a specified time horizon. It is part of the BUDGETING process. A detailed sales forecast, often based on historical data, is used as a starting point to plan the OPENING STOCK for each month. The assumption is made that to meet customer requirements there should be enough stock available to meet demand, plus a buffer stock which is needed to provide a choice. Taken together with existing commitments for the purchase of stock for that month, this can be used to calculate the OPEN TO BUY.

financial ratio A measure of company performance (or productivity) which is expressed in monetary units per unit of resource, and is based on figures drawn from company FINAL ACCOUNTS. Such ratios can be used to analyse changes in a company's performance over time, or to carry out an inter-firm comparison. This process is known as RATIO ANALYSIS. Financial ratios may be used by internal and external stakeholders to assess the company's performance. Certain ratios, such as sales per employee, sales per square foot and stock turnover help company management to monitor and control performance, whereas Return on Capital Employed (ROCE) can be used to examine profitability and efficiency. The latter will also be of interest to shareholders, who will use it in conjunction with Return on Shareholders' Funds and various investment ratios, such as Earnings Per Share, the Price Earnings ratio, the Dividend Yield etc. to assess the state of their investment. Corporate lenders in turn will be interested in the retailer's LIQUIDITY RATIOS and GEARING.

financial recording The documentation of all resource transactions taking place in the course of retail activities which can be expressed in money terms. A DOUBLE-ENTRY BOOKKEEPING system is used to facilitate the reckoning of debits and credits resulting from each business transaction. Accurate records must be kept in order to relate the appropriate revenues and expenses to each ACCOUNTING PERIOD.

financial statement A definitive record which describes an aspect, or aspects, of the activities of a retail organization in money terms. The most common financial statements are the INCOME STATEMENT, the BALANCE SHEET, the CASH FLOW statement and the funds flow statement. Financial statements draw on the DOUBLE-ENTRY BOOKKEEPING system as the source of information.

first in first out *See* FIFO.

fitment *See* FIXTURE.

fixed asset An item of value which has been acquired for long-term use within the retail organization. It is often purchased to support the ongoing retail activities. Fixed assets can be tangible or intangible. Examples of tangible fixed assets are buildings, computers, office furniture, a fleet of vans etc. An example of an intangible fixed asset is GOODWILL.

fixed cost An expense which does not change in value in the short run and for a given relevant range of activity. Shown on a graph, a pure fixed cost looks like this:

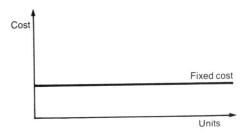

In a retailing organization, fixed costs typically include rent and rates, depreciation and the salaries of full-time permanent staff. At least in the short run, these costs are incurred whether or not the retailer generates any sales revenue at all. However, there are many costs which include a fixed element and an element for VARIABLE COSTS; a good example of this is the quarterly telephone bill, where the standing charge is fixed, but the cost of actual units used varies with the level of activity.

fixture An item of furniture,

COUNTER, SHOWCASE, display cabinet etc., used to store and/or display merchandise on the sales floor, and those articles associated with its use – SIGNAGE, hangers etc. Collectively, the items that are used within this context are described as 'fixturing'.

fixturing *See* FIXTURE.

flagship store The major shop or outlet in a CHAIN (usually located in the capital city), which is larger than the other outlets and carries a wider range of merchandise. It 'carries the flag' for the chain and may be the trial ground for new ideas. The store is usually furbished to a higher standard than the others and may have its own unique identity within the chain (e.g. Harrods in the House of Fraser group).

fleet management The control, administration and co-ordination of a substantial number of delivery vehicles. The fleet manager must balance the costs of a vehicle against the efficient use of the same asset in distributing merchandise. Vehicle costs divide into FIXED COSTS (manufacturing the vehicles themselves), and their VARIABLE COSTS (fuel, labour and maintenance). Larger retailers have tended to become more involved in the management of PHYSICAL DISTRIBUTION either by operating their own warehousing and transport fleets or by using the services of a THIRD PARTY. In each case, they incur an extra and substantial cost that was once the concern of the manufacturer/supplier.

The choice of transport equipment to use in distribution depends upon the nature of the task and the product. The standard vehicle is a 30 metre trailer drawn by one of a large number of 'tractor' units. Tractor units tend to be selected on the basis of their average cost per mile to the fleet owner.

flexible budget A method of relating planned levels of stock, debtors, creditors, cash, expenditure, revenue and profits to the expected sales volume, so that, in the short run, only certain costs of operating a retail business are FIXED COSTS, whereas others will vary with turnover. The flexible budget allows for rapid adjustments of the plan to the actual sales volume achieved, and eliminates variances (*see* VARIANCE ANALYSIS) solely related to volume. This is important in activities where there is a high level of VARIABLE COSTS. (E.g. for large food retailers a high percentage of CHECKOUT operators are part-time employees, and, as a result, wage costs will vary with the level of turnover.) SPREADSHEETS make the process of drawing up flexible budgets quick and easy, thus allowing management to draw up contingency plans as part of the budgeting process.

flexography A printing process, similar to LETTERPRESS, where the images to be printed are raised from the print roller. The raised parts are inked and the ink transferred onto the material being printed. Flexography uses rubber plates instead of the metal used in the letterpress. Flexographic printing is used for printing cardboard cartons or cases, and for plastic and cellulose films (e.g. crisp packets or biscuit film packages), where high speed is required but quality of print finish is less critical.

float A sum of money, usually of varying denominations, allocated to a cash point or specific operator, to facilitate the giving of change to customers at the time of purchase.

floor Normally an abbreviation of 'shop floor', being that area of the store to which customers have access.

floor space That area of the store designated to the particular or general sale of goods or services.

floor walker Individual responsible for dealing with customer queries and complaints, usually associated with large departmental stores. *See also* SHOP WALKER.

floppy disk An item of HARDWARE which allows the magnetic storage of information in a portable form. Floppy disks are transferable between different machines of a similar specification.

FMCG Fast-moving consumer good. A low-priced item which is used rapidly with a single or limited number of consumptions (as opposed to, for example, CONSUMER DURABLE or consumer service). An example would be a food product such as jam, or toiletry product such as shampoo. FMCGs are often the most heavily advertised products as manufacturers seek to develop brand character, loyalty and automatic repeat purchase. Retailer MARGINS on FMCGs are usually low and efficient STOCK CONTROL is therefore vital.

FOB *See* FREE ON BOARD TERMS OF SALE.

focus group A form of controlled DISCUSSION GROUP where the discussion is limited to very specific subjects and does not stray from them.

food court A mix of retailers, selling meals and snacks, located around a shared customer seating area (usually in an enclosed SHOPPING CENTRE). Food courts are becoming an integral feature of the 1980s and 1990s shopping centres as they provide a (attractive) focal point and are believed to increase the average length of time per centre user visit.

Food Retail Index (UK) A monthly statistic produced and published by the Central Statistical Office for the Department of Trade and Industry showing the volume of food retail sales.

food retailing A form of trading which sells edible products. It includes such diverse distribution channels as hotels, restaurants, supermarkets, health food stores, confectioners, bakeries, greengrocers and vending machines.

Food retailing represents the largest single retail sector. Traditionally it is subdivided into main subsectors: grocery (dry and packeted products), dairy (milk, butter, cheese), greengrocery (fruit and vegetables), meat (butchery), and many more. In France, for example, specialisms exist even today within meat retailing. However the general trend in food retailing has been for greater generalization, with supermarkets and hypermarkets aiming to sell all types of food and to include other food retail offers such as restaurants.

food science The study of the physical changes that affect the production and the consumption of edible products. Food science embraces the disciplines of chemistry, physics, engineering, biology, nutrition and home economics.

forecasting Systematic judgements as to the likely future state of nature, variables of interest etc. Judgemental forecasting concerns those techniques whereby current experts, or those having some knowledge of the field, aim to develop views of the future through mechanisms such as Delphi procedures, scenario writing. (These judgemental procedures are also sometimes known as technological forecasting.) Statistical forecasting methods concern those techniques such as LINEAR REGRESSION, TIME SERIES ANALYSIS, EXPONENTIAL SMOOTHING etc., which make use of established mathematical/statistical procedures.

form utility *See* UTILITY.

franchise An authorization granted by one person or enterprise (the *franchiser*) to another person (the *franchisee*) to use the franchiser's trade name, trade marks and business system in return for an initial payment and further regular payments. Retail franchises have included Circle K, the convenience store retailer, Bally Grove the shoe retailer and Tie Rack, but most high street franchises have tended to be services such as Budget Rent-a-Car and Kentucky Fried Chicken.

Franchising is said to offer the potential retailer an investment opportunity which encompasses the responsibility of managing an own business, but has the reassurances of a supporting network of similar business formats.

free-flow pattern A flexible arrangement of FIXTURES where, as opposed to a GRID PATTERN layout, customers are left to 'choose' their own pace and rate through displays. It is usually used within specialist or clothing DEPARTMENT STORES as it creates a more leisurely shopping experience for medium- to high-involvement goods which need some browsing space and freedom of appraisal.

free newspaper A weekly or daily publication which is provided without a charge to the reader. The cost of production and distribution is borne by the advertisers in the newspaper. It is sometimes called a 'free sheet', and usually has a local area circulation.

free on board terms of sale (FOB) Part of the contract of sale that determines the responsibility that the buyer and seller will incur in respect of transport charges, the control over movement of the shipment and the point at which title passes to the buyer. Should the goods be lost or damaged during SHIPMENT the FOB term of sale specifies who is responsible for claiming from the CARRIER. The decision to purchase 'FOB origin' places the responsibility for transport on the vendor and 'FOB destination' on the buyer.

free sheet *See* FREE NEWSPAPER.

free trial An inducement used in sales promotion to stimulate initial consumer demand for a product, or re-stimulate demand at latter stages in the product life-cycle. A treatment particularly used by those such as magazine publishers who would expect to generate a continuing commitment to sale purchase once the trial period had ended.

freehold (UK) A tenure, defined by the Law of Property Act 1925, by which real property is owned for an indefinite time period and can be inherited. The title to the property can be defended through 'real' legal action, which will result in repossession by the owner, rather than compensation to the owner.

freezer cabinet An insulated cold storage container designed for the purpose of storing goods at below $-18°$ C and maintaining them at the requisite temperature.

freezer case A transparent mounted cabinet, in which food items stored at below $-18°$ C are displayed for sale.

freezer centre (UK) A retail outlet specifically dealing with frozen foods (often in ECONOMY PACKS), but which may carry a few additional non-frozen lines.

freight forwarder Agent who arranges shipping and customs documentation of goods for import or export.

frontage 1. The area of space, facing a retail outlet, which is usually included in square footage measurement for the outlet, and is the responsibility of the retailer to clean and maintain. It is part of the site in law.
2. Facade of a retail outlet facing on to pedestrian walkway.

frozen food Edible product, preserved by subjection to a rapid fall in temperature, which is subsequently stored by retailers at below $-18°$ C, and is purchased by customers who would normally have a domestic appliance capable of storing the product at the required low temperature. The growth in freezer ownership and microwaves in the developed countries guaranteed a sustained rise in market share for frozen food products. By the 1980s frozen food was 6 per cent of consumer expenditure on food in Britain. The major product areas were the 'quick-frozen' products such as vegetables, prepared meals, deserts, rather than bulk products such as carcass meats, poultry and ice cream.

fulfilment house In MAIL ORDER, a business organization specializing in responding to customer orders through expertise in packing, posting etc., on behalf of a mail order company, magazine promotion etc.

full-line store A retail shop which stocks as broad a merchandise assortment as is expected for a shop of that type. For example, a full-line discount store would sell both HARD GOODS and SOFT GOODS, displayed in relatively inexpensive FIXTURES and building.

full service agency A business or other organization which provides a range of advertising activities including creative work, media buying, market research, public relations, direct marketing and sales promotion. The term is usually applied to a full service advertising agency to contrast it with one offering a single service, such as a media-buying independent agency.

functional discount *See* DISCOUNT.

G

gap The difference between desired and actual, or forecast, performance.

gap analysis The evaluation and interpretation of the difference between desired and actual performance so that strategies can be formulated which aim to close that difference.

garden centre A retail outlet often in a rural or suburban location, which specializes in selling horticultural products to (mainly) domestic users, and which utilizes a large outdoor selling area. Garden centres can vary greatly in the range of merchandise sold, and in size. Traditional centres still sell the core garden products (e.g. plants, seeds, compost, gardening equipment). However, there are also a number of leisure-orientated garden centres which have extended their product range to include aquariums, miniature railways, restaurants and pleasure gardens.

garment An article of clothing.

gas station (USA) *See* PETROL STATION.

gatekeeper Within a communications system, an individual, group or organization that is able to act as a valve controlling the flow of information between the transmitter and its intended final receiver. Because of the ability of such gatekeepers to influence the data and information received by final receivers they are often seen as having a major role in complex buying situations, such as those in trade or industrial marketing.

gearing The relationship between the two sources of financing any business – DEBT (borrowed money) and EQUITY (shareholders' funds). The gearing ratio is commonly expressed as total debt/shareholders funds. Low gearing means that the proportion of debt is small relative to the equity; high gearing indicates the opposite. The degree of gearing may influence the returns to the shareholder and the ability of the company to raise additional funding.

gender The social, cultural and behavioural distinctions drawn between the sexes on the basis of prevailing stereotypes ruling at any one time.

generic Applicable to, or referring to, a specific (retail) company or group of companies.

generic brand A name, not that of the company, under which a range of different products are sold, usually at a competitive price, in that company's outlets.

generic product A food good which is purchased as a commodity item. It is however also a term sometimes used to describe an OWN LABEL good presented in simple packaging and sold at a low price. Carrefour in France are credited with the first introduction of *produits libres*. In Britain, Fine Fare offered 'yellow pack' and International Stores 'white pack' lines to include basic products such as ginger biscuits, washing-up liquid and paper products. By the late 1980s generic products had virtually disappeared in British food retailing as companies moved their quality and price points for own label lines more in line with those of manufacturers' brands.

geodemographic targeting The identification of market segments based on geographic and demographic characteristics, used in systems such as ACORN and MOSAIC.

geodemographics The classification of consumers using demographic profiles for small areas, which utilizes census and market research data to look at particular neighbourhoods and types of housing. It is widely used for store location studies and targeting direct marketing activity. *See also* ACORN, MOSAIC, MONICA.

geodemography The study of the spatial distribution of populations and their characteristics.

geographical pattern The distribution of activities or objects over an area. Of special interest to retailing are the patterns presented by shops, population and transport. Regularity, clustering, linearity and randomness are the basic attributes of a pattern, and the scale of resolution may be at any scale from the world to the individual street.

gift coupon A certificate, often in the form of a greetings card, bearing a face value which is sold by a retailer etc. for cash and can then be redeemed or exchanged for goods and services at some future time, and which is intended to provide a suitable present to mark occasions such as birthdays, Christmas etc.

gift token *See* GIFT COUPON.

gift wrapping A service, often provided for customers who purchase goods as presents for others, whereby the purchased item is decoratively parcelled by the store assistant with greater care and attention than is the case for normal goods sold. Such a service is provided by stores on either a regular or seasonal basis (e.g. Christmas) to enhance the purchase decision. In mainland Europe this service is offered without charge or question for any gift purchased at any time of the year. In the UK, however, there is often a small charge.

giveaway An item offered cheaply by retailers to consumers. A product offered at a 'giveaway' price implies that consumers will almost be getting something for nothing.

global retailer A company which has, or seeks to have, a world wide presence, usually across a diverse range of economic, social and political environments (e.g. McDonalds, Benetton and Laura Ashley).

going-rate pricing A passive policy adopted by manufacturers and retailers who alone, or together, feel too small to influence price levels in a market. Such organizations are therefore obliged to take the 'going rate' as dictated by others in the market, often larger organizations, who could drive them out of business if they attempt direct price competition. *See also* PRICE.

gondola A free-standing fixture offering a variety of FACINGS for merchandising purposes.

gondola end The extremities of free-standing or fixed shelving which the shopper sees first and which is therefore often used for promotional purposes. Impulse purchases are reputed to be high from these positions.

good Used informally, especially in the plural, to mean any item of merchandise available for trade.

goods in transit Items of merchandise which have been dispatched by the sender but not yet received by the receiver.

goodwill In a company context, the (favourable) benefit which is derived from an existing reputation and customer base. A premium is often paid on the acquisition of a going concern in recognition of goodwill, which itself is listed as an intangible fixed asset in the BALANCE SHEET.

graphic *See* GRAPHICS.

graphics 1. Devices including illustrations, photographs and brand symbols which form an essential part of an advertisement. Graphics are com-bined with the copy to produce the advertisement which features both visual devices and words.

2. In computing, non-textual methods of presentation on a visual display unit. These may include dia-grammatic and animated images.

gravity model A mathematical rep-resentation of people movements which, in retail use, predicts the number of people who will use a par-ticular centre. The basic principle of the model is that the number of people attracted to a centre will be directly proportional to the size of the centre, and inversely proportional to the distance of shoppers from it. In various forms the gravity model is widely used for the prediction of turnovers and the delimitation of catchment areas.

green Formerly suggesting inexper-ience or immaturity. Now more likely to refer to the degree to which a com-pany or product is concerned with the conservation of the environment.

green belt An area of generally, but not necessarily exclusively, open land surrounding towns and cities in which there are severe planning controls and restrictions on new building development. Within Britain the establishment of green belts (around London since the late 1930s, and around major provincial towns and cities since the mid-1950s) have had both protectionist and positive objec-tives. The dominant protectionist element has been seen in terms of checking the physical extension of large towns and cities, preventing the merging of neighbouring towns and preserving the special character of historical towns. As such the green belt has been cited as a reason for the refusal of planning permission for new suburban and out of town shopping developments. The more positive objectives relate to increasing the recreational use of open countryside in urban fringe areas.

Green Shield Probably the best known example of a TRADING STAMP.

greengrocer A retail outlet or individual specializing in the sale of fresh fruit and vegetables.

grey market *See* SILVER MARKET.

grid pattern An interior design layout of a retail outlet, where the GONDOLAS and other display units are arranged to form a pattern of parallel aisles. Shoppers are thus encouraged to move towards the interior of the store.

gridiron pattern A street layout of regularly spaced, parallel straight streets, intersected at right angles by another set of parallel streets.

grievance procedure (UK) A statutory requirement under the EMPLOYMENT PROTECTION (CONSOLIDATION) ACT 1978 for companies to issue a written statement concerning an employee's rights to follow an agreed procedure designed to identify, communicate and resolve work related complaints. Employees have the right to raise grievances with middle and senior management as well as union representatives, provided that they have already given their immediate superior or manager an opportunity to resolve the complaint.

grocer A retail outlet, or individual,

specializing in the sale of canned or packaged food and associated household items.

gross domestic product (GDP) The total sum of all the goods and services produced within a country during a year, valued at the current market price.

gross margin The difference between the actual selling price of an item or group of items and the cost of that item or those items to the retailer. It may be expressed in monetary units (e.g. pounds, dollars etc.), in which case it is calculated as the selling price of the goods minus their cost. Alternatively, it may be expressed as a percentage, thus for a range of goods:

$$\frac{sales - cost\ of\ goods\ sold}{sales} \times 100\%$$

or for an item

$$\frac{selling\ price - cost\ of\ item}{selling\ price} \times 100\%$$

The total gross margin achieved must be sufficient to cover operating expenses and yield a profit for the retailer.

gross national product (GNP) The GROSS DOMESTIC PRODUCT adjusted to take account of foreign earnings (which are added) and income earned within the country by foreigners (which is deducted).

gross profit The difference between SALES REVENUE and COST OF GOODS SOLD for an ACCOUNTING PERIOD.

$$Gross\ profit = Sales - Cost\ of\ goods\ sold$$

See also GROSS MARGIN, PROFIT.

gross sales The total value of revenue from the conduct of ordinary business, plus exceptional items before allowing for special discounts, refunds on the return of goods etc.

group buying A process whereby a number of retailers gather together to purchase merchandise instead of doing so on an individual basis. Buying in this way often enables small retailers to enjoy economies of scale.

growth A complex organizational concept used most simply to describe an organization becoming larger, by reference to relevant variables such as sales turnover. The term is also used to identify increasing levels of complexity, ability, or maturity within an individual or organization. 'Personal growth' is in particular the development of any individual in terms of increased capabilities and attainments.

Organizational growth is often seen as being of two distinct forms: organic and inorganic. An organization is seen to grow organically when it develops by the use of its self-generated resources to continue in the direction originally determined for the organization. Inorganic growth is said to occur when an organization achieves a larger scale by the acquisition of other, pre-existing, organizations.

grudge purchase A product bought of necessity with no consumer enthusiasm. Also known as a 'distress purchase'. Examples include petrol for a car, fuel for central heating or a long-term commuter season ticket. The problem for retailers is that such products have no positive 'personality', and are subject to no, or low, brand loyalty. This can lead to brand, store or supplier switching by consumers as a result of small changes in price. Marketers (of, say, petrol) try to shift the emphasis away from the product itself to the whole service aspect associated with the product (i.e. the petrol station).

guarantee A formal assurance often given by retailers or manufacturers to consumers that a good or service will meet certain quality standards or specifications. If a good or service breaks down while under guarantee a consumer can often obtain a full replacement.

guppie Slang term for 'gay upwardly, mobile, professional person', indicating a certain type of lifestyle of a group of consumers.

H

haberdasher A retailer, or department in a larger retailer, which sells dressmaking requisites (e.g. patterns, fabric, buttons, pins, zips, hooks and eyes, needles and thread).

half-day closing *See* EARLY CLOSING.

hall test A market research technique used for trialing, in a central location, products, advertising or other items of marketing interest. It involves the recruitment of a sample of consumers who are brought into a conveniently located hall, where they are exposed to the product etc., and asked for their reactions to it.

hallmark *See* ASSAY MARK.

halo effect A bias in consumer response to a set of marketing research questions about a product, psychologically induced by the consumer's prior positive (or possibly negative) evaluation of the product or brand being researched.

handbill A sheet showing special offers or price reductions, which is given to shoppers, or delivered to houses in a particular CATCHMENT AREA.

handling charge Monies levied for processing payment or delivery of goods (e.g. a charge levied by a manufacturer for accepting retailer returns and passing them back to stock).

hard copy The contents of all, or part, of a computer file printed out onto paper so as to enable the user to take the printed pages away.

hard disk In a computer, an electromagnetic device which provides for the semi-permanent recording of SOFTWARE and DATA through the combination of a rigid rotating magnetic medium and a recording head.

hard good Literally, an item of non-food merchandise that is not soft to the touch. The term is used to describe items such as furniture, other household goods, electrical appliances etc. within a particular analysis of trade. It is particularly prevalent as a descriptor in the context of department stores and other mixed merchandise retailers. *Compare* SOFT GOOD.

hard sell A technique whereby consumers are subjected to persistent, relentless overcoming of objections, a presentation of options and a reluctance to take 'no' for an answer on the part of a salesperson. *Compare* SOFT SELL.

hard technology Seen in its widest sense as the application of any art or science to purposive behaviour, technology is described as 'hard' where the principal manifestation of such application is in the form of machinery, whether of mechanical, electro-mechanical, or electronic type. This is in contrast to SOFT TECHNOLOGY, which is the application of designed systems of interaction, such as management systems or reward systems to the purposes of an organization. The implementation of hard technology often has specific requirements for the development of soft technology at the same time within the implementing organization.

hardware Physical parts of a computer system, such as the central processing unit, DISKS, keyboard and printer. *Compare* SOFTWARE.

haulage The act of moving goods, especially by road.

hawker A person who travels from place to place selling goods, especially one who offers goods for sale at domestic premises.

head office The administrative centre, not necessarily the registered office, of a multi-site retailer.

health and beauty aids Goods and appliances sold specifically for personal grooming (e.g. cosmetics, perfumes, heated rollers, shavers, exercise machines).

Health and Safety at Work Act 1974 (UK) Legislation which lays down many of the employer's duties in relation to providing good, environmentally sound working practices. It also gives guidance on how to conduct the business in such a way that persons other than employees (e.g. customers) are not unreasonably exposed to health and safety risks. It states that entrances, exits and equipment in shops must be safe, and the employer should provide training and instruction for employees on health and safety. There are regulations in the Act controlling the handling, storage and movement of articles or substances. A retailer who employs more than five people has to provide a written statement of the safety policy and arrangements, and bring it to the attention of the employees.

Most other developed jurisdictions provide similar guidelines or requirements.

health bar Food and confectionary product made from cereals, dried fruit and sugar in the form of a small rectangular block.

health food Nutrition products and associated items, including dietary supplements, which are sold on the basis of a claim to being more wholesome than their mainstream equivalents. The rise in the importance of health food is a response to the changing focus of concern over the content of food and the correctness of diet: in the immediate post-war period this focus was on an adequate nutritional intake; more recently it has shifted to the balance of nutriments and the inclusion or exclusion of constituents such as roughage, polyunsaturated fat, sugar etc.

heat sealing Thermosetting plastic film for packaging, used to prevent air from circulating freely around a product in the pack. Heated jaws clasp the plastic film and join it by melting, thus sealing the product in. Heat sealing is used for food and non-food items and improves the appearance of many packs for display purposes. It can be used in conjunction with inert gas systems to improve the shelf life of prepared foods.

heterogeneous Consisting of unrelated parts, types or elements; used particularly in retailing to describe a type of mixed merchandising policy.

hierarchy An ordered, monotonic structure where each succeeding level in the structure is possessed of a greater measure or amount of the determining criteria for ordering (e.g. in a management hierarchy, each succeeding level of management possesses greater situational authority than lower levels).

high-order product See THRESHOLD.

high season The sales peak of the year. The particular time of year for a high season will depend on the product class. High season for ski wear is December-January, for swimwear it is June-July and for cars in the UK it is August.

high street (UK) A general term used to refer to the retail component of town and city centres (USA: main street). The pace and scale of retail decentralization has increased in many western countries, leading to widespread concern about the future of shopping provision within the high street, and the so-called 'doughnut' effect.

hinterland See CATCHMENT AREA.

hire-purchase (UK) A system of credit finance (now largely superseded by credit sale agreements), whereby the CUSTOMER takes possession of the GOOD after paying a deposit, and then pays the balance of the bill by a series of regular INSTALMENTS. The retailer owns the good until the final instalment is paid.

histogram A pictorial representation (chart) of a frequency, or percentage frequency, distribution, by means of rectangles (bars) whose heights represent the frequencies, and whose widths represent class intervals.

home market See DOMESTIC MARKET.

home shopping The ordering of goods/services directly from domestic premises, to which they are subsequently delivered by the supplier or agent; the buying process does not therefore involve a personal visit to a shop or office. Although traditionally seen as a somewhat DOWN-MARKET activity, more sophisticated and specialized customer targeting, facilitated by the development of computer databases, has allowed companies to move into UP-MARKET segments.

Information on products is provided through catalogues, advertisements, and direct sales techniques. Orders can be placed in four main ways: through agents, by mail, by telephone, or by an interactive telecommunication link (see VIEWDATA, TELESHOPPING).

homogeneous Consisting of related parts, types or elements; used particularly in retailing to describe uniform merchandising approaches.

horizontal blocking A merchandising

technique which extends the product presentation lengthwise along a fixture. *Compare* VERTICAL BLOCKING.

horizontal competition The predominant form of inter-firm rivalry for market resources (including customers). Horizontal competition can occur between similar institutions at any level of the distribution channel (e.g. between retailers and between wholesalers). Rivalry can also be described as horizontal competition when firms in ostensibly dissimilar markets are competing between themselves for the same economic resources of their customers, because of discretionary spending or the substitutability of goods (e.g. competition in the 'leisure' market, or competition between margarine and butter).

horizontal integration Process which occurs when a company develops activities which are directly complementary to its present activities. For example, if one clothing retailer acquires or establishes another, or sets up a chain of footwear shops.

house brand Merchandise or services distinguished by the application of names, marks or design features belonging to the distributor, especially retailers; a PRIVATE LABEL; those distinguishing marks used especially in instances to identify merchandise from an organization where that name is different from that of the organization (e.g. Sears 'Craftsman' power tools, Marks & Spencer's 'St Michael' clothing).

house style The distinguishing visual or other presentation of material related to a particular organization, in a manner designed to be consistent and to present the same identification to audiences over time.

house-to-house selling *See* DOOR-TO-DOOR SELLING.

household A family structure or group of people living in one unit of accommodation.

household appliance A tool, especially one that is powered, used in a domestic context to facilitate the execution of housework (e.g. vacuum cleaner, washing machine).

household debt The total of all monies outstanding to creditors by domestic borrowers in an economy.

household good 1. A tangible product sold to someone buying on his or her own behalf, or on behalf of his or her immediate family group.
　2. (*plural*) Those items of non-food merchandise, often sold through grocery outlets, of low unit price and high repeat purchase rates (e.g. washing up liquid, dusters, polishes), which are used extensively in the home.

housekeeping 1. The function responsible for the domestic upkeep of retail premises, especially cleanliness, maintenance and repair.
　2. More generally, the keeping of items, especially merchandise, in good order, or under adequate storage conditions.

housewife The individual, male or female, who is mainly responsible for shopping for food and everyday goods on behalf of a family or household. Where male, this individual is sometimes referred to as a 'house-husband'.

Huff's probability model A theory and formula for analysing the TRADING AREA of a SHOPPING CENTRE. It relies upon the footage in the centre and differential DRIVE TIMES for different classes of product to determine a probability that consumers will shop at a particular centre.

human resource People, especially the labour force of a particular firm and the management function chiefly concerned with their recruitment, selection, training etc. The term embraces the quantitative and qualitative characteristics of the labour force, and the methods, procedures and approaches designed to enhance the ability to promote customer service and operational efficiency.

hygiene management 1. Efforts to implement and control appropriate standards of housekeeping and cleanliness in a (retail) company. Particular attention is paid to the storage, handling and display of perishables, especially foodstuffs, and the avoidance of cross-contamination between cooked and raw foods.

2. The term of the occupational psychologist Dr Frederich Herzberg, referring to the positive measures which management needs to take in order to offset the tendency of employees expressing dissatisfaction about their material environment in such matters as pay, working conditions and fringe benefits. Hygiene factors are not able to produce satisfaction, but their absence or dissatisfaction causes demotivation.

hypermarket A very large store, usually over 50,000 square feet, on one level, situated on the edge of town or in retail parks, selling a wide range of groceries and non-foods. Stores selling only non-foods are excluded. The concept originated in France and spread throughout Europe, initially with French hypermarket operators offering expertise through joint ventures. The share of food sales through hypermarkets was estimated by the Corporate Intelligence Group, London, as about 20 per cent in the UK, France and West Germany, 17 per cent in Belgium, and 7 to 10 per cent in the Netherlands and Denmark in 1989.

I

image 1. A visual likeness of a person, scene etc. produced by an optical device, artist or illustrator.

2. The psychological perception of a commercial entity held by a (potential) consumer, derived from the prior experience of interaction, consumption of marketing messages and other inputs.

Commercial organizations are typically much concerned that the image held of them by significant others is both consistent and positive. To this end, organizations often employ extensive efforts (e.g. through ADVERTISING and corporate design programmes) to present consistent visual presentation and associate themselves with characteristics seen as desirable.

image analysis The structured evaluation of customer perceptions of an organization in terms of pertinent and salient characteristics relating to the generation of psychological representations of the firm. One particular common approach to image analysis is to produce MAPS of the customers' perceptual space, showing the relative positions of a firm and its competitors against salient characteristics and possibly an 'ideal'.

impact studies The systematic evaluation of the anticipated effects on existing patterns of trade of the introduction of a new retailer in a given location. While a wide variety of impact study methodologies have been used, a number of basic components can be identified, namely (i) identification of the potential catchment area of a proposed new retail development; (ii) analysis of the catchment area's socio-economic characteristics; (iii) estimation of consumer expenditure within the catchment area; (iv) estimation of consumer expenditure likely to be drawn to the new development; (v) estimation of the impact of the development on the viability and vitality of other shopping centres in the catchment area; (vi) advice on the acceptability or otherwise of the predicted levels of impact; (vii) recommendations as to how the benefits of the proposal can be optimized.

import 1. To bring GOODS or SERVICES into a country from a foreign country for sale.

2. Any product offered for sale in a country other than that of origin, viewed from the perspective of the receiving country. *Compare* EXPORT.

importer An individual or organization which brings goods into a country from abroad. An importer is often a specialist company acting with a view to the resale of such goods.

impulse good Product which is believed to attract buying by the customer without prior deliberation and is merchandised to encourage such buying (e.g. by being placed close to a CHECKOUT).

impulse line A product stocked, displayed and/or promoted specifically to encourage purchasing without prior consumer deliberation.

impulse purchase A consumer good bought unplanned, and not from a prepared shopping list, which can frequently be for immediate personal consumption. For retailers, such purchases provide an opportunity for extra sales, as illustrated by the food stores' 'checkout tempters'. Individual and multipack sweets and COUNTLINES are carefully graded by height of reach as children's, personal and family items. Gas stations use the same principle to merchandise food and non-food items to visiting motorists. *See also* IMPULSE PURCHASING.

impulse purchasing Activities of consumers in making unpremeditated buys. Studies have shown that there are various levels of planning purchase, and they have categorized impulse purchasing into: (i) *pure impulse* – a novelty purchase which breaks a normal buying pattern; (ii) *reminder impulse buying* – where a shopper is reminded of the need to buy a product when seeing it in a shop, or recalling an advertisement, or seeing it in a catalogue etc.; (iii) *suggestion impulse buying* – where a shopper sees a product for the first time and visualizes a need for it; (iv) *planned impulse buying* – where a shopper has a purchase in mind but leaves the actual decision to the point

of sale depending on price, special offers, sales person advice etc.

An important consideration for retailers designing a store or catalogue etc. is creating impulse purchases by using tactics of design, merchandising, store layout, sales personnel and promotional activity.

in-home retailing Sale to ultimate consumers which occurs in the purchaser's own domicile. *See also* HOME SHOPPING.

in-store bakery A department normally located in a SUPERMARKET or SUPERSTORE which produces bread and associated flour confectionery products from either the basic raw materials or from ready-prepared frozen dough.

in-store merchandising The arrangement of goods within a retail outlet in order to attract interest and invite purchase. Some retailers provide detailed plans from head office showing colour combinations and stock positions for a specific time period, while others leave the merchandising to store managers and staff.

in-store promotion Marketing communication activity which is specifically outlet-based, and which may involve sampling or tasting a product or products, supported by display material and (probably) a reduction in the normal price.

in transit Goods or documentation currently *en route* from one location to another.

incentive An encouragement to sell or to buy. In a customer sense (encouragement to buy) such incentives are more often termed SALES PROMOTIONS. Sales incentives for sales people (encouragements to sell) are intended to reward selling effort and encourage selling attention to particular products. In retail, opinions vary as to the value of such incentives. Although they are believed to encourage effort, they may lead to strong, or pushy, sales techniques which could conflict with the service objectives that many retail businesses pursue. Various systems for incentives are employed (e.g. cash bonuses or prizes).

income statement A document which shows revenues, expenses, losses and tax charges for an ACCOUNTING PERIOD. The balance derived from the subtraction of expenses, losses and taxes from total revenues is termed 'net income'. The form of the income statement may be varied to suit specific needs and the date of revenue and expenses may be reported in more or less detail.

independent retailer Any business, selling principally to those buying on their own behalf or on behalf of their household, whose form of legal organization, or pattern of ownership, is such that the business is controlled by an individual or (family) group deriving the benefits of ownership directly.

independent store *See* INDEPENDENT RETAILER.

Index of Retail Sales (UK) Published monthly by the Central Statistical Office, the index numbers of retail sales are presented in two ways. (i) Retail sales, by volume and value, are given in seasonally adjusted aggregate form for food, non-food and mixed retail businesses in Great Britain. The non-food retailers are categorized as 'Clothing and footwear', 'Household goods' and 'Other non-foods', and do not include the motor trade. (ii) A seasonally unadjusted series of aggregate sales value is given for the following retail sectors in Great Britain: grocers; dairymen; butchers; fishmongers; greengrocers/fruiterers; bread and flour confectioners; men and boys' wear; women's wear and general clothing; leather and footwear; furniture, carpets and household textiles; electrical and music goods; gas showrooms; hardware, china and fancy goods; DIY; electricity showrooms; TV and other hire and repair business; CTNs; off-licences; chemists; booksellers, stationers and newsagents; jewellers; toys, hobbies, sports and cycles; large mixed businesses; other mixed businesses; general mail order.

induction Process of providing individuals new to an organization or situation with a guide to procedures, modes of operation, culture etc., in a way such as to facilitate the individual becoming part of the organization.

industrial relations The quality of understanding (and the attempts to mediate it) that exists between groups of managers and employees within an organization. It may include the formal and informal mechanisms that promote that effective communication which is necessary to monitor and resolve issues of mutual interest.

inflation A reduction in the value of money over time, as a result of increasing national income without any corresponding increase in the volume of goods and services produced. Since inflation has the effect of distorting accounting information, current cost accounting is used to adjust the FINAL ACCOUNTS for inflation.

information technology (IT) The mechanisms and systems (especially electronic) which enable data to be stored, processed, transmitted and accessed through computer-based and telecommunication systems in order to create meaningful interchange between individuals, organizations etc.

ink jet printing A computer-driven reprographic device which produces an image on the paper, or other medium, by spraying a very fine stream of ink in the required shapes under the control of an electrically charged plate equipped with slits through which the ink stream passes. The stream, propelled by piezo-electricity, is discontinuous and the image is formed by a series of closely spaced dots. In packaging applications, types of ink jet printers are often used to add items such as date marks, batch numbers etc. that are frequently changing.

innovation The process of developing new products, or new forms of other elements of the marketing mix, and bringing them to the attention of the market place. More generally the process of developing new methods and approaches to any existing task, or the treatment of new tasks.

innovator 1. Generally, an individual involved in the process of the development of new ideas, processes, applications etc.

2. One of that small percentage of individuals in any given market who are likely to adopt a newly introduced product. This is a particular class of individuals within the DIFFUSION OF INNOVATION.

installment (USA) *See* INSTALMENT.

instalment Each of a regular set of payments, of normally equal amounts, which is made until the total amount owed is paid.

instalment plan (chiefly USA) A term relating to, or describing, CREDIT SALE arrangements.

insurance A contract whereby one part (the insurer) agrees to indemnify another party (the insured) against financial loss arising from the occurrence of the insured event (peril) on payment by the insured of a singular sum of money or series of payments (premiums). Such a contract for an event or peril which may occur is termed insurance, whereas if the event is certain to occur (e.g. death) the contract may be termed 'assurance'.

intellectual property Patents, trademarks, designs, and more recently copyright, 'know-how' and trade secrets. Intellectual property is property in the sense that all of the foregoing can be bought, sold, traded or otherwise licensed.

intelligent tills Electronic cash registers with added memory to handle large numbers of PRICE LOOK-UPS (PLUs) to analyse daily takings into departments and, within limits, to monitor stock levels. They are commonly used by small retailers prior to venturing into, or as an alternative to, full EPOS systems in their shops.

interactive video The provision of audio-visual materials in a format which permits the user to direct the presentation of fresh or additional elements at a pace, or in a pattern, which he/she determines. The chief method presently employed for achieving this is the combination of microcomputer and video disk player. The user controls the inter-action through the keyboard, keypad or touch-screen input. Interactive video is used particularly in training, educational and POINT OF SALE applications.

interior display Presentation of mer-chandise in-store (as opposed to the window displays) in order to create and sustain interest and stimulate purchases within the store. *See also* IN-STORE MERCHANDISING.

intermediary Any organization, indi-vidual or other body that functions as an element between manufacturer and ultimate consumer in the channel of distribution.

internationalization 1. The process by which retailers develop a trading presence outside their home markets. Two principal approaches are found: (i) the establishment of company-owned stores and/or franchise oper-ations using the same trading format; (ii) mergers/acquisitions/joint ven-tures with foreign companies, where trading formats are not necessarily replicated. *See also* GLOBAL RETAILER, MULTI-NATIONAL RETAILER.
  2. The spread between countries of trading formats, technologies, techniques, which may take place

independently of the physical expan-sion of individual retailers – for example, self-service, integrated shopping centres and consumer tar-geting strategies.

interpersonal skills Abilities (which can be acquired by an individual through training) to establish and develop relationships with other indi-viduals in society. Examples which are particularly important in a retail context would include the ability of a buyer to negotiate with a supplier and the ability of a sales assistant to question customers to find out what particular goods and services they may require.

interviewing A human encounter process designed to obtain relevant data or information for a constructive purpose (e.g. selection, counselling, market research).

intimate apparel Female underwear and sleepwear (esp. USA). *See also* LINGERIE.

intrinsic Wholly within, or belong-ing to any situation, object, or other circumstance. Specifically, used to describe those rewards accruing to activities of any kind including con-sumption activities.

introductory offer The initial con-signment of a new, repackaged, alternatively sized or otherwise altered commodity, which is on sale at a reduced price in order to create interest and stimulate sales.

inventory 1. *See* STOCK.
  2. A LIST of merchandise items held in STOCK.

inventory control The management

process of planning, measuring, monitoring and deciding upon the variety, scope and levels of stock of merchandise items to be held by a RETAILER or other CHANNEL MEMBER, in order to meet anticipated customer demand.

inventory management The activity of planning and administering the company's stockholdings, their storage and distribution. It is one of the most important and expensive functions within retailing and has a major impact on the standard of CUSTOMER SERVICE achieved.

Inventory management involves: determining the size, depth and location of inventories; housing and distributing them in the most effective way within certain constraints of time and cost; providing information to other departments, such as buyers, merchandisers and store operations to enable them to carry out their responsibilities

In retailing, the key to effective inventory management is achieving a proper balance between the sales of particular items and funds invested in them. Excessive inventories are expensive to maintain, tie-up capital and can lead to excessive markdowns and eroded margins. Inadequate inventories may result in lost sales and a poor customer perception of the company for reliability and service.

inventory turnover *See* STOCK TURNOVER.

investment appraisal The process of evaluating current options for the most effective application of capital sums available for long-term employment in a business. The techniques available for such a process provide a means of comparing the total cost incurred in carrying out a project with the revenue generated by the project over its expected life. The simplest and therefore most popular technique of this nature is the payback method, which is concerned with the number of years it takes to recover the costs of a project via its earnings. More sophisticated approaches are given by the 'net present value' and by the 'internal rate of return' methods, which are also known as 'discounted cash flow' methods. These take into account the fact that money owned in the present is worth more than the same amount receivable at a future date, by applying a discount factor to the anticipated cash flows.

invoice A document sent from supplier to customer containing details of the goods delivered, the cost thereof and payment required.

island display A free-standing presentation of merchandise, separate from other displays. It is sometimes central providing a focal point, or peripheral and used to divide departments physically.

island position Newspaper or magazine advertising space that is separate from all other advertisements.

isochrone A line or curve on a map which joins points of equal travel time from a centre by means of one form of transport. For retail purposes, isochrones usually refer to car travel. The shape of isochrones is never a perfect circle since they are elongated along routes where travel is faster. Isochrones are used in retail planning as a means of delimiting

CATCHMENT AREAS, where they are commonly linked to demographic data in order to establish, for instance, the number of people who live within an hour's driving of a particular location.

J

job description Formally, a document which specifically outlines the functions, duties etc. attaching to a particular post, possibly incorporating the requisite measures of performance.

job evaluation A rational means of ranking posts by reference to the component tasks according to their relative difficulty, responsibility and importance within an organization.

job grading The method by which a variety of different posts are evaluated and put in like groups, normally for the purpose of identifying appropriate salary scales and for assisting in future human resource planning.

job lot 1. A group of miscellaneous goods offered for sale as a whole, especially to a retailer (e.g. a job lot of household goods).

2. A group of similar items, but of variable quality, provenance etc., offered for sale as a whole.

job specification Formally, a document which identifies the qualifications, experience, attributes and personal qualities necessary for the successful discharge of the duties of the post, by its holder.

jobber 1. A WHOLESALER.

2. A dealer in commodities who buys on his or her own account.

3. Formerly, a dealer in stocks who dealt with brokers and not with the public direct. Now known in the UK as a MARKET-MAKER.

judgement sample A subset of a POPULATION selected on the basis of the personal choice of the researcher about the people/companies who are most likely to be representative of the population. The technique is commonly used in EXPLORATORY RESEARCH, and in business or individual research.

judgement forecast A prediction based on the personal assessment of an expert in the field in question.

jumble sale A retail activity which usually takes place in a community location (e.g. church hall or school), where old and unusual or unwanted items are exchanged for money. The proceeds of the activity are normally donated to a 'worthy cause' (e.g. a local football team, church funds or a charity).

jumbo pack An extra-large size of goods offered for sale at preferential price for promotional or money-saving purposes.

junk mail A derogatory term for

DIRECT MAIL, especially where poorly or inappropriately directed.

just in time (JIT) The production or delivery of merchandise items to the correct specification in the quantities needed by subsequent production processes or customers, at the particular moment they are required. The focus of JIT methods is on the elimination of inventory (work in progress) between members of the CHANNEL OF DISTRIBUTION (production departments) by co-ordinating the final stockholding rate with customer demand rate.

just in time inventory system *See* JUST IN TIME.

just in time stock replenishment *See* JUST IN TIME.

K

key account Any customer who represents a significant proportion of the sales of an organization. This is frequently the case for those who sell to the retail multiples. A key account is one which would significantly damage the business if lost and which, therefore, requires high-level attention within the company for negotiation and business maintenance.

keystone markup An increase on the wholesale or supplier price of a good whereby the retail price is double the cost price.

kickback A payment or gift made by a purchaser to a salesperson or vice versa to show 'appreciation'. It is unethical, and, in certain circumstances, illegal.

Kimball tag A punched ticket attached to a good to be removed or part removed at the POINT OF SALE. Information contained on such a tag (e.g. size, colour, style) will then be fed to a computer to aid further buying.

Kite mark (UK) A designating symbol used on goods to indicate compliance with the relevant standards, as approved by the British Standards Institution (*see* Appendix 2).

knock down (KD) 1. To offer for sale in disassembled form, requiring customers to provide final assembly themselves. The term is used especially of furniture and other large consumer durables.

2. The action of an auctioneer, of closing a sale of the specific item in an AUCTION by bringing down his or her hammer to signify that no further bids will be taken.

knocked-down A colloquial usage to suggest that goods or services are offered for sale at extremely reduced prices from those prevailing normally.

knowledge engineering In computing, the process of creating a base of expertise for use with an EXPERT SYSTEM or knowledge-based system. The process can be particularly difficult when the aim is to elicit specific knowledge or expertise from a human expert in order that it can be incorporated into a computerized system which offers informed advice.

known-value item (KVI) A basic food or household good, bought frequently by shoppers, the price of which is generally believed to be remembered by such shoppers. It is usually prominently featured in retail shops and is generally a high- volume low-profit-margin item (e.g. a packet of biscuits, coffee, sugar).

kraft Strong brown wrapping paper.

L

label A ticket, or sign, especially one of paper or card, attached to an item of merchandise indicating ingredients, composition, size, brand, marked price, computer code, sell-by date or any other combination of information pertinent to the customer. By extension, the term is also used to refer to such information when printed directly on the packaging, container etc.

lading The cargo carried in a vehicle of transportation, especially a ship.

laggard One of that small group of individuals identified by the DIFFUSION OF INNOVATION theory as being the last in a marketplace to accept or take up an innovation. More generally, those individuals or organizations who are the slowest to adopt new processes.

landed cost price The money to be charged for goods, together with transportation and unloading charges, used especially of goods shipped internationally.

laser scanner An opto-electrical device for reading product BARCODES. It directs an intense narrow beam of laser light onto product barcodes which are then 'read' by reference to the patterned reflection produced.

Some scanners are hand-held in the form of a wand (e.g. in bookshops or clothing retailers), whereas others are fixed for goods to pass over (e.g. in supermarkets or DIY stores).

last in first out *See* LIFO.

lay-away A GOOD whose purchase is secured through a deposit by a consumer, but which remains the property of the retailer until the payment is completed.

layout The spacial arrangement of fixtures etc. within retail stores and distribution facilities. The term is also extended to mean the pattern of display of merchandise on FIXTURES etc.

lead generation The initial activity, within the overall selling process, which seeks to stimulate potential buyers of products to contact supplying organizations in order to arrange for further sales visits. Such activities include press advertising, telephone canvassing etc.

lead time 1. The period that elapses between a supplier's receiving an order and having the ordered items available for the purchaser.
2. The period that elapses between the decision to carry out some activity and the individual or organization

being in the position to carry out that activity. (E.g. 'There is lead time of 18 months between site acquisition and opening a new store.')

leader pricing See LOSS LEADER.

leaflet Any printed message on paper, usually folded for distribution, especially for promotional purposes.

leakage The decrease in the value of stocks, cash income, profit etc. which is attributable to unknown causes, especially theft. Leakage is also known as stock loss or SHRINKAGE.

lease A contract between the owner of property and its occupier or user. The lease sets out the terms, conditions and period for occupation or use, rent etc. for that property. The term is used especially of contracts for the occupancy of buildings etc. and other capital assets (e.g. motor vehicles).

There are two main types of leasing agreements: the financial lease and the operating lease.

The *financial lease* is used as an alternative to loan finance. The lease cannot be terminated and the lessee bears the risk of the arrangement. The lessor aims to recover the full purchase price of the asset plus interest.

The *operating lease* leaves the risk with the lessor, as it can be terminated by giving notice. Operating leases are often used for assets which may become obsolete quite rapidly, but where a secondary market exists (e.g. operating leases may be used for electronic scales and cash registers). It is common practice for the lessor to agree to sell the asset to the lessee at the end of the lease for a nominal fee.

leased department An area where a retailer rents space to market his or her products within another retail outlet. (*See also* CONCESSION.) Leased departments are especially prevalent within DEPARTMENT STORES and other large retailers.

letter of credit A business document issued by a financial institution such as a bank, entitling the bearer to draw funds up to a specified maximum from that financial institution, its agencies or correspondents etc. The bearer is usually identified in the letter, as are the specific conditions which need to be met for the sum to become available. Letters of credit are widely used in international trade.

letterpress A traditional form of relief printing, where the shapes of the individual elements to be printed stand proud of the printing cylinder or plate. The advantages of the method are that it is relatively easy to change a small section of, for example, a printed page. However, it is generally slower and less flexible than processes such as FLEXOGRAPHY.

leverage The proportion to which a company's long-term financial structure is founded on DEBT on the one hand and on EQUITY on the other. A common way of calculating leverage is by using the following formula:

$$Leverage = \frac{Long\text{-}term\ debt + Equity}{Equity}$$

or its reciprocal. *See also* RATIO ANALYSIS.

liability A financial or other form of obligation which an organization or individual can be forced to discharge through the action of the courts. Such obligations can arise directly (e.g. through entering into a contract), or indirectly, through the application of statute or common law (e.g. the liability of an occupier for injuries caused to visitors through his or her carelessness). *See also* LIMITED LIABILITY.

life-cycle *See* FAMILY LIFE-CYCLE, PRODUCT LIFE-CYCLE.

lifestyle A form of classification of consumers by means of their style of living as opposed to segmentation by age, sex or social class.

lifestyle marketing The use of a system of MARKET SEGMENTATION according to group behavioural patterns. *See also* PSYCHOGRAPHICS.
  Various mnemonics have been applied to lifestyle groups (e.g. YUPPIE, DINKIE etc.). Retailers such as The Limited and Next in the 1980s have been successful by identifying with a particular lifestyle group at a particular period, believing that lifestyle segmentation gives them a broader picture of their target customers.

LIFO Last in first out. A method of stock valuation under which it is assumed that the goods most recently purchased are the ones immediately resold. In times of INFLATION the LIFO method is accurate in matching current costs and revenues, thereby resulting in a lower gross profit figure than FIFO. However, in the BALANCE SHEET an unrealistically low figure is assigned to stock as a result. This method is illegal in the UK but is legally acceptable in the USA.

lighting The design of, and the actual equipment used, to provide artificial illumination within a store. The nature of lighting used in a store is known to have an impact on customer behaviour. Variations in the illumination provided can play an important part in determining store ATMOSPHERICS.

limited function wholesaler A CHANNEL intermediary not selling to ultimate customers who has attempted to eliminate some of the functions associated with the typical pattern of operations of such intermediaries (e.g. a CASH AND CARRY wholesaler who is not involved with credit provision or delivery of goods to retailers).

limited liability 1. The containment of financial obligation to a predetermined sum.
  2. Specifically, a form of legal organization of companies where the extent of the ownership of the company by any individual is determined by the number of shares owned. In such circumstances the share owner's liability is restricted to the capital value of the shares owned.

line of credit The amount of money or monetary values that one party is prepared to advance or make available to another in pursuance of business relationships. (E.g. A supplier might make available to a retailer a line of credit of $100,000, thus allowing the retailer to purchase goods on account up to this sum.)

linear footage Measurement of the length of available countering and other fixturing etc. for the display of merchandise.

linear regression In its simplest form,

a statistical technique used for forecasting, which assumes a linear relationship between a dependent variable and an explanatory (or independent) variable. Examples are the relationship between the unit monthly sales of a product and the LINEAR FOOTAGE allocated to it in store, and the relationship between weekly energy costs and store square footage.

If a high CORRELATION exists, say, between linear footage and unit monthly sales, then a regression equation provides the vehicle for predicting unit monthly sales at different allocations of linear footage to the product (see below). The explanatory variable (in this case, linear footage) is a controllable variable (i.e. the retailer can determine the exact allocation of linear footage to the product over a given period), whereas the dependent variable (e.g. unit monthly sales) is a random variable whose value results from the net effect of many factors outside the control of the user. However, provided that a high correlation exists between the variables, the regression equation can be a useful management tool for predicting the effect, on unit monthly sales, of varying the linear footage.

For example, suppose that the regression equation has the form:

$$Sales = 45 + 310 \times Linear\ footage$$

If 10 linear feet are allocated to the product, then predicted monthly:

$$Sales = 45 + (310)(10) = 45 + 3100 = 3145\ units$$

Whereas, if 15 linear feet are allocated to the product, then predicted monthly:

$$Sales = 45 + (310)(15) = 45 + 4650 = 4695\ units$$

Given that sufficient existing data is available on the two variables, all statistical software and some SPREADSHEETS handle the computation of the appropriate regression equation. They can also handle the calculations associated with multiple linear regression, where the dependent variable is related to several, rather than one, explanatory variables.

liner conference A regular meeting of shippers who use established routes, to seek agreement on freight rates, shipping intervals etc.

lingerie Women's sleepwear and underwear, sometimes taken to include structured garments such as corsetry and brassières.

liquidation The winding-up of a business organization, prior to its dissolution, and the distribution of its assets amongst creditors and owners, after the discharge of debts (where possible). This winding-up can be on a voluntary basis, in which case a liquidator is appointed by the owners or creditors to supervise the process. In the case of a compulsory winding-up, the courts appoint an official to be in charge of the disposal of assets and payment of claimants. The precise processes to be followed in such procedures vary from jurisdiction to jurisdiction, but such procedures are formed wherever business law is developed.

liquidity The measure of, and ability to meet, short-term financial obligations (e.g. amounts outstanding to trade creditors) by turning CURRENT ASSETS, such as stock and debtors, into cash. The liquidity of retailers is usually very low. Especially in the grocery trade, high STOCK TURNOVER, combined with considerable power to extract favourable credit terms from suppliers, results in an excess of CURRENT LIABILITIES over current assets. Liquidity ratios (*see* RATIO ANALYSIS) are often calculated in order to compare the current liquidity of a company with historical figures and the figures of near competitors.

liquidity ratio *See* RATIO ANALYSIS.

list 1. Figuratively, the action of a retailer in placing the particular item of merchandise from a supplier on its roster of goods to offer for retail sale. *Compare* DELIST.
    2. The full roster of such items available for sale.

list price The amount to be charged for a product currently appearing in promotional literature etc., issued by a manufacturer. The term is used especially to denote the retail prices that manufacturers would wish to see charged for their products.

lithography A method of plano-graphic printing where the image and the base area are on the same level, and the distinction between them is created by chemical means, especially the antagonism of grease and water. Non-image areas are wetted to repel the grease-based inks that are generally used. The ink is transferred not from the image roller directly onto paper but via an intermediate roller called a blanket cylinder. This soft surface allows earlier transfer of the image and for faster printing times. Lithography takes several

forms. High-quality multi-colour printing is the norm in this most widely used printing process, which is used typically for long runs of print material, including packaging.

livery The physical design and visual appearance of an organization's vehicles and personnel uniforms. The term is used especially to describe the typical colour scheme, style, type-faces etc. used by organizations in presenting a consistent appearance to others.

load The consignment transported by vehicle.

loading The process of placing goods on a vehicle ready for shipment.

local advertising Paid-for insertions in mass media under clear sponsor-ship occurring within a town, village or restricted area. Local advertising contrasts with international, national, or regional advertising. Principal mechanisms for such advertising are local newspapers, radio etc.

local press Newspapers which are sold (as opposed to being distributed free) in a restricted area. In small countries such as England national press predominates in certain adver-tising areas, whereas in large countries like the USA local press predominates.

local rate A discounted charge for regionally restricted advertising levied by the owners of various media vehicles.

local station A radio or TV broadcas-ter with a limited transmission area, in distinction to nationally networked stations.

local store A convenience outlet situated in a residential area in order to serve the indigenous population.

location A place, site or area. A distinction can be made between *absolute location*, which refers to the exact location of a place identified by grid co-ordinates (e.g. latitude and longitude globally or the national grid reference system as in the UK), and *relative location*, which describes a place or site in relation to other similar places or sites and/or other relevant variables. Relative location is often used for example, to classify retail outlets (e.g. 'high street' shops are often contrasted with 'out-of-town' stores).

location strategy The explicit selection of sites for retail outlets within a given geographical area in accordance with predetermined objectives and criteria. Such selection must be seen as part of a more general corporate strategy reflecting both the company's objectives and trading policies and its assessment of such external environment factors as population characteristics, spending power and the location of its competitors. While many retail companies have developed their own characteristic locational strategy two general approaches can be identified: (i) the building of new outlets, (ii) the acquisition of existing retail companies' units or other premises and their conversion to the company's trading format. The relocation of outlets within existing trading areas is also a common characteristic of rapidly growing retail organizations.

logistics The systematic management and study of the planning, allocation and control of the financial, physical and human resources committed to PHYSICAL DISTRIBUTION, stockholding and service levels. It deals with all aspects of movement and storage facilities in the SYSTEM from the point of raw material acquisition to the point of customer consumption, for the purpose of providing adequate customer service at reasonable cost to the firm. Logistics differs from simple physical distribution or transportation in that it considers other factors such as packaging, stockholding costs and customer service, simultaneously with transport costs.

A second feature of a logistics approach is the recognition that a reliable flow of information from buyer to seller will ensure the efficient management of the LOGISTICS SYSTEM.

logistics system Any complete supply chain from manufacturer or grower to the consumer. Any retail business trading from store locations is part of the predominant logistics system to supply consumer goods to the customer. But other systems exist, such as MAIL ORDER and other forms of HOME SHOPPING. Each logistics system has its own inherent benefits and costs to the ultimate consumers, who will evaluate the real value to them when selecting one system in favour of another. The control of the logistics system, by the manufacturer or retailer, is an issue of concern to both parties.

logo A trademark, company emblem or similar device, used to identify an organization or its products. (An abbreviation of 'logotype'.)

loss The results of expenses for an ACCOUNTING PERIOD exceeding the

SALES REVENUE for the period. A gross loss is made when the COST OF GOODS SOLD is higher than the sales revenue. A net loss is made when the cost of goods sold added together with the expenses for the period exceeds the sales revenue in value.

loss leader An item put on sale at a low margin or below full cost in order to attract customers. Loss leaders are usually highly publicized and well known items. Where personal selling is used, salespeople aim to trade customers up away from basic loss leaders to higher value items.

lot An item, collection, assortment etc. of goods offered as an individual sale within an AUCTION.

low-involvement good Product which consumers spend little time considering prior to purchase. Usually such products would be frequently purchased, low-value items (e.g. matches, detergents).

low-involvement media Vehicles for marketing communication where the audience receives the message without any effort on their part to put themselves into a receptive position (e.g. television, transport advertising). This is to be contrasted with high-involvement media such as magazines, where the audience deliberately seek out media vehicles.

low-order product *See* THRESHOLD.

low season Period during the year when sales of specific products are below average. Often this is related to changes in the weather. *Compare* HIGH SEASON.

loyalty The attribute of continuing allegiance to, or preference for, a particular entity, or set of values. The term is frequently used in the sense of brand or store loyalty. The concept appears to be relatively simple, but proves to be difficult to operationalize. The high cost of acquiring a new customer compared to the cost of retaining an existing one, means that loyalty is a characteristic of customer behaviour much sought after by suppliers.

LUPIN database (UK) A collection of facts relating to shopping CATCHMENT AREAS, constructed from the results of a large domestic survey which sought to discover where consumers shop.

M

made-to-measure *See* BESPOKE.

magic pricing *See* ODD PRICING.

mail order A particular CHANNEL of retail distribution, distinguished by the absence of physical retail outlets (stores), as customer contact and delivery of merchandise is maintained through the post, telephones etc.

There are two principal forms of mail order: CATALOGUE MERCHANDISING and DIRECT RESPONSE ADVERTISING. In catalogue mail order, retailers distribute books containing illustrated guides to their merchandise ASSORTMENT and customers place orders for illustrated items by post or telephone directly, or alternatively through an AGENT, and goods are delivered by post, parcel services etc.

In direct response, individual items are advertised in mass media and customers place orders directly with the seller for those items, which are then distributed by post, parcel services etc.

Mail Order Protection Scheme (MOPS) (UK) An arrangement set up by publishers which offers certain safeguards for consumers who buy through DIRECT RESPONSE ADVERTISING.

mail shot A promotional activity (or the materials generated by such activity) which involves the use of the post to send (personalized) letters, brochures, leaflets etc. to individuals in an attempt to stimulate demand. Such materials are described disparagingly as JUNK MAIL.

mailer 1. (USA) A company that uses post as an essential means of contact with customers or as a major element in other aspects of activity (e.g. lead generation).

2. (USA) A lettershop. *See* FULFILMENT HOUSE.

3. Any item of paper, card etc. designed specifically for postal transmission, either to provide protection to contents, or to provide a facilitating means of reply etc.

mailing list An ordered collection of names and addresses used as a basis for planned postal contacts with existing or potential customers, or other publics of interest. Mailing lists are developed which are characteristic of certain types of consumers or business groups (e.g. a mailing list of doctors or a mailing list of all DIY stores). Such lists can be obtained, either to buy or rent for specific purposes, from specialist supplying organizations (list brokers).

Mailing Preference Service (UK) A

113

scheme whereby members of the public can state their wish either to be excluded from, or added to, current MAILING LISTS. Similar schemes operate in other countries.

mailing response analysis The process of evaluation of the replies received from an audience after that audience has been sent an initial personal communication, especially promotional. The process is used to measure the effectiveness of campaigns and to plan future mailings.

main street (USA) *See* HIGH STREET.

maintained item A good that is always kept in stock in a merchandise ASSORTMENT (e.g. a black tie in a range of ties).

maintained markup The difference between net sales and the gross cost of merchandise sold, where the price of items of merchandise has varied at different points in time. The term is synonymous with cumulative markup.

management information system (MIS) A computerized communications network (based on the idea that information is a valuable corporate resource) which is designed to convert data from internal and external sources into meaningful material upon which managers can act. Outputs from such systems are normally structured management reports, period reports on, for example, store sales by PRODUCT LINE, and exception reports. In addition to reported facts, the system may include simple analysis of the information to support, for example, sales forecasting or stock ordering.

manager An individual responsible for the control of a specific operation or set of operations, who is probably charged with the organizing, control and monitoring of the output of subordinates.

mannequin 1. A person who wears the clothes exhibited at fashion shows.
2. A life-size DUMMY used for display of clothes in-store or in a WINDOW DISPLAY.

manufacturer The producer of a physical or tangible good for sale. Production is accomplished by taking either raw materials and/or semi-finished materials and processing them to add value.

manufacturer's agent An organization or individual working on behalf of the producer of goods to sell or merchandise such goods to members of the CHAIN OF DISTRIBUTION. Such agents are often used by a manufacturer to distribute products in other countries where the agent will have local knowledge and expertise.

manufacturer's brand The uniquely identifying name, mark, symbols etc. applied by producers to their products, especially where such names etc. are capable of evoking a desired response from consumers.

map Graphical representation of spatial DATA, especially in two-dimensional form, particularly where certain relationships and/or variables are selected for emphasis (e.g. distances, relief etc.).

mapping The graphical presentation of spatial information.

margin That proportion of SALES REVENUE which is CONTRIBUTION. It is the usual practice to differentiate between GROSS MARGIN and NET MARGIN.

marginal costing An approach to the determination of the increased charges incurred by producing one additional item of output. It thus identifies only the direct costs of a product or activity and is used to determine the CONTRIBUTION that item or activity makes towards fixed overhead and profit. *See also* ABSORPTION COSTING.

mark A sign placed on an item to convey information such as quality or character. *See also* ASSAY MARK, KITE MARK.

markdown A downward revision of a previously set retail price. It is a way of adjusting a price to bring it into line with the customers perception of a lesser value, hopefully to achieve prompt sales.

Although markdowns may be caused by buying and pricing errors, in which case they may be seen as devices to correct a previous error (*'correctional' markdowns*) there are two other forms of markdown which need not be viewed negatively. (i) *Operational markdowns* are used to clear merchandise which have become unsaleable at normal prices as a result of normal handling; examples are shop-worn or display goods, fabric remnants and individual items from sets being sold separately to clear. (ii) *Promotional markdowns* may be used to meet price competition or increase sales by increasing store traffic through temporarily reduced prices.

One common form of markdown is the twice-yearly sale by which companies can clear out their stocks. By this means a retailer can maintain a high-class appeal for most of the year but clear its stock by attracting bargain hunters at a time when the regular clientele is less active.

market 1. An event (often regularly occurring) designed to provide the opportunity for individuals and organizations to meet for the purpose of buying and selling merchandise. The range of merchandise to be offered for sale at a particular market may be narrow (e.g. livestock) or the market may be general in its coverage.

2. A place, especially an open square or other arena within a town where such merchandise sales take place.

3. More figuratively, the provision of a mechanism for buyers and sellers to meet or contact one another in the process of exchange.

4. The total demand amongst consumers/customers for a particular line of merchandise or particular service (e.g. the market for shampoo).

5. Business or trade in a particular commodity (e.g. the lead market).

6. The trading opportunity provided by a particular group of people or segment of customers.

market day A designated time within a week, or other calendar period, when provision is regularly made for buyers and sellers to meet for sales of specific or general types of merchandise. Traditionally market day is linked to specific days within towns designated for the sale of livestock and produce.

market development A method of

expanding business by finding new consumers to purchase the current range of goods and services offered by an organization. (One of the four generic strategies of ANSOFF'S MATRIX.)

market hall A roofed building dedicated to the buying and selling of merchandise, usually either open to the public and dealing in a wide range of household goods, or conversely dedicated to certain lines of trade at a wholesale level, in which situation such buildings are often designated by titles such as cloth or draper's hall etc.

market leader 1. An organization which has the largest share in volume or value terms of a particular merchandise sector.
2. An organization which tends to set the pattern for the rest of the organizations in the same sector (e.g. by being the first to raise its prices).

market-maker A wholesale dealer in a range of shares who aims to make a profit on the bid-offer spread of the shares. In this process the price of the shares traded is continuously adjusted according to changes in the demand-supply equilibrium.

market map A graphical representation of the spatial distribution of consumers' perceptions of brands, stores, or products within a perceptual space defined by reference to the most salient criteria. *See also* IMAGE ANALYSIS.

market niche A 'space' within the total (i) pattern of demand or (ii) pattern of supply for a particular product which is not occupied by

current providers, thus affording opportunity for a supplier to meet the demand from a particular segment of consumers.

market penetration A method of expanding business by increasing sales of current products among current purchasers or those similar to them. (One of four generic strategies suggested by ANSOFF'S MATRIX.)

market positioning 1. The location, by reference to salient characteristics, that an organization adopts in presenting itself and its products to relevant groups of consumers.
2. That location that arises as a result of an organization's historical marketing policies.

market pricing Charging for a product what relevant consumers are prepared to pay without reference to (in the short run) cost or other considerations.

market profile A description of the key characteristics of the total pattern of demand for a product in such terms as volume, value, growth, consumer segments, overall structure etc.

market research The systematic scientific gathering, recording and analysing of data concerning all aspects of an organization's concerns with its exchange relationships with customers and with the aggregate levels of demand etc. generated by exchange participants in particular areas, lines of business etc. or in general.
Consumer market research focuses on the attitudes and behaviour of the consumer. 'Trade research' focuses

on the distribution channel members (including retailers). 'Industrial' market research (often referred to as 'business- to-business research') concentrates on manufacturing or service companies who supply non-consumer markets.

Most market research is commissioned from, and carried out by, specialist market research agencies working on behalf of the client company.

market saturation *See* SATURATION.

market segment Any clearly identifiable customer group, where characteristics of members of the group are relatively more HOMOGENEOUS that those between different groups. The term is specifically used to describe customer groups that offer an adequate return to a marketing organization when addressed as a whole.

market segmentation The process of dividing consumers, customers, users into homogeneous subsets, each of which shows similar internal behaviour or taste characteristics but are dissimilar from one another.

In order to be defined as a segment the customer grouping has in some way to be measurable, accessible by marketing channels and marketing communications and viable (i.e. big enough to justify developing a specific marketing mix).

Market segmentation is one of the fundamental concepts of MARKETING. Its value lies with the notion that most markets are segmented, and not uniform, and that by recognizing this more customers can be satisfied profitably.

Various systems for segmentation are available, for example DEMOGRAPHICS, SOCIO-ECONOMIC CLASSIFICATION, behavioural or LIFESTYLE characteristics or regional differences.

In retailing, segmentation is recognized in particular by the 'niche' operators who target a relatively narrow segment with a specifically directed offer.

market share The proportion of the total period sales of a product (by volume or value) enjoyed by any individual manufacturer, supplier etc.

market skimming A pricing technique designed to take advantage of the willingness of a limited segment of customers able to pay for conspicuous exclusivity.

market stall The structure (at its simplest boards and trestles) on which merchandise is displayed within the context of a public arena for the sale of goods, especially those occurring in the open air or MARKET HALLS. In more permanent markets the structure may be of a fairly complex type, akin to, for example, a kiosk.

market structure A description of the number, composition and relationships etc. of buyers and sellers within a particular arena with respect to particular products.

market test The process of conducting an experiment with respect to the MARKETING MIX, in a defined, limited consumer arena.

marketing 1. (chiefly USA) The activity of shopping.

2. One of the chief business functions, concerned with directing an

organization's resources to address continuing exchange relationships with selected groups or customer segments, especially in distinction to production, operations, finance and personnel functions.

3. The study of those voluntary exchange processes between social actors through which value is created and maintained for mutual and/or societal benefit.

marketing communication Persuasive and informative messages directed at ultimate consumers or intermediaries in the CHANNEL OF DISTRIBUTION, designed to emphasize the behaviour of the target audience in the directions desired by the transmitter.

marketing concept An approach to business which holds that the fundamental task of a business is to identify those benefits sought by those particular consumers whose needs, wants and desires the organization is best able to meet in order that the long-term success of the business can be assured. The adoption of such a 'concept' is seen as being central to a MARKETING ORIENTATION.

marketing department That section of an organization which has responsibility for guiding and developing the mutually beneficial exchange relationships between the organization and its customers. Many so-called marketing departments in retail organizations concentrate only on the promotional activities in the MARKETING MIX.

marketing map *See* MARKET MAP.

marketing mix The set of those controllable variables that a company can blend to achieve the required response from its target customers. It has classically been identified as the Four Ps – product, place, price and promotion, which can be combined with varying emphases by marketing management. A description of the scope of each is given below.

Product – the combination of goods and services offered to the market, including the actual product and a range of benefits including packaging, delivery and after- sales service.

Place – the activities which make the product available to the consumer, including the distribution network, stores, agencies etc.

Price – the amount of money and/ or value the customer must pay to obtain the product, after accounting for discount, credit terms etc.

Promotion – activities that communicate the benefits of the product and persuade the target market to buy it, including advertising, public relations activity, price promotions etc.

The marketing mix has been extended and redefined for retailing as the 'retail mix'.

marketing orientation The attitude adopted by an organization and its employees in putting the customer at the centre of all its decisions.

marketing plan A guide to future action, based on an analysis of the current situation, to direct the application of the organization's MARKETING MIX to current and potential MARKET SEGMENTS in order to achieve organizational objectives.

marketing strategy Those elements of the executive control of a firm which relate principally to the definition of target customer segments to be served, and to the mix of product, pricing, promotional and distribution measures to be chiefly employed in the context of mutually beneficial exchange relationships, when considered against the background of competition and the general environment. *See also* CORPORATE STRATEGY.

marketplace 1. The physical space made available for the conduct of the public sale of merchandise in the form of an arena etc.

2. Figuratively, the demand for a particular item, line of merchandise, good or service, particularly in reference to the characteristics of such demand.

markon *See* MARKUP.

markup The difference between the cost of merchandise and its retail price. It can be used in connection with a single item or a group of items.

For example, if an item is bought for £5 and sold for £8, the markup is £3. If a consignment is bought for £30,000 and sold for £50,000 the markup is £20,000.

There are three further terms relating to markup: (i) *initial markup* (or *markon*), which is the difference between the cost of goods and their original retail price; (ii) *cumulative markon*, which is the difference between the total cost and total original retail value of all goods handled to date (i.e. since the beginning of an accounting or trading period); (iii) MAINTAINED MARKUP (or MARGIN), which is the difference between the gross cost of goods sold and net sales (i.e. the prices actually received for goods sold during the period and the actual cost of those goods).

markup percentage That proportion of the COST OF GOODS SOLD which is added to the purchase price of an item in order to determine its selling price. The practice of determining selling price in this way is known as MARKUP or COST-PLUS pricing.

marque A term of French origin denoting a brand of product, especially a car (e.g. Porsche).

marquee Large tent used for exhibitions, functions etc.

mart A marketplace. A term used mostly in connection with sales of SECOND-HAND goods (e.g. car mart, AUCTION mart).

mass media Communication vehicles which reach large audiences, namely newspapers and magazines, television and radio, cinema, posters and transport advertising. The term is used chiefly to describe those media where individual audience members are not pre-identifiable.

mass merchandiser Any retailer, or other CHANNEL intermediary, whose business is concentrated upon supplying relatively uniform standard goods to a chiefly undifferentiated market (e.g. F. W. Woolworth).

master budget The key statement about expected income and outgoings in an ACCOUNTING PERIOD, which, when combined with historical accounting data, enables the drawing up of budgeted INCOME STATEMENT and BALANCE SHEET.

The budgeted income statement serves to show the expected change in the financial position of the business over the budget period. The budgeted balance sheet shows the financial position the business will be in at the end of the budget period if all goes according to plan.

MasterCard One of the two principal international CREDIT CARD systems, to which individual card issuers may belong. The existence of the international system provides for mutual recognition of other issuers' cards, centralized clearing facilities and other merchant benefits. From the consumer's point of view, the system's existence provides greater flexibility and patronage of card usage.

mature market Those arenas for the sales of goods and services in which the pattern of trade and product features have been relatively stable over time and there has been little growth in sales volume.

maturity That phase in the PRODUCT LIFE-CYCLE when demand for product or product class is static or is either growing or declining only slowly. This phase is usually seen as occurring after a period of introduction and initial growth.

maximization The process of taking the value of a selected variable to the extreme high attainable value of the variable. Under restrictive assumptions, and constraints, mathematical MODELS can be devised, which, for example, will suggest a pricing policy for a retailer to achieve maximization of sales value, where, quite literally, sales cannot be made higher by any other policy. In practice, the concept of maximization in such applications may be an ideal, and businesses will realistically aim for targets which differ from the theoretical maximum.

Mazur plan An approach to the management of a retail store, once adopted by many DEPARTMENT STORES, particularly in the USA, whereby the management of the organization has four basic functions – merchandising, publicity, store operations and accounting/control.

mean *See* AVERAGE.

media (*singular* medium) Channels of communication employed by retailers, manufacturers etc. to convey messages to their customers, potential customers and society at large.

The main media are print (newspapers, magazines, leaflets), commercial television (broadcast and cable), cinema, radio and outdoor media (posters, buses, taxicabs etc.). This list, though, is far from comprehensive. Retailers have used such media as theatre tickets, waste bins, banners, sandwich boards, customized carrier bags, delivery bicycles and their own product packaging as vehicles for customer communications. Of particular importance in retailing is the medium of interpersonal communication.

median *See* AVERAGE.

memorandum buying An arrangement for the purchase of merchandise whereby the retailer does not pay for items until they are sold, but does take on the legal title at the time of shipment. The retailer can normally return unsold goods within a specified period of time.

memorandum terms A form of indefinite DATING where the legal title of goods passes to the retailer who then assumes responsibility for damages.

mercantile 1. Relating to the economic theory of mercantilism.

2. Relating to, or the characteristics of, merchants, trade or traders.

merchandise 1. The ASSORTMENT of goods sold by a retailer.

2. Any item offered for sale by a retailer of goods.

merchandise   assortment   *See* ASSORTMENT.

merchandise center (USA) Buying and administration offices, located in a large city, which are used for regular contacts between retail buyers and manufacturers.

merchandise cost The purchase price of goods for resale, less discounts, plus transportation charges (if paid by the retailer).

merchandise ranging The process of determining the ASSORTMENT of products within particular product categories in order to ensure adequate WIDTH and DEPTH.

merchandise return *See* RETURN.

merchandiser 1. A stand on which stock is displayed and which allows easy selection (e.g. greeting cards).

2. A person who allocates stock to branches or who displays stock on sales fixtures within a store.

merchandising 1. In-store layout and display; shelf and fixture space allocation; restocking empty shelves and fixtures and implementing promotional activity at the point of sale.

2. Ordering or reordering goods from suppliers once they have been selected by buyers; managing the

supply chain; planning and implementing distribution and stock levels; progress chasing; maintaining the information base on which the buying and replenishment process depends.

In practice, the word 'merchandising' carries a wide variety of usages and varies from retailer to retailer. In one, for example, it may relate to the entire process of distributing the merchandise, including replenishment ordering, stock control, warehousing, transport and in-store display. In others, the emphasis may be on the positioning of goods in-store, shelf and fixture layout and replenishment and point of sale promotional activity. In mail order, the layout and presentation of goods in the catalogue may be included.

merchandising allowance A reduction in price offered to a retailer by a manufacturer to compensate for retailer incurred costs during a product promotion.

merchant 1. One who buys goods to sell subsequently, especially engaged in trade, or in supply of bulk commodities (i.e. MERCHANT WHOLESALER).

2. Of a bank, when used to describe those activities relating to group 'wholesale' financial activities, or of an organization explicitly established to supply such services.

merchant wholesaler A CHANNEL intermediary who buys goods for resale, taking title and then selling on to retailers etc.

merchantable Saleable or marketable; specifically, of a quality such that the good is fit for ordinary purpose, and any defects are visible to any careful buyer, or are particularly identified (if not visible) prior to sale.

merger Amalgamation; the coming together of two or more commercial firms to form a new organization, or the absorption of one or more firms into another. The term is used when such coming together or absorption is of firms that are of approximately similar sizes, or where the absorption or amalgamation takes place by mutual consent.

metro area *See* METROPOLITAN AREA.

metropolitan area The economically contiguous/homogeneous region surrounding a central or core city.

Metropolitan Statistical Area (MSA) (USA) One of 323 areas, classified by the United States Bureau of the Census, which are drawn around a central urban area with 50,000 or more inhabitants. *See also* ENUMERATION DISTRICT.

microcomputer An electronic device for data storage and transformation, under the control of appropriate SOFTWARE. Silicon microchip technology forms the central processing unit. A microcomputer is physically small, relatively inexpensive, and is often employed for personal use. In retailing, microcomputers are used, with appropriate business software, to fulfil day-to-day clerical and accounting tasks. In addition, they are increasingly being used for specific retail-related applications (e.g. DPP analysis). Microcomputers can act as remote terminals giving access to a large (mainframe) computer. As microcomputer capacity has increased, microcomputer based

EPOS systems are being developed. This will make EPOS installations affordable for small, independent retailers.

middleman Any member of a chain of distribution who stands between a manufacturer and the retailer, especially used of wholesalers.

minimum stock *See* SAFETY STOCK, INVENTORY CONTROL.

Mintel (UK) A commercial research firm publishing a wide range of market reports. (The name is an abbreviated form of 'Market intelligence'.)

mission A statement of the aims, scope and posture of an organization, often phrased in terms of its products, competitive standing and its role in society.

A clear mission statement is said to guide people in the organization so that they can work independently yet collectively towards overall organizational goals and objectives. However, many mission statements are also written for display purposes and not as a guide to action.

missionary salesperson One whose responsibility is to provide representation for an organization in an area or market not previously addressed by his or her employing organization. The term is used especially of those who are the first to attempt to sell an organization's products in a new market.

mix 1. MARKETING MIX.
2. Within the field of marketing, those activities that show similarities to the overall process of marketing in requiring the combination of indi-

vidual elements under management control to achieve particular effects in the marketplace (e.g. retail mix).

mixed merchandising *See* CROSS-MERCHANDISING.

mixed retailing 1. The provision of a number of sellers in different lines of trade at any grouping of OUTLETS, especially shopping malls.
2. The activities of a seller of merchandise at the household level in providing a wide RANGE of such merchandise, often without any clear linkage between the merchandise groups offered (e.g. DEPARTMENT STORE retailing).

mobile shop A van, lorry or converted bus which goes from place to place selling goods. It is characteristic of areas of low population densities and low income where the potential market is too small to support a conventional shop.

mode 1. Current fashion or style.
2. *See* AVERAGE.

mode of transport The medium used in the movement of goods. There are five main modes – road, rail, air, ship and pipeline.

model 1. A person employed to display clothes by wearing them. *See also* MANNEQUIN.
2. A figure used in shop WINDOW DISPLAYS, also called a mannequin.
3. A physical, visual or mathematical simplified representation of a complex system. For example, an INVENTORY CONTROL model allows decision-makers to estimate appropriate stock order quantities, and periods, according to a much simpli-fied, mathematical, representation of product supply and demand; a London Underground map is a visual model of the Underground system which enables passengers to make journey decisions.

model stock An INVENTORY that contains a satisfactory ASSORTMENT at the time when customers want to purchase. For example, in fashion retailing, the percentage of sales in each size, style, colour and price may be calculated in order to enable the buyer to plan stock levels and purchases.

model stock plan The 'ideal' situation of INVENTORY holding which can then be compared with actual.

modified task buying A purchasing situation where an organization either (a) has to repurchase a type of good where one or more decision parameters has changed, or (b) make a purchase of a new good which is closely allied to purchase activities carried out before (e.g. purchase of vehicle fleet where a previous model has been replaced, or purchase of vans after previously buying automobiles).

monetary policy That area of government action concerned with the monitoring and control of cash aggregates or dimensions of the economy. Most commonly this concerns the level of interest rates, the overall supply of money and the level of lending or indebtedness in the economy. This contrasts with fiscal policy, which is the government's concern with raising taxes. Monetary policy is a crucial area to be monitored because of the impact on trade that interest rates and credit policies can have for many sectors of retailing.

money-back offer A cash incentive to purchase a product, whereby the cash can be reclaimed by proving purchase.

money shop A non-bank financial outlet which offers credit and savings facilities. Such shops are required to be registered under the CONSUMER CREDIT ACT 1974 through the OFFICE OF FAIR TRADING as licensed credit brokers. Money shops tend to be placed in high street and high traffic locations in order to offer a more user-friendly environment than the banks.

MONICA (UK) A classification of consumers by age and household or family structure based on forenames, designed by CACI for use with ACORN. The system is mainly used for targeting households in DIRECT MARKETING campaigns.

monopoly A market when there is only a single seller of a good or service, and therefore no competition between providers.

monopsony A market when there is only a single buyer of a good or service.

monthly sales index A comparative measure of the revenue in each calendar period, where each month's sales is divided by average monthly sales and expressed as a percentage. It is a guide to sales seasonality used mainly in the United States.

MOSAIC (UK) A GEODEMOGRAPHIC classification system developed by CCN Systems. It uses census statistics, housing, financial and demographic data collated to identify 58 types of residential area.

most favoured nation (USA) In trade with the United States, the situation of a country in not being subjected to tariffs or discriminatory trade practices.

motivation A driving force or urge which moves an organization or social entity into action towards the achievement of a goal.

multi-channel marketing system A method of distribution which employs parallel distributors to move products from supplier to the MARKET PLACE.

multi-client survey A research investigation commissioned by a group of purchasers who share an interest in the findings.

multi-dimensional scaling A multivariate statistical technique in which respondents make pair-wise judgements as to the similarity/dissimilarity between two of the many items of interest (e.g. retail stores), using scales which relate to the salient characteristics of those items (e.g. service levels).

The responses are pooled and are used to generate a MAP showing the relationships, in proximity terms, between the items of interest as measured on the salient characteristics. The technique is particularly used in MARKET POSITIONING studies.

multi-national retailer A supplier of goods and services to ultimate consumers who has stores or other outlets in more than one country.

multi-pack A product offered for sale, usually on a promotional basis, where a number of individual items are grouped together, usually within one outer, for a single sale (e.g. multipacks of different flavoured crisps/potato chips).

multi-sector retailing A business strategy whereby a seller of products to ultimate consumers elects to sell a diversity of such products drawn from unrelated markets through outlets based on product type (e.g. a retailer having grocery, domestic appliance and fashion outlets.)

multi-stage sample *See* SAMPLING METHODS.

multiple retailer A seller of products to ultimate consumers who has more than one outlet, especially those firms which tend to predominate in concentrated retail markets. *See also* CHAIN.

N

national brand A manufacturer's TRADEMARK, characteristic product etc. which enjoys distribution across a wide market, and has a high level of consumer recognition.

National Bulk Mail System (USA) An organization of postal centres and supporting facilities which is used for the distribution of large volume post from commercial and other organizations throughout the USA.

national retailer 1. Within a given domestic market, a firm having a large number of branches at a wide number of locations throughout the particular country.

2. Occasionally, a retailer who, despite not having such a number of branches, enjoys a wide national reputation.

national zip code area (USA) The specific geographic location identified by a particular five-figure USA postal cypher. *See also* ZIP CODE.

necessary good *See* NECESSITY GOOD.

necessity good Fundamental product which meets a CONSUMER's everyday needs (e.g. pair of shoes, bed, bread).

need 1. The innate awareness of the individual of the physical body's minimal requirements (including physiological and psychological) to sustain life.

2. Any input necessary to the continuation of the existence of a system.

negligence A legal term which describes a civil wrong committed by a defendant against a plaintiff. UK law states that a manufacturer has a duty or care to consumers when producing products. If a consumer is injured by that product the manufacturer may have been in breach of that duty (i.e. may have been negligent and damages could be awarded to a plaintiff).

negotiation To bargain with; to confer with for the purpose of coming to an agreement or arrangement.

In retailing, the most common form of negotiation takes place between a retail buyer and supplier. The precise details of the areas discussed in a retail negotiation vary from one organization to another. However the topics included might be an overview of historic sales trends and forecasts for existing products and ranges, new product opportunities, advertising spend, distribution considerations and merchandise allocations. A produce buyer, for example, may be involved in many different negotiations which have specific titles: (i) a *general business negotiation*, which takes place with more important suppliers once a fortnight, and in which the buyer and seller discuss general business activity, sales, promotions and new lines etc.; (ii) an *overrider negotiation*, which also takes place with larger suppliers to negotiate bonuses and discounts for long-term trading; (iii) *central distribution negotiations*, which negotiate the financial implications of the withdrawal of the supplier's merchandising support from the retailer.

Three distinct phases have been identified: (i) the *prenegotiation phase*, when information is collected by both parties, objectives are set and detailed arrangements made for the negotiation; (ii) the *meeting phase*, when the actual discussion takes place and an outcome is reached; (iii) the *post-negotiation phase*, when the details of the outcome of the negotiation are passed on to relevant parts of each party's organization and action points are consolidated.

neighbourhood shopping centre A minor concentration of retail activity, often in the form of a STRING STREET or parade of shops, meeting the day-to-day purchase requirements of households for groceries, newspapers etc. This type of centre is viewed as the third level in the hierarchy of shopping centres below REGIONAL SHOPPING CENTRE and DISTRICT SHOPPING CENTRE. *See also* CENTRAL PLACE THEORY.

net The result arising from the reduction of a gross amount by appropriate and applicable expenses, returns etc.

Net Book Agreement (UK) A registered price-fixing arrangement which permits book publishers to fix the net selling price of a book and to print it on the book's cover, and obliges the booksellers not to undercut it.

The Restrictive Trade Practices Court in the UK accepted the argument that to discount books would seriously restrict the availability of technical and academic texts, as large volume booksellers would discount and drive smaller booksellers out of business. This would restrict true competition and eventually the availability of texts. The agreement was also allowed to stand under the Resale Price Maintenance Act of 1963.

The Net Book Agreement is under attack from the European Community; some large UK booksellers are also citing examples of free competition in France and the USA.

net dating An agreement whereby the retailer pays the total amount for the purchases by the end of the DATING period.

net lease A contract for the occupation of property by a retailer which requires that the maintenance expenses for the store are to be paid by the retailer.

net margin NET PROFIT expressed as a percentage of SALES REVENUE.

$$Net\ margin\ =\ \frac{Net\ profit}{Sales} \times 100$$

Net margin can be influenced through the CONTROL of GROSS MARGIN and/or the expenses of the business.

net profit The excess of GROSS PROFIT over the OPERATING COSTS for an ACCOUNTING PERIOD. For purposes of historical and inter-firm comparisons it is often expressed in the form of a FINANCIAL RATIO, the NET MARGIN. *See also* PROFIT.

net purchases Total expenditure less returns to suppliers.

net sales Total revenue for a period after returns from customers and special discounts have been deducted.

net terms Payment of an INVOICE is to be paid in full, with no discount for cash.

net worth That part of a retail organization which is owned outright by the proprietor or shareholders. It is calculated by deducting all LIABILITIES (current as well as long-term) from the total value of the ASSETS of the business.

never-out list A record of high-selling items which warrant separate planning and control from those on the MODEL STOCK PLAN, in order to minimize the probability of STOCKOUTS.

new lines committee A group of individuals, sometimes from a number of functional areas, who meet on a regular basis to discuss the adoption of different products to the range.

new product development (NPD) A method of expanding business by investing money in cultivating and fostering novel goods or services to interest consumers (in contrast to MARKET DEVELOPMENT). There are several different stages associated with the development of a new product. Typically they would include idea generation, idea screening, business analysis, testing and commercialization. *See also* ANSOFF'S MATRIX.

new store opening The launch of a retail outlet, usually incorporating all activities involved in the lead up period such as layouts, merchandising, advertising, staffing, recruitment and training. The activity is often considered as being of sufficient importance to warrant specialist departments, staff etc. being designated to control it.

new task buying The purchasing, by a retail buyer, of items which have never previously been bought by the retail organization. *See also* MODIFIED TASK BUYING, STRAIGHT REBUY.

newsagent An individual or store selling newspapers and magazines, commonly in association with confectionery and tobacco, known in the UK as CONFECTIONERY, TOBACCONIST, NEWSAGENT (CTN).

niche retailing The action of one who sells to ultimate consumers in specializing in the needs of a very small market segment and serving its particular needs more effectively than more generalized companies. The niche can be defined in many ways (e.g. demographic characteristics, special interests, psychographic characteristics, or location). The niche may be served either by a cost-led strategy (i.e. serving that niche more cost-effectively) or a differentiation strategy (serving the niche more appropriately).

Niche retailing was especially popular in the UK during the mid-1980s, with companies such as Next, Sock Shop and Tie Rack successfully exploiting niches in the clothing market.

Nielsen rating The estimate of the size of a television audience relative to the total group sampled, expressed as a percentage. The estimated percentage of all television households or persons tuned to a specific station.

Nielsen retail audit *See* NIELSEN RETAIL INDEX.

Nielsen retail index A highly accurate continuous monitor of consumer sales and in-store conditions.

Nielsen scantrack An EPOS-based service offering precise weekly analysis of sales, price elasticity and promotional effectiveness.

Nineteen-ninety-two 31 December 1992, the date declared in Milan in June 1985 for the completion of the SINGLE EUROPEAN MARKET by the heads of state of the 12 member countries of the European Community. Although the Treaty of Rome signed in 1957 outlined the long-term goal of creating a single European economy based on a common market, the impetus for progress came when the Single European Act was signed in December 1985. It committed the Community members to attaining six objectives by 1992 – (i) completion of a large frontier-free market; (ii) increased economic and social cohesion; (iii) a common scientific and technological development policy; (iv) further development of the European monetary system; (v) the emergence of a European social dimension; (vi) co-ordinated action in the environment. These objectives would be achieved through various types of COMMUNITY LEGISLATION which would aim to remove physical, technical and fiscal barriers to trade

within the European community. Although few of the measures being taken will directly affect retail organizations there are a number of issues that have indirectly affected their activities, particularly in relation to standardization and harmonization of goods and services between member states. The relaxation of physical barriers to trade has led to an increase in merger activity and UK retailers looking to source innovating products from other countries.

no-back window A glazed area, especially a frontage, for display in a store that is open on the store side, thus permitting passers-by to see directly into the store. Such windows may or may not contain WINDOW DISPLAYS.

no-returns policy A contractual arrangement, whereby a supplier grants an increased DISCOUNT to a retailer if the retailer undertakes not to send back to the SUPPLIER for credit damaged or defective merchandise.

non-durable goods Goods that require frequent replacement, as they do not last long in normal use (e.g. groceries).

non-executive director One elected to the board of a limited company by a vote of the shareholders, who does not hold a full-time management appointment with the company. Whatever the detail of such relationships with the business, non-executive directors are generally expected to bring certain benefits to the firm by their not being as closely involved as executive directors in the day-to-day workings of the business. Frequently they are themselves executive directors of other companies or prominent

figures in society. Their value to the executive directors stems from having wide experience and by being able to see the business from a different perspective. In the context of retailing, a large company entering a period of change might appoint a non-executive director with experience of the business area or activity concerned. A small retailer may appoint someone with experience of large-scale retailing who would be well placed to comment on areas such as stockholding, merchandising and training.

non-price competition The attempt to secure customers against the efforts of suppliers of similar goods and services through the application of MARKETING MIX variables other than price. Within retailing, non-price competition might take the form of superior in-store design, additional customer facilities, higher-quality products or better customer service (often implemented through CUSTOMER CARE programmes).

non-selling area That part of a retail outlet concerned with stock and inventory reception, preparation and storage; administration and staff facilities.

non-store retailing Selling to ultimate consumers carried out without the use of a traditional shop premises.

The principal forms of non-store retailing are MAIL ORDER, VENDING, DIRECT SELLING and informal retailing.

notions department (USA) A department within a DEPARTMENT STORE or VARIETY STORE which carries haberdashery goods such as needles, ribbons and cotton reels.

nutritional labelling On food products, the process of indicating on the PACKAGING, by means of tables etc., the composition, constituents, chemicals etc. contained in the product.

In the UK the Food Labelling Regulations (1984) was an attempt to regulate the terms used in such labels. The regulations and subsequent amendments, and the voluntary guidelines published in 1988, provide a framework for manufacturers and retailers of own brands. The guidelines foresee three levels of nutritional labelling: (i) details of energy, fat, protein and carbohydrate; (ii) the proportion of saturated fat; (iii) levels of sodium and fibre and the proportion of carbohydrate as sugar. The UK provision is indicative of systems used elsewhere, especially the USA; it may be subject to revision in line with recent European Community proposals.

O

observational research Methodology for scientific investigation based on DATA which is collected only by sensory perception (e.g. pedestrian or vehicle flows), and which does not involve verbal or oral communication with respondents.

odd-even pricing *See* ODD PRICING.

odd pricing The practice of fixing the money to be paid for an item at an amount other than a round number. For example, instead of pricing a shirt at £8.00 a retailer may charge £7.95, based on a view of consumer psychology which assumes consumers will see the price to be closer to £7.00 than £8.00 and therefore better value for money.

oddment End-of-line item, and other singular items of merchandise available for sale, usually placed in retail SALES.

off licence (UK) A retail outlet, or designated part of a larger store, devoted almost entirely to the sale of beers, wines and spirits for consumption away from the premises. For this purpose, a licence is granted by an appropriate authority. (USA: liquor store, bottle shop)

off-peak Times other than those of the highest demand for services (e.g. off-peak air travel). Such times may relate either to seasons of the year, or particular times of day.

off-price store A discount retail outlet which sells better-quality, nationally known (often designer-label) brands at prices below those of DEPARTMENT STORES, and other regular outlets.

off-retail markdown *See* OFF-RETAIL PERCENTAGE.

off-retail percentage A reduction in price expressed as a proportion of the original.

off-sale date A day applied to products, especially foodstuffs, to indicate the day by which time the product should either be sold or removed from sale.

off season Within the tourist trade and other similarly affected areas, forms of merchandise etc. (e.g. swimming costumes), the description applied to that part of the year that does not constitute the peak selling period.

off-the-page buying *See* DIRECT MAIL.

off-the-peg In clothing retailing, goods that are ready to wear by the

consumer and bought from amongst stock in the shop. (*Compare* BESPOKE, where items are tailored to individual customer's sizes etc.) By extension, the term is used of any situation where the solution for a particular problem is obtained ready-made (e.g. computer SOFTWARE) rather than being designed specifically for that situation.

off-the-screen sales *See* DIRECT MAIL.

offer 1. The action of a seller in making products available for sale.
2. (UK) Legally, the action of a potential customer in indicating to a potential seller a willingness to purchase. Such an offer is the first of the four elements – offer, acceptance, valued consideration and capacity to contract – required to make a legally enforced contract.
3. That sum of money proposed by a buyer to a seller as being the amount at which a bargain should be struck.

Office of Fair Trading (OFT) (UK) A government agency, created in 1973, which is designed (among other things) to help the consumer in five main ways: (i) assisting the public, through publicity, on their rights and obligations; (ii) encouraging the introduction and maintenance of voluntary codes of practice; (iii) interpreting information received so as to advise government on areas of concern; (iv) actively pursuing persistent offenders, taking them to court if necessary; (v) carrying out the licensing provisions of the CONSUMER CREDIT ACT 1974.
Although the OFT is not normally concerned with individual complaints, it responds to situations where a number of complaints reveal either a weakness in the legislative controls or the apparent inability of traders to act fairly in their dealings.

Offices Shops and Railway Premises Act 1963 (UK) Legislation concerned with the health, safety and welfare of employees in the workplace. It states that all shop premises, where assistants are employed for more than 21 hours each week, are required to register under this Act and may be inspected by the local authority to ensure compliance. The main requirements of the Act relate to the cleanliness of the premises, temperature controls and ventilation, toilet and washing facilities, the provision of cupboards and lockers and a first-aid box. The Act also specifies minimum seating requirements and catering facilities. It states that floors, stairs and gangways should be kept free from obstruction. *See also* HEALTH AND SAFETY AT WORK ACT 1974.

oligopoly A market in which there are only a small number of sellers of goods or services.

oligopsony A market in which there are only a small number of buyers of goods or services.

omnibus research A regular survey which is undertaken using the same sampling techniques and size each time and for which clients pay for individual questions to be added to the survey. Thus, a single survey may contain several different sets of questions from different clients. Clients pay only for their own questions, and the costs of the fieldwork are therefore spread across a number of users.

on-label game A contest used for promotional purposes where the purchaser scratches off sections of a bottle label to reveal multiple choice answers or prizes.

on-pack Describing the extension, or addition, of materials to the normal form of wrapping, especially to provide LEAFLET, PROMOTION, premium etc.

on-percentage That proportion of an original price which is calculated when there is a series of discounts on an item of merchandise. For example, if an item has a 20 per cent discount (wholesale discount), followed by a further 10 per cent discount (cash discount), then the on-percentage is 0.8 multiplied by 0.9 = 0.72 or 72 per cent. The final net price is calculated as the on-percentage (i.e. 72 per cent) of the original list price.

on-sale date The day on which a publication, such as a journal or child's comic, is actually placed on sale at a retailers, as opposed to the day which appears on the cover of the publication.

one-cent sale (USA) A promotional offer where two items of a certain class are sold together at a price of one cent more than the price of a single item.

one-stop shopping The provision of a wide range of goods and services at a single location such that a consumer or household is able to satisfy all purchase requirements in a single visit. It is normally associated with edge-of-town hypermarkets where households may obtain all their grocery needs, including packaged and frozen foods, fresh foods, non-edible groceries and non-foods from one store rather than visit a number of small specialist stores such as grocers, greengrocers, bakers and chemists.

one-time buyer A customer who has made only a single purchase since an initial contract. It is important for MAIL ORDER retailers to identify such customers in order to encourage further purchases, or eventually delist.

open account An arrangement for the supply of goods on credit, instigated by a retailer or other individual with a supplying organization, which is subject to a predetermined credit limit, but which is still in the state where that credit limit has not yet been reached.

open code dating *See* OPEN DATING.

open dating The practice of printing in uncoded form so that the customer can read them, the time of manufacture of a product, the day by which an article must be sold or the day before which it must be used. This process is particularly common with foodstuffs.

open-front store A type of retail outlet which is usually found within the controlled environment of a shopping centre or mall where during trading hours the normal type of frontage is dispensed with in order for customers to gain easy access. Outside trading hours, the frontage is closed by means of shutters, movable glass screens etc.

open market 1. An area, physical or virtual, for trading, which has no restrictions on those who can buy or sell within it.

2. A collection of stalls etc. trading on a regular basis in a street, or designated area of a town or city, which is unroofed, and usually under the control of a town council etc.

3. The translation of *market ouvert*, a legal term defining certain retail outlets etc. (all shops in the City of London, some MARKETS), where, providing a purchase is made in daylight hours, the BUYER gains good title irrespective of the seller's title to the article.

open stock Merchandise items which can be sold individually or as part of a set (e.g. crockery, glassware).

open to buy The budgeted difference between planned purchases for a period and purchase commitments already made by a buyer at any point during that specified period. It is the amount the buyer has left to spend and is reduced each time a commitment is made. It is normally recorded at cost prices.

'Open to buy' enables the company to maintain a fixed relationship between stock and planned sales, should avoid underbuying and overbuying, and tells the buyer how to adjust purchases if factors such as sales, stock levels and MARKDOWNS change.

Many buyers find it advisable to hold back part of their 'open to buy' figure to allow them to take advantage of special deals, replace merchandise that sells better than expected, and purchase new products.

opening balance That sum on an ACCOUNT at the start of an ACCOUNTING PERIOD.

opening bid The first OFFER to be put

forward for consideration in a negotiation or auction.

opening hours The trading times of a retail outlet.

opening inventory *See* OPENING STOCK.

opening stock The value of merchandise held for resale etc., as at the beginning of an ACCOUNTING PERIOD. Except for a new business start-up, this is identical with the value of CLOSING STOCK at the end of the previous period.

operating budget The anticipated level of expenditure on those items necessary to an organization's functioning with respect to clients, expressed in a systematic and planned way. The plan is based on a forecast of the likely sales and expenditure for a specific period.

operating cost Any expenditure associated with retail activities that relate (ultimately) to providing the means of contact with the customer, with the exception of the cost of purchasing goods for resale (*see* COST OF GOODS SOLD). Operating costs include such items as wages, DEPRECIATION, rent, heat, light, administration, at unit level. These are deducted from GROSS PROFIT in the profit and loss account to show operating profit or loss.

operating expense *See* OPERATING COST.

operating profit *See* PROFIT.

operational research (OR) The application of the scientific method to problems of management decision-making. Textbooks tend to emphasize the mathematical models of linear programming, queuing (waiting line) theory and INVENTORY CONTROL. However, more recently, and particularly in the UK, greater emphasis is being given to what is termed 'soft OR', which uses methodologies and processes such as cognitive mapping and soft systems, which have evolved from the behavioural sciences.

The OR units employed by MULTIPLE RETAILERS and MAIL ORDER companies work on, for example, STORE (and DISTRIBUTION CENTRE) LOCATION models, demand forecasting, manpower planning, and the monitoring of advertising/promotions.

operations That department of the retail or other firm concerned with the day-to-day pursuit of its principal business functions (to be distinguished from, say, marketing, finance, personnel etc.). Within service industries in general, including retailing, the operations function is one that encompasses many of the activities that would elsewhere be, for example, part of marketing (e.g. the design of stores and the type of layout to be used within them may well be operational questions, but because of their impact on the consumer they might elsewhere properly be considered marketing).

The nature of the operations function in service businesses has been widely studied, and has given rise to the subject of operations management/marketing.

operations research *See* OPERATIONAL RESEARCH.

opinion A positive or negative attitude, held by an individual, towards any psychological object such as issues, persons, 'facts' etc. Surveys of consumer opinion are carried out in order to help determine the stance to be adopted by an organization towards the marketplace.

opinion leader An individual who influences the attitudes of others by being regarded by them as a likely trendsetter, or authoritative source.

opportunity cost The notional price paid in foregone potential revenues etc. incurred in accepting any particular pattern of commitment of resources rather than undertaking any other available course of action. (E.g. a retailer who chooses to use investment cash for a store refurbishment cannot at the same time undertake a new store opening with that same cash; the store assistant being trained in customer care away from the shop floor cannot serve customers. Both are loosely opportunity costs.) The usefulness of the concept is in requiring an analysis of the TRADE-OFF involved in selecting any particular course of action.

option The granting, by a seller to a potential purchaser, of the right to complete the sale etc. at a future (specified) date, and possibly, price. Potential buyers sometimes purchase such a right.

Oracle (UK) TELETEXT service available on independent television, providing news, travel, weather and other information. *See* VIDEOTEX.

orange good A consumer product that Aspinwall ranked in the middle category of all of his five classification parameters: replacement rate, gross margin, adjustment, time of consumption, searching time. A loose match to SPECIALITY GOOD – product for which consumer search may be undertaken and which may be durable in nature. *Compare* RED GOOD.

order 1. The document requiring a supplier to provide a particular range of goods or services, sent by a buying organization.
2. The process of issuing such documents.

order margin The residue remaining per item of merchandise, after deducting the total of product selling and delivery costs, but excluding promotional expenses. The calculation is used particularly in direct response MAIL ORDER to determine ADVERTISING budgets and target profitability.

order number A reference code applied to documents requesting the supply of products, which is used to facilitate administration.

order-taker A category of sales personnel whose function is limited essentially to writing down the requirements of the people who have a predetermined list etc. in mind when arriving at the point of sale. The order-taker is distinguished from, for example, MISSIONARY SALES-PERSONS or sales-getters.

ordering Requesting or calling for goods to be supplied by a supplier.

organizational buying The process of purchasing goods and/or services on behalf of a business, firm, local authority, or other entity, in order to facilitate the work of that organization. The topic of organizational buying has stimulated considerable debate and it is frequently viewed as a 'rational' decision process. *Compare* CONSUMER BEHAVIOUR.

organizational climate The atmosphere created within a business firm or other institution largely in response to the prevailing managerial style. The dimensions of organizational climate are often seen to be those factors in an organization which relate particularly to the style of interaction between management and staff, especially in such areas as participative decision-making etc.

organizational marketing The process of identifying the needs, wants, and desires of decision-making units in control of purchasing in business firms, public institutions etc., and satisfying those needs, wants and desires on a mutually beneficial basis in an economic context.

OSCAR (UK) Outdoor Site Classification and Audience Research. A service to advertisers providing the identification of particular POSTER sites, and estimates of the opportunities to see such sites.

outdoor advertising Paid-for insertions under clear sponsorship in the mass medium provided by POSTER sites and transport vehicles, especially trains and buses.

outer The packaging which encloses a number of saleable items, which are themselves further packaged (e.g. the cardboard boxes used to contain multiples of many grocery items).

outlet Any building, kiosk, caravan,

stall etc. which offers/sells GOODS or SERVICES direct to customers.

outside buying organization A business firm, or other third party with whom a retailer contracts for that party to undertake to purchase merchandise for resale by the retailer.

outsize 1. Garments produced to cater for those individuals substantially larger, taller etc. than the general population.
2. A department within a traditional retailer, or an independent operation – e.g. Evans (womenswear), High & Mighty (menswear) – selling such items.

over-the-counter 1. Goods selected by individual customers, which are weighed, packed and priced (as required) by staff prior to being passed to the customer for payment at that point, or subsequently at a cash point.
2. Pharmaceutical products which can be sold by a pharmacy direct to customers, without a doctor's prescription.
3. Any good or service available for direct sale without modification or specific work, especially where an element of such work might be expected (e.g. replacement/exchange gearboxes).

overage State of INVENTORY where a physical stock check reveals a higher stock than that listed in the BOOK INVENTORY. The opposite of SHORTAGE.

overrider An allowance or discount given to a retailer etc. who meets a large volume sales or profit goal over a long period. It is common for suppliers to pay retailers 'overrider' rebates annually.

overwire hanger A type of banner suspended from the store ceiling as a means of in-store promotion or providing customer information.

own account The purchasing of the title to goods by an intermediary in a chain of distribution prior to resale (as opposed to operating as an agent working on a commission basis, where title is never acquired).

own brand A synonym for OWN LABEL, though this designation may be misleading as the products may not in fact show all the characteristics of true BRANDS.

own label The designation applied to products developed or purchased by a retailer, wholesaler or other channel intermediary exclusively for sale through their outlets. The 'label' may bear the same name as the channel intermediary or it may bear another title (e.g. Marks & Spencer's 'St. Michael' goods, or Sear's 'Craftsman' range of power tools).

P

pack 1. A pre-wrapped item or items, normally bearing a description, content details, weight or number and sometimes price.
2. To place items in a bag or other container.

package 1. The container(s) into which goods are placed for the purpose(s) of transportation, distribution, merchandising and/or display.
2. To place items into containers.
3. Informally, to bring together, and prepare for use, a number of disparate and/or related items, actions, processes etc. in order to achieve some unitary purpose (e.g. computer package, franchise package).

packaged good Any item placed in containers or wrapping materials for protection during handling/transit etc., especially items of a non-food nature for sale in grocery outlets.

packaging Any form of covering for an item of merchandise, designed to perform the primary function of protection. For many products it also has a major secondary function of providing an intrinsic component of the product, particularly by providing brand recognition, and customer reassurance (e.g. brand recognition of packaged grocery products, reassurance through perfume packaging).

The primary protective function can be achieved using a wide variety of materials (e.g. paper, board, plastic, film, metal or wood). The secondary features of design and promotion require the portrayal of consistent design themes across all promotional materials – ADVERTISING, SALES PROMOTION and packaging design. Packaging designs can be registered and protected, as is the Heinz 'shield' design.

Retailers' interests in packaging have intensified due to OWN BRAND and OWN LABEL products, and the designs often emanate from a dedicated in-house design department.

packing list A document bearing details of the variety of items placed in a specific container.

packing slip A docket bearing details allowing for future identification of the place, and possibly date, of preparation and packing of an item.

pallet A platform device, normally constructed of wood, used for moving and storing goods, particularly by means of a fork lift truck. A typical pallet is a softwood platform of approximately 1×1.5 metres in size and standing approximately 100 mm high. Pallet loads can vary tremendously but the materials required to support the required weights may need to change in specification. Specialized pallets in metal for strength, or plastics for light weight, can also be used. Many retailers now receive palletized loads of bulk items which require mechanical handling equipment in storage areas, and the means to break the loads in order to put the products on sale.

pallet configuration A description of how a PALLET is laid out in order to remain stable in transit and to support its own load and any loads to be stacked on top of it in a multi-pallet combination.

Pallets may be strapped or bonded using PVC or metal strapping to help retain their configuration and to remain stable. They can additionally be shrink-wrapped for protection from moisture or dust.

palletization The use of PALLETS, especially in a consistent manner throughout a CHAIN OF DISTRIBUTION, with a view to improving efficiency etc.

pantry check See PANTRY INVENTORY.

pantry inventory Market research technique which involves a researcher visiting a consumer's home to study and list the contents in 'the pantry' (more usually today the refrigerator and household cupboards), to examine the particular brands, items, quantities etc. held in stock by the household.

part-time staff Employees who work for less than the standard weekly full-time hours.

party plan selling A method of direct distribution in which a householder acts as a host to a group of invited potential customers to whom representatives of the distributor (often the manufacturer) make presentations and take orders. The invited customers tend to be friends or relatives of the householder, and thus the informal social setting is felt to be conducive to selling. Party plan selling is used for consumer goods including plastic kitchenware, cosmetics, lingerie.

party selling See PARTY PLAN SELLING.

passing off A legal term normally understood to mean the wrong committed by someone who presents products as if they were those of another. Passing off is not covered by any formal written law in the UK and decisions rely therefore upon precedent rather than on the interpretation of statutes. A key issue is often the logo and packaging design used by competing companies for similar products. Examples exist of quite blatant copying of such 'get-up' in addition to the copying of physical products themselves. Passing off could be an issue in the production and marketing of OWN LABEL products, where the retailer might choose a packaging shape, a product name and colourways similar to those of the brand leader. If the similarity causes confusion, then an action for passing off is likely. A feature of a legal challenge on passing off is that, should the courts decide there is a case to answer, the commercial position is frozen at the point just prior to the alleged offence (possibly the day the copy was launched) until the full hearing (possibly six months later).

patent A grant, given by government,

to the 'first and true inventor' of an article or process, of the exclusive right to sell such articles, or use such processes, within the government's jurisdiction for a limited term. In the UK, an initial grant of patent is, for example, for 20 years. There exist international agreements to facilitate the granting of patents in other jurisdictions besides that first sought by the inventor. Patents form one of the most important classes of articles within the area of INTELLECTUAL PROPERTY.

patronage A formal term for adoption or use of an outlet or supplier by a customer, especially where such usage is frequent or repeated.

payload Cargo, or part of a cargo, which produces income.

peak time That part of the period where an item is available or offered for sale corresponding to the highest demand. Specifically, in the case of television airtime, that period when TV viewing audiences are at their highest during the day. In periods of peak time, prices for space, service, travel etc. tend to be at their highest.

pedestrian flow The number of people walking (or moving in wheelchairs etc.) along a street or shopping mall within a given time period, in a given direction (usually expressed as an hourly rate). Measurement may be made by either manual means (e.g. hand counters), or mechanical means (e.g. pressure pads). Data can be collected locally or remotely (through using video recording or time-lapse photography). The data can be combined with information on pavement/mall width to produce a measure of pedestrian density. Pedestrian flows can be viewed as a simple measure of potential shopping activity (the more people passing a given point, the greater the possibility of expenditure), and are therefore often used to help determine shop rents.

peddler Itinerant retailer selling small goods in low quantities, especially in the street.

pedlar (USA) *See* PEDDLER.

peer group 1. That collection of individuals who are similar to a given person by reason of status, age, background etc.
2. That collection of significant individuals whose status, values, beliefs etc. provide a reference point for any person in terms of guiding his or her behaviour, especially in matters of consumption.

penetration An approach to new MARKET SEGMENTS for an organization which aims to cement the organization in a segment by securing high market share in a relatively short time. The objective can often be achieved by having a low initial price for the product at the launch, backed up by heavy promotional support. It is particularly appropriate to markets where high volume is essential for profitability due to high FIXED COSTS or high competitive barriers (e.g. periodical publishing, where advertising revenues can only be attracted by high sales and readership and, as sales increase, the proportion of revenue from the sales price of the magazine or newspaper can be exceeded by the proportion attracted from advertisers).

percentile The value below which a specified percentage of items in a statistical POPULATION falls.

perception The psychological process by which sensory stimuli are converted into meaningful interpretations of the external world.

perceptual map A representation, in graphical terms, of the psychological 'space' into which consumers place BRANDS, retailers, suppliers etc., using those dimensions or attributes that are discovered to be pertinent through research. *See also* IMAGE.

performance 1. The act of presenting information to the public, especially for the purposes of entertainment.
2. The levels of attainment reached, especially against preset targets, such as budgets, turnover or profitability.
3. The capacity to achieve high levels of attainment (e.g. performance cars have a high power to weight ratio).
4. The act of carrying out or discharging duties.

performance setting The establishment of a target plan to be achieved, normally within prescribed times and budget.

periodical A publication appearing at (usually regular) intervals. Retail examples include: *Retail Week*, *Retail Marketing and Management* and *Journal of Retailing* (*see* Appendix 4).

perpetual inventory The process of maintaining a current valuation of stocks held by retailers, on the basis of a valuation of initial stocks and a programme of continuing adjustments due to sales, deliveries etc.

personal selling The presentation of products, and associated persuasive communication to potential clients, employed by the supplying organization. It is the most direct and longest established means of PROMOTION within the promotional mix. Skilled sales people can be a highly effective means of communication because the desired message is selected and adapted to the customer's specific character and needs. Personal selling is, to a large extent, a learnable skill with a distinguished history of training.
    In retailing, where SELF-SERVICE and SELF-SELECTION have become widely used, there is less emphasis on selling skills and more on the more widely defined CUSTOMER SERVICE.

personality The totality of all those behavioural, social and psychological traits which make up each unique individual. The term is also used attributively of retail stores to describe the way in which their 'personality' is perceived by store visitors.

personnel Collectively, the individuals employed by an organization.

personnel management The process of planning, organizing and controlling the human resource aspects of an organization.

personnel manager The individual responsible for the human resource aspects of an organization, especially recruitment, selection, training etc.

petrol station (USA: gas station) A retail sales point for lubricants, fuel and other services associated with the motor car.

physical distribution The transportation of goods from the supplier to the retailer (and where applicable, from retailer to customer), particularly where the transportation is under the control of one of the contracting parties.

From the retailer's viewpoint physical distribution is about getting the goods to the store (if a store-based retailer) or to the customer's home (if mail order) or to the point of sale (for vending machine operators, for instance). Increasingly this activity is a joint effort between manufacturers and retailers through a network of warehouses which may be owned by either party, using transport which may operate on behalf of either.

Another alternative which is frequently used is to employ a specialist warehousing or transport contractor.

Physical distribution may involve a number of activities – consolidation, ordering, planning, warehousing, materials handling, inventory control, transport, load planning, safety and security. It is perhaps the third largest cost incurred by retailers and offers opportunities for efficiency and profitability improvements if planned and executed effectively.

Two recent trends in retail physical distribution should be noted.

First, large multiple retailers have been centralizing their own warehousing and transport facilities during the 1980s, removing their control from the manufacturers who traditionally operated these facilities. Retailers thus have greater control over distribution costs and the timing frequency and quantities of deliveries to stores.

Second, many large retailers have contracted out their distribution functions to THIRD PARTY specialists. The main advantages of using contractors are the ability to exploit their specialist expertise, lower capital investment requirements and the reduction in retailer management time devoted to distribution. Furthermore, retailers who have opted to use third parties also claim increased working flexibility, a reduction in stockholding, savings in setup time and fewer industrial relations problems as additional benefits, without a reduction in the level of service achieved.

physical inventory The actual tangible amount of stock held by a retailer at a point in time.

physical vertical marketing system Those integrated and related elements of a SUPPLY CHAIN which are involved with the movement of goods from manufacturer to CONSUMER.

picking The process of assembling items required for an order from larger stocks prior to dispatch to the point of supply.

piece good Textile fabric, such as cotton materials, which is sold at retail by the yard or metre and payment is made for the quantity sold – 'piece'.

pilferage The process of stealing in small quantities. In retailing, pilferage is the theft of the company's goods or property from the shop floor, stockroom, warehouse, transport vehicles etc. by customers, employees or agents working on behalf of the company. *See also* SHRINKAGE.

piloting 1. The process of testing a questionnaire (or other data collection procedure) to identify weaknesses in wording, structure, layout, sampling procedures and data handling techniques before the full-scale survey is undertaken.
2. Testing any new product, including store formats, by means of trial marketing an early version. *See also* MARKET TEST.

pin ticket A label or TAG which is fastened (by means of a small clip etc.) to a PRODUCT to show price, size and other relevant information such as colour or STYLE.

placard Any written or printed notice, especially one written on thick, stiff card, used to inform the public, especially at point of sale or elsewhere in the store.

place utility *See* UTILITY.

plan 1. A simplified model or representation of reality, particularly of an object, organization, building etc. Such a model is used to provide the basis for orienting activities with respect to the object etc.
2. A document containing an outline of anticipated decisions, drafted to indicate likely courses of actions and intentions to those within an organization.

planning gap analysis A study of the differences between a forecast of likely business performance and the desired business performance (declared in the corporate objectives). Causal elements of the reasons for the planning gap (e.g. low market share or poor profitability) can be identified, and then analysed and addressed.

planogram A diagram or picture detailing the layout of goods in a section of a FIXTURE or area of the sales floor.

point of indifference *See* GRAVITY MODEL.

point of purchase *See* POINT OF SALE.

point of sale 1. The particular place where customers purchase a product, especially where payment is exchanged for goods or services.
2. As used of materials which promote products and which are located at the place of transactions (e.g. free store catalogue available to customers at cash points).

point scoring *See* CREDIT SCORING.

policy 1. A preselected line of conduct, for areas of strategic significance or operational importance, whereby individual decisions are made and co-ordinated.
2. The contract, terms and conditions of an insurance agreement.

poll An investigation into the attitudes, opinions, interests etc. of a target POPULATION of interest, usually conducted through the use of a sample of people from the population.

pooled buying A purchasing operation, used by INDEPENDENT RETAILERS, where separate (small) orders are grouped together to take advantage of the possibility of quantity DISCOUNTS. *See also* VOLUNTARY GROUPS.

population 1. *See* SAMPLE.
2. The total number of inhabitants

of an area, or of people within a particular group.

Porter's generic strategies A recent and influential attempt to define the principal broad forms of business policy with respect to markets, which has been much criticized. Michael Porter proposed three generic strategic approaches which could be successful in outperforming other firms in an industry by coping with the five basic competitive forces – competitors, suppliers, substitutes, potential entrants, buyers.

(i) *Overall cost leadership* This involves the achievement of overall cost leadership in an industry through a set of functional policies aimed at this basic objective. This requires aggressive cost minimization and cost control throughout the firm's operations.

(ii) *Differentiation* This strategy is to differentiate the product offering of the firm to create something which will be perceived as unique industry-wide, ideally giving several different dimensions. Such dimensions may be design, brand image, technology, product features, customer service, store size, location etc.

(iii) *Focus* The strategy of focusing on a particular group, segment or geographic market rests on the premise that a firm is able to serve its particular target more effectively or efficiently than more broad-based competitors. This may be achieved either by differentiation in meeting the needs of that market sector, or by lower costs in serving this target, or both.

portfolio analysis The consideration of all the products of a business organization as a collectivity so as to ensure that the salient variables (risk etc.) constitute a blend likely to lead to the continuance of the firm.

positioning By analogy, the notion that the perceptual space of target consumers, with respect to a market and the brands and products within it, can be viewed as being a MAP, and that business organizations may choose to locate their offerings as a particular point (position) on the map.

The expression is particularly used of *product positioning* or of *brand positioning*. However, while there is a tendency to speak in terms of reinforcing an existing position, or repositioning, as the map exists in consumers' minds, organizations seldom have sufficient data in fact to be able to do this, even if the effects of the business organization's activities were to be predictable (which they are not).

possession utility *See* UTILITY.

post-purchase behaviour The activities, overt and covert, physical or psychological, of an individual or DECISION-MAKING UNIT, occurring after and stimulated by a buying occasion. Such behaviour may include evaluation of the purchase (resulting in satisfaction or dissatisfaction), changes in attitudes and beliefs, complaining and recommending the purchase to others etc.

post-purchase dissonance A psychological state, arising from the consequences of buying actions, where divergence or incompatibility is perceived between prior expectation of the product and PERFORMANCE in use. *See also* COGNITIVE DISSONANCE.

postcode Any system, defined by a mail authority, to designate a particular address or group of addresses by means of a cypher. In the UK there are six to ten addresses per postcode. Postcodes generally have become an important marketing tool through the growth of GEODEMOGRAPHICS. *See also* ZIP CODE.

poster 1. A (normally) outdoor panel, ground-based or fastened to a building, which bears advertising messages printed on large sheets of paper which are hand pasted onto the panel. These sheets are usually arranged to form a single message. Panels vary in size and the size is often referred to as 'x' sheets, these sheets being the largest size of paper a printing press used to be able to hold.
  2. Printed, eye-catching, promotional or informational message on paper or card, which is displayed inside a store or outlet.

postponement An agreement between a retailer and supplier, whereby delivery of an order is staged, and the retailer can delay an intended delivery at a particular stage according to the level of sales.

power The capacity to undertake work; in a social setting, the ability of any actor to obtain the compliance of other actors in achieving outcomes of his or her desire, with little or no regard for the desires of other actors; the possession of control authority or influence over others.

pre-approach That phase of the selling process which takes place before the sales interview. At this time the salesperson will assess the customer's background and needs.

pre-customer contact That phase of the retail PERSONAL SELLING process which occurs prior to approaching the potential client. The skills of anticipating and 'sizing up' clients to be approached, and to some extent the manner of approaching the customer, can be developed. Non- verbal cues from a customer can be read and the selling approach tailored corresponding (e.g. is he or she timid or extrovert, positive or undecided?). Pre-customer contact procedures can be taught but tend to be the product of experience rather than formal training.

predatory pricing The situation where losses are planned and accepted initially by a market player, in the expectation of greatly enhanced profits subsequently (from increased prices) as competitors are forced out of the particular market. May be attempted by larger retailers to reduce competition from smaller retailers.

present value The current monetary worth of the expected revenues accruing to an investment or project etc. It is the basis of discounted cash flow methods of INVESTMENT APPRAISAL which are based on the 'time value of money' concept.
  The projected cash flows resulting from a capital investment project are converted into their present value through use of discount factors. The appropriate discount factors are calculated using the formula:

$$\frac{1}{(1 + r)^n}$$

where r = the discount rate expressed as a proportion
n = the number of years after the investment in which the cashflows are generated

presentation 1. The art of displaying merchandise so as to convey appropriate messages to customers, store visitors etc.
2. A performance, demonstration etc. by an individual or group which conveys messages to a specific (usually small) audience. Presentations may employ various techniques and supporting media, such as video, overhead projectors etc.

press The main printed media, including newspapers, journals and magazines.

press release (PR) A document prepared by an organization in order to achieve editorial coverage for the story or news contained therein. Such releases are usually sent to all relevant media, including broadcasting, rather than simply PRESS.

price 1. The monetary amount at which the supplier of a traded product is initially prepared to conclude a bargain with a buyer.
2. The monetary amount at which a bargain is struck between a buyer and seller.

price audit 1. The careful, systematic evaluation of the charges made by an organization for its products, especially when carried out as an element of the marketing audit.
2. The checking of the charge made for a product item by a retail outlet. This is carried out by either the manufacturer (to check that prices charged are in line with expectations) or by the retailer's head office (to ensure conformity with company policy). Such checks may also be carried out by MARKET RESEARCH organizations as part of their ongoing services to subscribers.

price band A notional group or segment where products cluster naturally together by reason of similar charges, though not for reasons of product similarity (e.g. 'Christmas Gifts' – £7.50 to £9.99).

price control The activity of determining the retail charge to be made for an item of merchandise by the manufacturer of the item or government, or other authority, responsible for the jurisdiction concerned. Generally speaking, attempts to control retail prices are unlawful in many jurisdictions, except where expressly permitted.

price competition The situation in which sellers, or suppliers, of a traded product seek to attract buyers and conclude bargains by offering to accept less money for a product than others in the same MARKET.

price cutting The actions of a retailer in reducing retail charges, usually in response to competition, in an attempt to increase trade. Such actions may be undertaken either as a tactical response to a particular situation, or as a basis for strategic action in a given market.

price discrimination The deliberate act of differentially charging two or more market segments for a product. Examples include discrimination by individual customer (e.g. for 'trade-in' allowances on a car), by time (e.g. peak and off-peak prices), by physical location (e.g. seats in the theatre) or by minor product variations which do not reflect cost differences. The discrimination is intended to reflect the value customers place on the product in their circumstances reflecting their strength of need. If price discrimination is done clumsily, it can be seen as unfair and may lead to customer resistance.

price elasticity The ratio of the relative change in demand for (or supply of) a product to the relative change in the monetary cost of that product.

For most products, the price elasticity of demand will be negative (i.e. an increase in price results in a decrease in demand). Conversely, the supply elasticity is usually positive. By convention, however, each of the above elasticities are usually represented as positive numbers. By this convention, elasticities higher than one (where supply or demand changes relatively more than price) are known as 'relatively elastic'; similarly, where the ratio is less than one they are 'relatively inelastic'.

The concept, originally introduced to economics by Alfred Marshall, is widely used and of considerable importance. Readers requiring a more technical treatment should refer to the economics literature.

In a retailing situation, food is believed to be relatively inelastic, whereas luxury products are elastic in demand terms – this, however, is a gross over-simplification as the elasticity of any product will vary according to price.

price label A paper ticket affixed to an item of merchandise to indicate to the customer (sales assistant) the retail cost of that item. Price labels used in SELF-SERVICE outlets have to be tamper-proof, and in such situations the self-adhesive label is most common. Such labels use gun delivery systems, where the labels fragment if tampered with. EPOS systems reduce the need for product labelling, in favour of shelf-edge pricing.

price lining The use of particular charges for the sale of items of merchandise where the level of such charges is viewed as being established through expectation and custom. *See also* PRICE POINT.

price list A summary document showing product costs or charges published by a manufacturer or trader, which will be used as a basis for transactions for a period of time. Price lists may be rigidly applied or merely treated as an offer to begin negotiation depending upon the attitude of the trade concerned.

price list order form (PLOF) A document used by VOLUNTARY GROUP members for ordering goods from their wholesale distributor. Although used primarily for stock replenishment, other useful information is contained on each page (e.g. price of goods, pack size etc.).

price look-up The facility on an EPOS (or EFTPOS) system which allows CHECKOUT operators, or other store personnel, to interrogate the retailer's database to establish the amounts to be charged for an item of merchandise.

price maintenance The process of

upholding a suggested or desired final charge to the customer, by the original manufacturer or supplier. Price maintenance has been legally unenforceable in the UK since the abolition of *resale price maintenance* in the 1960s, except in a few cases. The situation is to some extent similar in the USA and other jurisdictions, though there may be controls on PREDATORY PRICING. It is considered to be a restrictive trade practice in the UK if a manufacturer attempts to withhold supplies to retailers who cut prices to below the recommended retail price.

price marking The process of applying a suitable indication to show the retail charge for a particular item of merchandise.

Price Marking (Bargain Offers) Order 1979 (UK) Consumer protection legislation relating to the application of retail charges for merchandise. The law lays down regulations for the period of time merchandise must have been on sale in a store before it can be sold as having been reduced in price, or sold as a sale item. More details relating to the issue of pricing are given in the CONSUMER PROTECTION ACT 1987, which replaces a number of areas of the Order.

price point Those particular charging levels, for an item of merchandise, that are believed to be psychologically important to consumers (e.g. for everyday blouse, a maximum of £12.99). *See also* PRICE BANDS.

price range The spread of the retail costs of merchandise charged to consumers within an outlet, or across a particular merchandise category.

price ring An illegal conspiracy to maintain the charges to be levied for work or items of merchandise, or the money that will be paid for certain kinds of merchandise, at a higher or lower than normal level, by agreement of suppliers or purchasers not to undercut or compete with each other. A particular example is at AUCTIONS where dealers refuse to compete against each other in bidding and dispose of wanted products outside the auction between themselves.

price tag *See* PRICE LABEL.

price war An aggressive confrontation between marketers who compete overtly on the basis of charging the lowest amount for a given item, service etc. Price wars are normally avoided because ultimately they drive profit margins down for all participants in the market, although customers benefit in the short term. Price wars are sometimes used by large companies to drive out weaker competition, ultimately worsening the deal for consumers. Such tactics may attract the attention of regulators.

Prices Act 1974 (UK) Consumer protection legislation designed to ensure that prices are clearly and accurately marked on goods prior to purchase by consumers.

pricing The process of determining the charges to be levied on its customers, undertaken by any business organization. Specifically, within the MARKETING MIX, an organization would need to select those policies with respect to PRICE that are consistent with all other aspects of their strategic positioning. For many retailers, given that there is an easily identifiable item cost, there is a temptation to use crude mechanisms such as MARKUP, rather than considering pricing more strategically.

primary data Basic measurements and/or impressions collected by original field research for a specific purpose. *See also* SECONDARY DATA.

prime time That period on the commercial television networks which is most in demand by advertisers, because it enjoys the highest audiences. Television contractors charge a premium for advertising space at prime time.

private brand A consumer product produced to the specifications of a retailer and bearing that retailer's identifying TRADEMARK, design etc. *See also* OWN BRAND.

private label A consumer good bearing the TRADEMARK (or other design etc.) of a retailer, which is not necessarily the same as the TRADING NAME of the retail organization. *See also* OWN LABEL.

pro forma 1. An invoice sent to a BUYER, prior to the shipment of the GOODS, to allow for preparation of documents and payment prior to receipt of goods. (This is used particularly for new ACCOUNTS.)

2. A document prescribing a set layout or procedure (e.g. for a BALANCE SHEET or PRICE LIST).

probability An expression of a belief regarding the level of uncertainty associated with an outcome or event in the absence of precise knowledge of such an outcome or event. The formal mathematical or statistical approach represents an attempt to measure the level of uncertainty on a scale of values which varies between 0 (impossibility) and 1 (certainty). The higher the probability (nearer to 1), the more likely the event will occur.

The classical definition of probability says that; 'The probability of a favourable outcome is f/n, where n represents the number of possible, mutually exclusive and equally likely outcomes, and f is the number of favourable outcomes.'

The classical definition is one of three approaches to the measurement of probability. It would be appropriate, for example, to the calculation of the probability that a particular respondent (to a direct mailshot) will win the lottery scheme incentive. It would assume a random selection of lottery numbers, knowledge of the number of winning tickets, game rules etc. A second approach, appropriate in QUALITY CONTROL methods, is based on relative frequencies found from, usually, historical data. For example, if 2 per cent of items from a batch process have been found to be defective, the probability that a specific item is defective is said to be 0.02. The third, and most controversial approach is known as subjective probability where an individual, or group, is required to use expertise and experience to generate a value on the probability scale. An example (in retail SITE location) would be where the research team is asked to estimate the probability that a store located in a specific position will meet company sales and profit targets.

Despite the potential difficulties in probability measurement, a large number of scientific and management techniques (e.g. decision theory, BAYESIAN STATISTICS, computer simulation, risk evaluation, manpower planning) have foundations in probability theory.

process technology *See* BATCH/CONTINUOUS PROCESS.

process theories Any of that class of explanations, models and hypotheses which explain the outcomes of social and other situations through reference to the activities of the social or other system occurring over time, rather than through the structural elements of the system.

procurement The purchasing of items required to further the interests of a business. In retailing, the term covers merchandise for resale, equipment and sundry items necessary to conduct the business (e.g. counters, scales, lorries, checkout equipment, carrier bags etc.).

The precise range of procurement activities depends on the nature of the retailer, but could include buying, transport, manufacturing, storage, order processing, stock control, quality control and back door procedures for receiving goods.

produce Greengrocery: fruit and vegetables, flowers, house plants.

product A good or service offered to a MARKET. In a MARKETING context, such offerings are capable of satisfying the needs, wants and desires of a target MARKET SEGMENT through attention, acquisition, use or consumption. In this context, the notion of product is extended to include activities, personal, locational, or ideas etc. *See also* MARKETING MIX.

product characteristic An attribute or feature of a good or service which is salient and can be easily identified by a potential consumer or user, especially when making a purchase decision (e.g. the product characteristics of a chair might be the number of legs it has, its colour and the material from which it is made).

product knowledge The understanding a person has of the nature and characteristics of a good or service. Product knowledge is an important requirement both for consumers and those in employment roles, such as salesperson, BUYER etc. A 'cheese buyer' with good product knowledge, for example, would know all of the different types of cheese available, how they are manufactured and stored, as well as how they taste.

product life-cycle By analogy, the idea that a good or service offered for sale is likely to pass through a number of phases, representing stages in life, during the period it remains on the MARKET. Marketing theorists have suggested that a product goes through five stages during its life: product development, introduction, growth, maturity, decline.

Product development is the process of generating new ideas and developing them; sales are zero, investment high and returns negative. As the product is being introduced, resources are invested in sales growth and market share, sales grow slowly and losses are made. Growth is a period of rapid acceptance and increasing profits. Maturity sees a slowing of sales growth, and profits level off or decline as competition is attracted and marketing expenditure is required to defend sales. Finally,

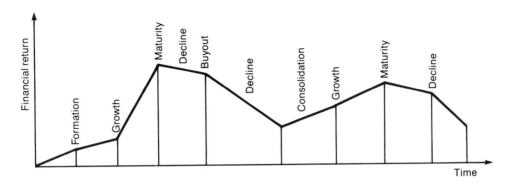

decline is the period when sales and profits fall; some firms leave the market, while others may decide to plough on and harvest returns, or eventually relaunch in a modified form.

The idea is intuitively appealing but has not always been supported empirically and has proven to be difficult to use in practice. One thing that is essential is that those wishing to make use of the concept are able to define precisely what is meant by 'product' (i.e. the level of analysis is clear).

product line A group of goods (or services) falling into a specific category (e.g. pet foods, shampoos, insurance). Within the category, the products can have a variety of brands, sizes, prices, widths and depth etc.

product management A method of organizing marketing which provides for the specific attention of one person to be given to a single item or brand, or to a relatively narrow range of related items/brands. It was introduced by Proctor & Gamble in the 1920s in the USA. It encourages internal competition between product managers who 'compete' for cen-

tral marketing resources, such as ADVERTISING or SALES PROMOTION.

The product or brand manager is held responsible for the sales performance of his/her product without the overt authority to demand cooperation or help from field sales, advertising, distribution etc. Some organizations consider that such 'competition' leads to wasted effort.

product/market scope *See* ANSOFF'S MATRIX.

product mix The combination of goods and/or services that a company has within its portfolio. The company may have a mix which is wide but focused (e.g. Heinz with food), or highly diffuse (e.g. Unilever with frozen foods to washing powder). In retailing terms, product mix is usually associated with product ASSORTMENT or variety of assortment.

product positioning *See* POSITIONING.

product quality A combination of two sets of variables (which, in the minds of many, should be separated) relating to the extent to which a good or service conforms to user requirements and the extent to which that same good or service conforms to

STANDARDS appropriate for that class of good or service.

product range The ASSORTMENT of GOODS and/or SERVICES a company offers to a particular MARKET. Retailers are frequently differentiated from each other by consumers on the basis of the WIDTH of product (merchandise) range they offer.

product specification A delineation, particularly when formally expressed in writing, of all those characteristics of a good or service which are necessary to ensure the conformity of output to the purchaser's or consumer's requirements.

productivity The ratio of the values of outputs to inputs of a business, or other system, expressed in terms capable of economic analysis (total productivity), or as the efficiency of the utilization of any particular factor or element in the system (factor productivity, e.g. labour).

profile See MARKET PROFILE.

profit 1. The excess of the selling price of a product above the cost of providing it.
2. The increase in the net ASSETS of a business in an ACCOUNTING PERIOD, after allowing for capital adjustments such as capital injections, rights issues etc., where appropriate.
Gross profit results from the excess of the value of sales in an accounting period (adjusted for RETURNS and allowances) over the cost of goods (services) sold in that period. A *trading profit* (or *operating profit*) arises from the subtraction of additional operating expenses from gross profit. *Net profit* is trading profit further

reduced (or increased) by the application of other income and/or expenses for the period.

profit and loss account A particular form of INCOME STATEMENT required by tax authorities in many jurisdictions, which summarises turnover, allowable expenses, profits and taxation.

profit planning The actions carried out in an attempt to ensure that the price charged for goods is sufficient to cover fully all relevant costs and, in addition, achieve the required level of financial gain.

profitability The measurement, using appropriate ratios etc. of (generally) the excess of income over expenditure, as a proportion of the ASSETS etc. employed in the business (e.g. return on capital employed, profit per pound of labour wage). *See also* RATIO ANALYSIS.

promotion Any particular form of communication and activity which an organization undertakes to make its target audience more aware of, and favourably disposed to, its products. The major forms of promotion used within the MARKETING MIX are PERSONAL SELLING, SALES PROMOTION and ADVERTISING. The inclusion of PUBLIC RELATIONS under this heading is seen by some as contentious.

promotion mix That particular or specific combination of forms of persuasive communication, such as PERSONAL SELLING and ADVERTISING, used by an organization to support its business objectives. *See also* PROMOTION, MARKETING MIX.

promotional discount A reduction in

the usual unit price of a product offered to customers in order to stimulate increased purchases.

proof of purchase A piece of evidence (often an element of the PACKAGING) which demonstrates to a promoter that a PRODUCT has been bought by a consumer etc., in order for a participating consumer to claim promotional gifts offered.

psychographics The description of the behaviour of consumers or buyers through the application of approaches designed to highlight their attitudes, interests and opinions by means of quantitative rather than qualitative techniques.

public enquiry A formal investigation, convened by local or national government into issues of general concern, whose deliberations are open to all comers and whose results are published. For the retail sector, those that are most relevant relate to planning applications for new stores and transport developments.

public house (UK) A form of retail outlet which has a licence to sell alcoholic (and non-alcoholic) beverages to its customers for consumption on the premises (a bar). They are commonly referred to as 'pubs'. Many public houses retail food at lunchtime and in the evening and snacks such as crisps and peanuts at other times of the day. Opening hours are restricted by legislation.

There are three major categories of public house, differentiated from one another because of the relationship they have with the brewery companies who supply their major product lines. These are tenanted house,

managed house and free house. The lessee of a *tenanted house* pays a rent to a brewer who owns the pub and takes a margin in the products sold from beer, spirits and soft drinks through to food and fruit-machine takings. A *managed house* is owned by the brewery and managed by an employee. A *free house* is one where the owner has no contractual relationship with any brewer in terms of ownership.

public relations (PR) The process of actively cultivating positive goodwill and mutual understanding between an organization and significant interest groups (e.g. customers, staff, central and local government agencies).

Less formally, it is the pursuit of the media for favourable publicity, which, unlike ADVERTISING, is not paid for directly. Tools used for this purpose include the PRESS RELEASE, the press conference and the publicity event, the latter of which is often used to launch new products or ideas. The media, and in particular the trade press, are often content to take information from press or media releases to compile details of new products or industry events.

Public relations is also used in a defensive sense where the Public Relations Officer (PRO) acts as spokesperson to defend an organization against adverse criticism or to show a positive response to potential external threats.

pull strategy The attempt to stimulate consumer demand through PROMOTION to the point where consumer requests for a product are at such a pitch that intermediaries feel compelled to stock the item.

Such a strategy requires resources

to be pumped into expensive consumer advertising and also to a lesser extent to trade advertising, and is not available to smaller companies. *Compare* PUSH STRATEGY.

purchase 1. To obtain goods or services by payment.
2. A good or service obtained by payment.

purchasing 1. The process of obtaining goods and/or services for payment.
2. *See* PURCHASING DEPARTMENT.

purchasing department The section of an organization responsible for obtaining goods and services required by the organization in exchange for payment.

push strategy The attempt to motivate the retailer (and wholesaler where applicable) to stock a product believing that, once the product is on sale, then its POINT OF SALE and display impact will cause the product to sell. A push strategy relies on the power of DISTRIBUTION availability to generate sales. *Compare* PULL STRATEGY.

pyramid selling A type of distribution whereby the originator of a product grants the rights to sell the product to a number of different levels of distributor. Within succeeding levels there are fewer and fewer distributors, culminating in the originator him- or herself. Each higher-level participant in the pyramid thus created earns commission based on the sales made by the lower levels. As the system is open to abuse by the originator, such activities may be controlled by law in various jurisdictions.

Q

qualitative research That group of investigative techniques which seek to answer the question 'Why?'. Such research is usually conducted using small groups of respondents recruited for some predefined characteristic (for example, they have young children, buy a particular product, or share a particular occupation). The group is not sampled on a probabilistic basis and hence is not necessarily representative of a given POPULATION.

The focus of qualitative research is on careful attention to responses as providers of insight into participants' behaviour, attitudes, motivation and interests. Qualitative research is therefore usually either exploratory or diagnostic (i.e. it may be used to generate ideas, explore motivations and discover why people behave as they do in situations where formal questionnaire-based approaches would be inappropriate).

There are three main types of qualitative research technique: DIS-CUSSION GROUP, individual non-directive or depth interview, and 'projective techniques'. The latter use a wide variety of approaches rooted in clinical psychology in an attempt to explore attitudes by encouraging the respondent to 'project' his or her real motives onto a third party, using, for example, cartoons, sentence com-pletion, role plays and fantasy situations.

The analysis of qualitative research is a highly skilled task usually under-taken by specialists with a back-ground in the behavioural sciences. There are a large number of qualitat-ive MARKET RESEARCH agencies.

quality Generally applied to the per-ceived attributes of a good or service provided by a retailer. Is most com-monly associated with price but can equally relate to the 'fitness for use', or 'meeting agreed customer require-ments'.

quality assurance The identification and eradication of defects at source; the application of right-first-time design techniques (e.g. Marks & Spencer product design).

quality control Those management procedures of various kinds utilized in the attempt to ensure that all prod-uct output conforms to specification and STANDARD and fully meets cus-tomer requirements. As a topic, qua-lity control has recently received growing attention particularly in re-sponse to the developments made by the Japanese on the basis of post-war American advice. This attention has presently culminated in the elaboration of systems of total quality management, whereby the output of any element, department etc. of an organization is viewed as a product which must meet the needs and requirements of the 'customers' in the next element, department etc.

quantitative research That group of investigative techniques that is characterized by the use of statistical techniques to summarize, reduce or analyse numerical data relating to (large) samples.

Typically, quantitative MARKET RESEARCH will be used, via a structured QUESTIONNAIRE, to estimate from a sample selected from a target POPULATION, what proportion of the population possess a specified attribute (e.g. those who own a car) and to provide confidence levels associated with such an estimate.

Other quantitative research techniques (e.g. LINEAR REGRESSION) may be used to explore relationships between variables of interest.

questionnaire A structured interrogative document addressing a single topic, or set of related topics, which seeks to elicit data from respondents. The term is also used to describe batteries of attitudinal statements, items etc., with which respondents are asked to agree or disagree.

Question items within such a document should be subject to careful design procedure in order to meet technical standards (e.g. the elimination of bias, and non-response error etc.). They are often laid out in a sequence which routes the respondent through the schedule on the basis of his or her responses to particular items.

quick response system (QRS) A co-operative network between a retailer and its suppliers whereby EPOS data from the retailer is transmitted directly via ELECTRONIC DATA INTERCHANGE to suppliers so that they can use the data to provide timely, appropriate restocking to meet customer demand. It is particularly effective when used with items such as swimwear or T-shirts, where, because of seasonal or fashion trends, the merchandise is required on the sales floor as quickly as possible. It is estimated that a quick response system can reduce the time from purchase order to the selling floor from five weeks to one week.

quota bonus A compensation plan whereby a salesperson is paid a basic wage plus a COMMISSION on sales in excess of a predetermined sales figure, often expressed in volume/item terms.

quota sample *See* SAMPLING METHODS.

R

rack jobber A supplier of certain classes of merchandise, which are sold on a SELF-SELECTION basis, who not only supplies the merchandise but undertakes stock replenishment and display of the fixturing ('racks'). The precise contractual relationship (e.g. ownership of merchandise) between jobber and retailer varies. Goods often sold in this way, especially through SUPERMARKETS, include records, spices and books.

random sampling A (simple) procedure for selecting a subset of a POPULATION where every element of the population has an equal chance of inclusion in the subset.

range 1. The ASSORTMENT of categories of merchandise offered for sale by a particular retailer. Also, within a particular category, the number and variety of lines offered.

2. The maximum distance a customer is prepared to travel to purchase goods and services of a particular kind. It is one of the concepts underpinning CENTRAL PLACE THEORY.

rate of turnover *See* STOCK TURNOVER.

rates (UK) A tax levied on a property, based on its notional rental value. Until 1990 the rates were the principal form of local taxation, and their value was set by local authorities. In 1990 the Uniform Business Rate superseded the old system for property in business use, the rate being set by central government.

ratio analysis A tool for the investigation of financial data relating to the operations and stock market quotation (if any) of a company.

Ratio analysis focuses on the four areas of LIQUIDITY, profitability and efficiency, GEARING (*see also* LEVERAGE), and investment performance. Various models exist which aim to improve control through the use of ratios.

Examples of liquidity ratios are 'current ratio' (current assets/current liabilities) and 'acid test' (liquid assets/current liabilities), where manufacturing norms are in the region of 1.5 to 2, and 1.0, respectively. In retailing, lower values are often found because retailers' stocks are more 'liquid' (i.e. easily convertible to cash), than the case in manufacturing. The principal profitability ratio is 'return on equity' or 'return on capital employed', where the manufacturing norm is in the region of 0.05 to 0.15.

Gearing is the ratio of debt to capital employed in a business, and can vary widely. Low gearing is in the region of 0.2, high gearing may be over 1.0. Investment performance may be measured by the price–earnings ratio (market price per share/earnings per share). Typical values (say 8 to 12) may vary between stock markets. Such ratios are also affected particularly by market sentiment.

Because of the wide variation in ratios typically encountered in different industries and markets, comparisons should probably be restricted to those between firms in similar situations.

readership The number and characteristics of the individuals who peruse newspapers, journals and magazines, as distinct from those who actually buy, or subscribe to, such publications.

ready-made Products that are sold for immediate consumption or use etc., which require little or no adaptation by consumers prior to use.

ready meal Prepacked and pre-prepared food dish which merely requires heating by consumers prior to consumption.

ready-to-wear 1. Clothing made to a specific size, but with no individual in mind, as opposed to made-to-measure, or BESPOKE garments.

2. Especially when in the French, *prêt-a-porter*, used to distinguish designer ranges of clothes produced for immediate sale rather than 'couture' garments produced for a specific customer.

receipt 1. The act of taking possession of goods, cash etc. on the occasion of their delivery.

2. A document which records the money, goods etc. involved in a transaction and is issued as a record of such transaction, especially by means of a retailer's TILL.

recommended retail price (RRP) The monetary amount attached to products sold to consumers that a manufacturer or wholesaler of the products strongly suggests be charged by the organization responsible for the final sale to consumers. It is often referred to in retailer–supplier negotiations to enable the retailer to estimate the amount of profit which will be generated from the supplier's products.

record A basic element, containing pieces of information which are specific to that element, which, when taken with other elements, make up a DATABASE file. For example, the record of a particular customer of a newsagent may contain customer name, address, daily newspapers taken, Sunday newspapers taken, payments due, payments made. This record, together with those of all other customers, would make up a customer file.

recruitment The process of attracting and selecting new staff to undertake identified duties and responsibilities for a specific post.

red good Consumer product having the following characteristics as selected by Aspinwall. It has a high replacement rate, but rates relatively lowly on his other four parameters, namely gross margin, adjustment, time of consumption, searching time. Such goods are broadly CONVENIENCE GOODS.

redemption A voucher which a customer may trade in to obtain a free gift or money off the normal price of a GOOD. It is usually obtained in the course of a SALES PROMOTION, which may be mounted by a manufacturer and/or retailer etc.

reference group Any collection of individuals sharing some salient characteristics such as age, social status, lifestyle values etc., which is regarded as an arbiter of those products, attitudes, activities etc. which are acceptable or desirable to any particular person (e.g. sports stars, members of Rotary, others in the same profession). *See also* PEER GROUP.

refund The money (and the act of giving such money) returned to a customer in exchange for goods previously purchased, where such goods have in some way been unsatisfactory.

refurbishment The redecoration and/or renovation of a STORE or SHOPPING CENTRE.

regional shopping centre 1. Any major conurbation acting as a focal point for the provision of retail services within an extensive hinterland. *See also* CENTRAL PLACE THEORY.
2. A planned and purpose-built development which integrates at least 500,000 square feet of retail floorspace embracing a wide range of stores, service outlets and catering and leisure facilities, in a spacious and weather-protected environment. Such centres are designed with car parking facilities and a location on high-capacity road links.

registered design A representation of a particular good or service with respect to physical appearance, style, colour, function etc., which has been lodged with the appropriate authority in a jurisdiction in order to provide a protection against PASSING OFF and the infringement of the rights of the owner.

registered trademark/name The style and title applied to goods by which a particular supplier's goods are recognized or known in the market place, and which is given a degree of protection from imitation by the process of submitting the designating marks etc. for scrutiny by the government authority for the jurisdiction, and having such marks etc. placed on file as being identified with the particular company. In some jurisdictions the distinction is maintained between TRADEMARKS, which apply to goods, and service marks, which are applied to service products exclusively.

regression analysis *See* LINEAR REGRESSION.

reject Any item of merchandise identified as being of less than acceptable quality, possibly for minor reasons such as surface blemishes, which is not sold through the regular channel of distribution. A SECOND.

reject shop Retail outlet selling SECONDS and other similar items of merchandise, such as over-orders, at prices below those pertaining for first-quality goods.

reminder line A small promotional item, such as a pen or matchbook, bearing a company or PRODUCT name which serves as a continuing vehicle for the re-presentation of that name to the user.

remnant The fabric left over after fulfilling an order or completing regular sales, which can itself then be sold at a DISCOUNT. ('Fent' is a synonym.)

reorder level *See* REORDER POINT.

reorder point That quantity of stockholding to which inventory falls, which triggers a request for new supplies. *See also* INVENTORY CONTROL.

repeat order A requisition which is placed with a supplier, for a second or subsequent delivery of merchandise etc. with minimum changes from the previous occasion. Such orders may be placed automatically, using appropriate systems, for standard lines.

repeat purchase The occasion on which a product is bought for a second or subsequent time, by a consumer. Retailers and manufacturers both strive to develop customer loyalty, namely the habitual behaviour patterns of shopping in the same store, or the automatic repeat purchase of a brand or product without wider comparisons.

repositioning *See* POSITIONING.

resale The action of any channel intermediary in concluding a contract for the purchase of merchandise by other intermediaries further along the CHANNEL.

resale price maintenance *See* PRICE MAINTENANCE.

resident buying office A department responsible for a company's purchasing activities which is in a central location other than the HEAD OFFICE,

especially in cities such as New York, London or Hong Kong.

resource file A document containing information compiled by a retailer on all potential suppliers of particular classes of merchandise (e.g. information on the reliability, new product developments, product quality, and speed of response of the suppliers).

response rate That number of people who react to the stimulus of a DIRECT MARKETING activity, usually expressed as a percentage of those to whom the stimulus was directed. This figure is used as a measure of the effectiveness of the activity.

resumé (USA) *See* CURRICULUM VITAE.

retail To sell goods or services directly to final consumers, or those buying on behalf of such consumers (general public, households).

retail accordion theory The suggestion that dominance in the patterns of merchandising alternates between general-line, wide assortments and specialized, narrow-line assortments over time. (Also known as the general–specific–general process.) This variation in merchandising is seen as the basis of the varying character of competition between institutions at a given point in time. *See also* WHEEL OF RETAILING.

retail audit A MARKET RESEARCH technique for monitoring and tabulating the pattern of consumer purchases from outlets. A SAMPLE of stores is selected to represent the sector or product classification of interest.

Auditors visit the stores at regular intervals to count stocks, record deliveries and gather other information such as display, price and promotional activity. Sales through that outlet since the previous visit may then be calculated using a simple formula:

Sales = Stock at last visit + Deliveries

− Stock this visit

The DATA is then grossed up to represent the national or regional universe which the sample was designed to represent.

Most retail audit data is available from specialist agencies who offer syndicated data to manufacturers, wholesalers and retailers on a subscription basis. The best known company in this field is A. C. Nielsen.

Retail audits can provide data for individual brands or product groupings, such as sales, deliveries, retail stock levels, prices, display, product availability, combinations of brands stocked and more sophisticated analyses such as forward stock cover, marginal stockists and cumulative distribution.

The data may also be used to show retailer and manufacturer market shares by type of outlet, retailer-type and region.

In recent years, the adoption of EPOS technology has made it possible to provide much of this data without the need to visit stores and count stock. If retailers agree to make their sales, deliveries, pricing and stocking levels available to auditing companies via electronic means, costs can be reduced and the speed with which the data is made available increased.

retail design Those activities involved in the totality of the visual presentation of shop outlets etc., especially as they relate to the FASCIA and other exterior elements, the interior FIXTURES and finishes, colour schemes etc. The visual design and components of an outlet have a considerable impact upon its ATMOSPHERICS.

retail employment The total of those individuals, either salaried, wage-earning or self-employed, who are wholly or partially engaged in the sale of GOODS or SERVICES to the general public.

retail enterprise Any business organization engaged in the sale of goods and services to ultimate consumers, or those buying on behalf of such consumers.

retail industry Those organizations which, when taken collectively, constitute those concerned with the supply of goods and services to ultimate consumers, or those buying on behalf of such consumers.

retail information system A holistic view of the network which provides for the transfer of data, and its interpretation, between the component elements of a DISTRIBUTION CHANNEL. The information interactions include those which occur within the retail organization (e.g. EPOS data used in SPACE ALLOCATION), and those which occur between retailers and outside organizations such as suppliers (using EDI), financial institutions (using EFTPOS), or research organizations (via, for example, RETAIL AUDITS).

retail marketing Those activities, and the management thereof, involved in the mutually beneficial exchange occurring between organizations supplying goods and services to ultimate consumers and those target segments they seek to serve, particularly in respect of the elements of the RETAIL MIX.

retail mix Those elements of an organization's offering to a final consumer which are seen as being (a) under the control of the organization's management, and (b) having an impact, individually or in combination, on the customer's perception of the organization's offer. The elements may be seen as consisting of the retail product (i.e. merchandise sold and trading style), location, physical facilities and number of outlets (place), pricing, promotion (including the use of sales assistants), services (e.g. delivery, after- sales, credit etc.), organizational factors and the use of and type of personnel employed.

The concept of blending the elements of the mix to achieve the desired response from the target market is borrowed from the MARKETING MIX.

retail operations Within a store format business organization, those activities connected with the running of stores, particularly as involves the day-to-day conduct of business and the definition of systems to be followed in the conduct of such business. *See also* OPERATIONS.

retail outlet *See* OUTLET.

retail park An area, usually on the edge of a conurbation etc., created or designated for the sale of a wide range of GOODS and SERVICES to the general public via OUTLETS of different types, and which normally incorporates extensive parking facilities.

retail pricing The process for determining the charge to be made to the customer for an item of merchandise or service purchase. Pricing in a retail firm is, in the strategic sense, no different from pricing in other sectors. The objectives of price setting may be expressed in terms of sales, profit, competition and market position. The element peculiar to retailing is the extent, nature and visibility of price adjustments, which therefore assume a significance in retailing not reached elsewhere. The mechanisms by which prices are determined (MARKUP, competitive pricing, vendor pricing) receive extensive consideration, as do adjustments (MARKDOWN, DISCOUNTS).

retail promotion Activities designed to stimulate demand for a product among final resellers. Such promotions are used by manufacturers and wholesalers, particularly in the context of INDEPENDENT RETAILERS.

retail sector That part or division of total trade represented by the value and/or activities associated with the sale of goods and services to ultimate consumers or those buying on behalf of such consumers.

retail strategy *See* CORPORATE STRATEGY.

retail value The monetary worth of the sales within a particular non-industrial and non-wholesale context.

retail warehouse Normally, a free-standing, single- storey OUTLET selling non-food goods, with a minimum of 1,000 square metres of floorspace, occupying an industrial- type building ('shed') and having on-site car parking facilities. Although such stores occupy industrial-style premises, they are clearly retail outlets selling directly to the general public and as such may be distinguished from storage depots, which do not sell to the public, and from wholesale warehouses, which deal primarily with the retail trade.

Retail warehouses can also be distinguished from hypermarkets and superstores which sell both food and non-food goods, but which concentrate on the former. Retail warehouse operations had their origins in the late 1960s but they have become a common feature of the retail scene in the UK and elsewhere since the mid-1970s. This style of retailing is dominated by MULTIPLE RETAILER groups. Initially three types of retail warehouses were generally recognized – electrical goods, furniture and carpets, DIY (home improvement) products. A much wider range of products, including toys, children's goods and motor accessories, is now sold by such outlets.

Many of the early developments were housed in converted factories and warehouses, but companies today operate from new purpose-built units. Retail warehouse operators tend to favour 'out-of-town' and 'edge-of-town centre' sites rather than traditional shopping centres. These retail warehouses are increasingly found clustered together in RETAIL PARKS.

retailer Any business enterprise, or individual, involved in the sale of goods and services to ultimate consumers, or those buying on behalf of such consumers.

retailer co-operative A group of final resellers who combine to buy basic products from suppliers in order to enjoy the potential benefits of quantity DISCOUNTS. *See also* VOLUNTARY GROUP, POOLED BUYING.

retailer credit card *See* CREDIT CARD.

retailing Process of selling goods and services to ultimate consumers, or those buying on behalf of such consumers, particularly when carried out through store outlets and, when further specified, MAIL ORDER etc.

retention The length of the time period that the medium bearing a message, such as an advertisement, can be stored by the recipient. While press (advertising) and DIRECT MAIL can, in theory, be kept permanently, other MEDIA such as radio, TV, POINT OF SALE and POSTERS rely on the repetition of the message as a means of substitution for the ability to be stored.

return 1. Merchandise sent back to a retailer for REFUND by a customer, usually because of faults or a failure to suit the customer's purpose. *See also* RETURNS POLICY.

2. Unsold, damaged or defective stock sent back to a SUPPLIER for credit by a retailer.

return on capital employed *See* RATIO ANALYSIS.

return on investment Return on equity. *See* RATIO ANALYSIS.

returnable A container such as a bottle, for which an allowance is made on return, or a charge levied on the failure to return.

returns *See* RETURN.

returns policy A retailer's operating code or guidelines for accepting goods back for credit or REFUND after purchase. In most jurisdictions customers have the right to return defective merchandise, but the retailer may, in addition, grant customers the option of returning merchandise merely because it proves unsatisfactory.

revenue 1. The income earned as services are being performed, or the cash received in a period.

2. The net income received in a period after the deduction of appropriate expenses.

revolving credit A facility for deferred payment for products up to a preset limit which, once agreed, continues until cancelled, or the preset limit is breached.

risk capital *See* EQUITY, VENTURE CAPITAL.

risk reduction The search for higher levels of certainty by those engaged in decision-making, particularly when it concerns purchase decisions.

Robinson–Patman Act (USA) A federal law which prohibits price discrimination by manufacturers for products of 'like quality'. The Act is intended to encourage competition.

role The characteristic behaviours etc. deployed, or expected by others to be deployed, by one occupying a particular position, family place etc.

route planning The selection (or calculation) of the optimum modes of transport and journey pattern to be followed for the shipment of goods from supplier to retailer.

routine buying The purchasing of goods, commonly and frequently bought, such as milk and potatoes for consumers, and standard raw materials for suppliers, by habit or convention rather than by a fresh decision-making process on each purchase occasion.

routine selling The practice of a SALESPERSON in approaching a potential customer and offering assistance with the purchase decision.

royalty The agreed proportion of the total income received from the sale of a book etc., or from the use of a patented invention, which is paid to the owner, author or inventor.

S

safety stock The additional inventory which must be held, over and above that required to meet anticipated demand, to ensure that there are no (or few) occasions on which the seller is unable to supply the merchandise. *See* INVENTORY CONTROL.

Sagacity A system of consumer classification, developed by Research Services Ltd, based on the hypothesis that people have different aspirations and behaviour patterns as they go through their life-cycle. The four main stages of the life-cycle that are defined are subdivided by income/occupation groups: (i) dependent, (ii) pre-family, (iii) family and late, (iv) white and blue collar.

salad bar A temperature-controlled counter, normally in a supermarket or large food section etc., devoted to the display and sale of pre-prepared combinations of fresh vegetables, nuts, fruits, cheeses, meat etc. in dressings such as mayonnaise, for SELF-SELECTION by the customer, and consumption without further preparation.

sale 1. The point at which the contract for a supply of goods and/or services is completed when the customer gives good consideration and his/her OFFER is accepted by the seller.

2. A retail promotional event which seeks to stimulate trade by offering, for a limited period, price reductions on regular merchandise etc., or goods purchased specifically because they are viewed as offering excellent value for money. Such events are traditionally associated with the end of a fashion or clothing season or the period prior to model changes.

Sale of Goods Act 1979 (UK) Legislation which determines that a retailer must sell goods which are:

(i) *of merchantable quality* Should the goods be sold in this condition? E.g. a new car with scratched paintwork is not of merchantable quality, whereas a second-hand car may well be.

(ii) *fit for the purpose* Are the goods suitable for their usual use? E.g. if a new car will not run properly it is not 'fit for purpose' (nor is it of merchantable quality).

(iii) *as described* Do the goods correspond exactly with the description applied to them by the retailer, or any description attached to the goods by whomever applied, which is present at the point of retail sale? E.g. if a car is sold as 'the latest model' but is in fact from a previous year's production, then it would not be 'as described'.

The Act gives the dissatisfied party the right to claim compensation from the other party involved in the exchange if the law is broken. Any retail transaction which involves the seller exchanging goods for the buyer's money (cash, credit card or instalments etc.) is affected by the legislation.

sale or return A term of trading offered by a supplier to a retailer whereby the products are paid for only if sold by the retailer; if unsold they are fully credited to the retailer when sent back to the supplier. Sale or return offers a strong incentive for retailers to stock a new or risky product, as the stockholding and risk is financed by the manufacturer or supplier.

sale room *See* SALES ROOM.

sales 1. The monetary amounts (in total) derived from or generated through the supply of goods and/or services to customers.
2. The function, department etc. of a business firm with responsibility for and control of the company's representatives.

sales aid Equipment, literature, video, model etc. used to support the presentation of goods and services to prospective clients by a supplier's representative. Sales aids help the customer visualize the product and its benefits more powerfully than the salesperson's words alone could do.

sales analysis A systematic examination of revenues and volumes of products purchased by customers from an organization, department etc. in order to identify significant

patterns which can indicate potential opportunities or problems. Sales can be analysed by, for example, customer size and type, region, salesperson, product group or any other meaningful division. Computer analysis of sales results can give access to considerable detail but may provide too much data unless exceptions analyses are built in to identify significant or unexpected results.

sales area *See* SELLING SPACE.

sales assistant *See* SHOP ASSISTANT.

sales budget 1. A planned amount of money set aside to finance the costs anticipated to be associated with personal representation, and other promotion, used to stimulate purchases by customers.
2. *See* SALES FORECAST.

sales call A visit made by a representative to a customer. (A telephone-based sales contact may be part of the selling process but is usually not considered to be a full sales call.) Representatives are often appraised, in part, according to the number and types of sales calls they make. Examples of sales calls include new business calls, repeat business calls, service or follow up calls and technical support calls.

sales campaign A specific drive to increase customer demand for a particular product or group of products by means of promotional techniques. Such campaigns are used particularly for the launch of new products and are often accompanied by the provision of special incentives for the SALES FORCE.

sales clerk (USA) *See* SHOP ASSISTANT.

sales force The group of representatives employed by an organization who go out and seek orders from customers. In the retail situation, those SHOP ASSISTANTS who deal directly with customers in seeking orders may be regarded as the sales force.

sales forecast A prediction, usually based on a systematic or statistical procedure, of expected income levels for a determined period in the future.

sales incentive An inducement or encouragement to representatives or agents of an organization to achieve higher levels of customer orders or purchases than the norm. (E.g. a competition with a prize for reaching a given sales target, a percentage of the sales turnover as sales commission.)

sales lead An indication of a potential customer who might be more likely, or more willing, to purchase a product. Salespersons generate leads by progressively working with potential customers in their territories and also by asking existing customers for information about others they know who might need the same products. Leads also arise independently through customer enquiries generated from ADVERTISING and PUBLIC RELATIONS.

sales pitch 1. For a market trader, or street hawker, the physical space occupied by the trader, especially when established through custom or contract.

2. The (slightly derogatory) term for the oral presentation of a promotional or persuasive message used in support of the effort to secure customer orders by representatives.

sales promotion Inducements or incentives, offered for a limited period as additional benefits to stimulate customer demand for goods or services (e.g. price reductions, extra quantity offers, bonded packs, COMPETITIONS, gifts with products, paid-for gifts with the product – self-liquidators – and free samples). The objectives behind sales promotions can be grouped into three broad areas: (i) encouraging trial, (ii) encouraging loading or extra quantity sales, and (iii) encouraging loyalty and regular repeat purchase.

Sales promotions are essentially viewed as short-term measures to clear stocks or reach sales targets. The seasonal SALES are classical sales promotions which are well understood in all retail operations. With sales promotions there may be a dip in sales once the promotion ends, and this must have been exceeded by the extra sales during the promotion period for it to be deemed to have succeeded.

sales quota 1. An allocation of market share in a situation where demand exceeds supply. It is in effect rationing of sales. An example is the 'gentleman's agreement' that governs the market share of Japanese-built cars in various markets.

2. *See* SALES TARGET.

sales representative An individual employed by an organization who is charged with the responsibility for securing orders etc. from customers. (Many titles exist for this role, ranging from 'commercial traveller' to sales executive.)

sales revenue Income received from customers for the supply of goods and service.

sales room That part of a building, particularly an AUCTIONEER's premises, that is used for the conduct of AUCTIONS, as distinct from rooms used to display LOTS. Also, any other part of premises set aside specifically for the conclusion of bargains.

sales target An expression of the desired or expected level of incomes to be generated through the supply of goods and services to customer. Such targets are often built into SALES FORECASTS and SALES INCENTIVES.

sales terms *See* TERMS OF CONTRACT.

salesperson That individual who communicates a promotional message directly to a buyer or customer, or receives their orders. Many multiple retailers now use fewer salespersons, where SELF-SERVICE or SELF-SELECTION dominates.

sample 1. A subset of a statistical POPULATION. A population consists of all items within a scope of study; for example, all sales assistants employed by a retail company, or all sweatshirts of a particular style provided by a supplier. A sample consists of some, but not all, of the 'members' of the population. A sample of a small number of the supplier's sweatshirts may be examined, for example, for QUALITY CONTROL purposes. The decisions made on the basis of sample information are supported by the application of STATISTICAL ANALYSIS and STATISTICAL TECHNIQUES AND TESTS.
2. Specimen part of, or example of, merchandise offered for sale (e.g. a section of carpet), which is indicative of the overall quality and pattern of the complete item, or a typical or representative item such as a garment.

sampling methods Those procedures for choosing representative subsets from a specified POPULATION (sampling frame). The particular sampling methods to be utilized for, say, a MARKET RESEARCH survey, would normally be chosen after consideration of the following:
(i) *Simple random sampling* A procedure whereby every member of a population has an equal choice of being included in the sample. In theory, to achieve a simple random sample (*see* RANDOM SAMPLING), all members of the population need to be identified and numbered, and the sample members are picked by random (or pseudo-random) number generators (the equivalent of drawing numbers 'out of a hat'). This procedure may be practical in, for example, selecting a sample of employees from a personnel file, but may be inappropriate on economic or logistical grounds for many market research surveys.
(ii) *Systematic sampling* When a population is organized in a systematic way (e.g. invoices filed according to date received), then the sample may be selected by picking every kth member of the (ordered) population, after selecting the first member by random number. This can prove more convenient and economical than simple random sampling, but care must be exercised in choosing the value of k.
(iii) *Stratified sampling* In cases where a population is very large, heterogeneous and/or geographically widespread, it is often useful to divide it into subpopulations or strata. For example, in the grocery sector,

companies may be subdivided by type (multiple, co-operative, independent), by nationality, by level of turnover etc. In a customer attitude survey, the population may be subdivided by criteria such as age, gender, socio-economic group. After the strata have been chosen, random samples are selected from each stratum, the sizes of which may be determined by prior knowledge of the relative proportions of each stratum within the total population. For example, if a sample of 500 customers is to be selected from a population believed to consist of 70 per cent female and 30 per cent male, then the sample should include 350 randomly chosen female customers and 150 randomly chosen male customers.

(iv) *Multi-stage sampling* Where personal interviews are required of a sample of people from a wide geographical area, cost and time constraints would prevent a rigid application of simple random, systematic or stratified sampling methods. Therefore, initially, the locations for the interviews, rather than the interviewees, are chosen by random methods over a series of stages. Once the locations are known (and considered to be suitable for an economic interviewing schedule), then random or stratified sampling methods can be employed to select the interviewees. A retailer gathering customer views on merchandise range and display may, at the first stage, select a sales region, at the second stage a sales area within the region, and at the third stage, a sample of old-style and new-style stores within the area. A stratified sample of the customers of each chosen store may then be selected.

(v) *Quota sampling* The members of the sample are selected only on the basis of some agreed prior percentage of the full sample (e.g. when interviewers are given quotas – certain numbers – of people to interview with given characteristics; age, gender, and are instructed to achieve the quotas within a specified time period). The method is used to obtain some of the benefits of stratified sampling at a lower cost. However, the consequence is that the results may contain unknown (interviewer and other) biases.

sandwich board Two pieces of supporting sheet onto which a promotional or other message is pasted, connected by shoulder straps which is worn by a man or woman, who then parades in a public place.

satellite store A smaller, physically separate outlet, often offering a restricted merchandise range, which is under the control of management in a nearby 'host' store, rather than reporting directly to HEAD OFFICE. Such a store may provide a solution to the problem of obtaining additional floorspace in a particular centre where there is not the option of extending the original store.

satisfaction A measure, estimate or belief relating to the extent to which a product has met the criteria expressed by the user or consumer of the product.

saturation The position when a product has been purchased by all likely potential customers in a MARKET. It is usually thought to occur during late maturity within the PRODUCT LIFE-CYCLE. Saturation particularly affects CONSUMER DURABLES which generate only replacement sales, after most households have purchased (e.g. TV sets).

scale A machine for determining the weight of an item of merchandise, consignment etc.

scanner *See* LASER SCANNER.

scanning The POINT OF SALE process by which product BARCODE data is fed into a computer, often by means of a LASER SCANNER. The resultant EPOS data can be converted into retail management information. The ostensible potential benefits of scanning for customers at the point of sale are said to be speedier service and payment, and itemized receipts.

scrambled merchandising The result of a policy decision, or haphazard outcome, whereby the goods on offer in a particular OUTLET are not necessarily coherently related, one with another (e.g. the sale of clothing in a food superstore).

screen 1. A surface on which images are shown.
2. The process of selecting, often at an early stage against predetermined criteria (e.g. screening respondents).
3. In printing, the fine mesh used as the carrier for an image which is to be transferred to the paper etc. by squeezing ink through the appropriate unblocked areas of mesh. (Used especially for printing POSTERS.)

screen printing *See* SCREEN.

seal A form of closure, on a pack or container, which is used to exclude air and/or retain fluids, often in order to preserve the contents.

season That period of a year conventionally considered appropriate for the sale of certain types of merchandise (e.g. swimsuits).

seasonal discount A promotional price reduction, offered at certain times of the year, to stimulate demand, especially in LOW SEASON or out of season.

seasonal merchandise STOCK which is sometimes offered for sale only at particular times of the year (e.g. skiwear, sun tan lotion, Christmas decorations).

seasonal promotion A short-term sales inducement specific to a given period of the year, especially used in HIGH SEASON or mid-season.

seasonal variation The cyclical pattern of troughs and peaks of sales, and other (retail) variables, at different times of the year. *See also* TIME SERIES ANALYSIS.

second An item of merchandise that has been found faulty (not up to defined standards) which may then be sold, as such faults as are present are not sufficiently serious to render the item useless. Independent outlets have been quick to seize the opportunity to sell 'seconds' of branded goods at discount prices.

second-hand Goods that have been previously owned, which are then offered for resale.

second-line merchandise Goods offered for sale by a manufacturer, retailer etc. which do not bear that organization's regular or best known BRAND, TRADEMARK etc. (e.g. Tudor brand watches from Rolex). Not to be confused with SECONDS.

secondary data Information that has already been collected (analysed etc.) for another purpose, and is available to the researcher (e.g. existing reports, articles, company sales data etc.).

seconds shop A retailer selling slightly imperfect merchandise, end-of-lines, clearance items and cancelled orders, at a DISCOUNT on regular prices.

sector The particular division of retail trade into which a good, service, operator etc. falls (e.g. the fashion sector, the wholesale sector).

security The protection of property, goods, money, documentation or personnel, from harm or theft.

segment See MARKET SEGMENT.

segmentation See MARKET SEGMENTATION.

selection 1. A range of goods that are available for sale within a particular category of merchandise.
2. The act of choosing, by retail BUYERS, the merchandise to be held in STOCK.

selective distribution The situation where a manufacturer, agent etc. chooses only a limited number of the possible appropriate retail OUTLETS to carry his or her PRODUCT, especially where such retail sales are subject to particular contract conditions.

selector A person who makes decisions on merchandise to be bought. See also BUYER.

self-regulation The provision of rules, principles or conditions which will determine the behaviour and procedures of members of an association which are imposed by the association itself (and not by the law). Examples of self-regulatory bodies are the British Franchise Association and National Advertising Review Board (see Appendix 2).

self-scanning Any system whereby the (supermarket) customer takes the responsibility for all those processes required to input product BARCODE data into the retailer's EPOS system. The idea is currently at the experimental stage with retailers, such as AHOLD (see Appendix 3) in Holland, trying out systems where self-scan units are attached to specially designed customer trolleys. The units consist of a hand scanner, 'add' button, 'subtract' button and an electronic display, and the trolley gives an alarm signal if an item of merchandise is not scanned first. The goods are paid for at a special checkout desk where the self-scan unit can be linked to the cash drawer and EPOS unit.

self-selection A selling method where goods are displayed on racks, fixtures and counters allowing customers to choose, without assistance, those goods which they wish to purchase and take them to the nearest cash point for wrapping and payment. Self-selection is the sales process in most department and variety stores.

self-service The absence of retail sales assistants and the work undertaken by them, where customers themselves select goods and take them to a till point in order to pay.

The development of self-service is one of the most important features of post-war retail development, reducing the number of store employees required, and allowing economies of scale to be tapped, though with an increase in theft. The term is used particularly of the operating system of supermarkets etc.

sell 1. To offer a product for purchase by customers.
   2. To inform, listen to, interpret for, and ultimately persuade, the customer of the merits of the product in meeting his/her needs. Much debate persists as to whether selling is a natural attribute or a learnable skill.

sell-by date A day stamped or printed on the containers of foodstuffs and other perishables, to indicate the time by which the product should have been sold.

sell-in The activity of promising special DISCOUNTS or PROMOTIONS undertaken by manufacturers to persuade retailers to stock their products.

sell-out The situation where all tickets for a theatre play, football game etc. have been purchased in advance of the event, or where a retailer has no remaining stocks of an item.

sellers' market A situation where demand for a product exceeds supply of that product which thus allows those having the product in stock to command high prices for a short time.

selling space That proportion of the area of retail premises which is given over to the display of merchandise available for purchase, particularly in distinction to stock and other such areas.

semi-variable cost An expense incurred by a business, changes in which are not directly proportional to changes in sales. Staffing costs are an example of a semi-variable cost in a retail context: regardless of sales levels, the retailer is committed to the payment of the salaries of many employees; however, the increasing use of part-time staff means that there is also a variable element. At busy times the wage bill will be higher than at slow times.

sensitivity analysis A considered examination of the predicted variation in an output of interest in response to a known change in the level of an input variable. For example, the profitability (output) of a new retail venture will depend upon sales volume, site costs, purchase prices, staff, and other operating, costs (inputs). The profitability calculation would be sensitive to any changes in the input variables to different extents. If profitability was indeed highly sensitive to one particular factor then management would need to pay particular attention to that factor.

serial number One of a series of consecutive codes applied to, for example, cars, bicycles and electrical goods, as a means of identification of the individual item of production, or to books or magazines as a means of classification of the general category.

service A benefit-producing activity and/or provision of a facility which may incorporate the use of facilitating goods (e.g. dry-cleaning, merchandise returns policy, shopping mall signage, insurance). Within this definition are encompassed entire industries such as retailing, tourism, banking, transportation etc.

Services, where they are traded in advanced economies, account for the majority of employment and GROSS DOMESTIC PRODUCT. By 1980, for example, 70 per cent of the USA labour force was employed in services. While services encompass a diverse range of activities, some common features of the nature of service outputs can be observed. Service output is abstract (intangible, in major part); cannot be stored or inventoried; involves buyer/seller interaction during the 'production' process; and is usually highly specified to the requirements of a particular buyer, thus leading to heterogeneity (the Three Vs – variety, variability, variation) of output.

service area A location alongside a motorway or highway which normally affords fuel and car repair services, and refreshment, telephone, toilet and shopping facilities for travellers.

service centre 1. The office or section within an organization which has the responsibility of maintaining machines or equipment in proper working order.
2. The section of a car dealership or gas station to which cars are sent for regular maintenance or repairs.
3. Any retail outlet specializing in the maintenance or repair of particular types of goods, especially ones so designated by a manufacturer (e.g. Sony Service Centre).

service department The unit within a

retail or manufacturing organization which provides the after-sales assistance, advice or repairs for customers (e.g. for cars, television sets).

service desk The clearly identified COUNTER etc. of a store which deals with, for example, returned goods, credit requests and payments, and gift vouchers.

service level See CUSTOMER SERVICE LEVEL.

service mark See REGISTERED TRADE-MARK/NAME.

service station A unit which sells petrol (gasoline) and oil for motorists, and which often provides car repairs service, toilet facilities (rest room) and a basic assortment of goods for sale to travellers. Some service stations offer CONVENIENCE GOODS for sale for 24 hours a day.

share A small part of limited value, in the issued capital of a limited liability company; stock.

shed See RETAIL WAREHOUSE.

shelf A horizontal board or similar structure, solid or meshed, attached to a wall or fitment, on which goods are placed.

shelf barker A notice, attached to the boards carrying merchandise, giving information on the product displayed thereon, normally for promotional purposes.

shelf display Goods positioned on a board attached to a FIXTURE etc. in such a manner as to encourage customers to purchase.

shelf edge label A small ticket, slotted in a horizontal rim of a FIXTURE, which contains the description, price, weight etc. of items of merchandise located immediately below, or above, the particular rim. The use of shelf edge labels has, for many SELF-SERVICE retailers, replaced the practice of individual pricing of items of merchandise. The updating of labels (after, say, a price change for an item) is still a manual process, whereas at the POINT OF SALE, the same price change is made via the computer. Any lack of integration between the changes will cause a mismatch between price displayed and price charged with, possibly, serious legal consequences for the retailer.

The development of electronic shelf edge labelling systems, where a price change entered into the computer will automatically change the price on the shelf edge label, is believed to be one of the major information technology challenges of the 1990s.

shelf edging That part of the merchandise-carrying boards etc. attached to a FIXTURE which is nearest to the customer and which often carries temporary display or product information.

shelf filler An individual responsible for the placement of goods on FIXTURES for display and sale.

shelf life The period, especially but not solely where perishable goods are concerned, after which it is recommended that an item is no longer acceptable to the purchaser, or will not perform as well as when recently manufactured (e.g. paint, adhesives).

shelf talker *See* SHELF BARKER.

shelving Loosely, the FIXTURES installed in a store.

shift 1. Any time period within a day for which employees are contracted to work.

2. A group of individuals working in a unit for a specific period, on a regular basis (e.g. the night shift).

shift worker An individual who is part of a group, working for a specific period, on a regular basis, or one whose pattern of hours of employment moves on a regular basis between different periods of the day.

ship 1. Any large sea-going vessel.

2. To transport, or dispatch, goods, especially long distances, by any means of transport but especially sea-going vessels.

shipment A consignment of goods either about to be, in the process of, or recently transported by, ship, or other means of transportation (road, rail, air).

shipping 1. The act of sending goods by sea-going vessels, or other modes of transport.

2. The industry involved in the transportation by sea of goods, passengers etc.

shop 1. A fixed, permanent building used for the purpose of selling goods and/or services to customers by RETAIL.

2. A vehicle converted to serve such a purpose (mobile shop) which is taken to the areas where customers reside.

3. The activity of visiting retail premises in order to acquire goods and/or services.

shop assistant An individual employed in a retail outlet to undertake tasks related directly to customer service, shelf filling, order taking etc.

shop fitting 1. Equipment utilized in a retail outlet such as COUNTERS, display FIXTURES etc., normally of a fixed nature.
2. The art of installing such equipment.

shop floor 1. The sales area (SELLING SPACE) of a retail outlet.
2. Employees of a non-managerial kind, especially collectively as in shop-floor (workers).

shop front That part of a retail building, usually provided with display windows, that faces onto the primary street location of the outlet.

shop-soiled Describing goods which have been damaged or become dirty, because of storage or display within a retail outlet. Shop-soiled goods may be offered for sale at a reduced price.

shop theft The removal of property from the retail owner with the intention of permanently depriving the owner of the property without the owner's consent or payment therefor. The principal categories of persons stealing from retailers are employees and customers.

shop walker An individual responsible for dealing with customer queries and complaints, usually associated with large departmental stores. See also FLOOR WALKER.

shoplifting Theft by a customer of merchandise from a retail outlet.

shopmobility scheme A set of provisions for continuing access to, and facilities for, the disabled in their use of retail outlets and SHOPPING CENTRES.

shopping centre A planned, architecturally uniform, retail location containing a managed tenant mix occupying a number of different outlets within the scheme. Such centres may be covered schemes associated with on-site car parking (*shopping mall*) or merely strip developments in suburban locations (*shopping parade*).

shopping good See YELLOW GOOD.

shopping mall See SHOPPING CENTRE.

shopping parade See SHOPPING CENTRE.

Shops Act 1950 (UK) A (controversial) piece of legislation which controls the opening and closing times of shops, and conditions of employment in retailing. The latter provisions have in many circumstances been overtaken by the OFFICES SHOPS AND RAILWAY PREMISES ACT 1963. Parts 1, 2 and 3 of the Shops Act deal with the general opening and closing hours and early closing days. Part 4 deals specifically with Sunday trading.

short change That situation where a customer receives less than the correct amount of money owed by the retailer, when a purchase has been paid for by a tendered amount greater than the sum required.

short delivery A consignment of goods which contains less than that stated in the documentation or other agreement.

shortage The amount by which actual physical INVENTORY is less than the value of the BOOK INVENTORY.

show A specially organized promotional event for a specific range of GOODS or SERVICES for sale (e.g. flower show, motor show, holiday show).

showcase An item of furniture in the form of a FIXTURE with glazed sides and/or top, which is used to display merchandise within a retail outlet, especially where the merchandise is of high intrinsic value (e.g. jewellery). In a figurative sense the term is used to describe any outlet, location, exhibition etc., that serves as the epitome of a particular style, class of merchandise etc.

showroom An area within a building devoted to the display of merchandise, whether for sale by retail or wholesale.

shrink wrapping Plastic film, normally transparent, which is stretched over goods, holding the contents tightly in position for subsequent handling/transportation. The film is normally either heat sealed or self-adhesive.

shrinkage The monetary difference that arises between the value of INVENTORY received, at retail selling price, and retail sales in a period, when adjusted for opening and closing stocks. Up to 5 per cent, perhaps, of the total retail value of merchandise may be lost to shrinkage due to known causes such as in-store damage, stock passing its SELL-BY DATE etc., or to unidentified causes such as PILFERAGE, inefficient stock-recording methods etc.

sign A graphic device used to convey information, whether by means of writing, pictogram etc., especially for the benefit of users and visitors to buildings, facilities etc.

signage Those graphic information devices used within the retail setting to convey informational and promotional messages to customers and store visitors.

silent salesman A VENDING MACHINE.

silver market The proportion of the population who are over 60 years old and who have both reasonable disposable income and specific needs.

simple random sample *See* SAMPLING METHODS.

simulation model A simplified representation of reality, usually with a mathematical basis, which mimics or imitates the functioning of a physical system. Such models can provide a relatively inexpensive means for experimenting with potential changes to the operation of the physical system, but with little or no actual disruption. For example, the potential customer queues associated with a new arrangement of superstore CHECKOUTS can be estimated by experimenting with a computer simulation model of the superstore. Potential bottlenecks can be identified without causing actual customer inconvenience.

Single European Market The concatenation of the individual, national economies of the member states of the European Community under a consistent set of regulations for the sale, exportation etc. of goods and service. It is intended to come into force on 1 January 1993 as a result of joint agreement by EC governments to remove all restrictions on the internal market of the European Community. In the case of the UK this change originates from the Single European Act of 1985. The Act enshrines basic principles of a customs union and the free movement of goods, services and capital throughout member states. It does not promote harmonization as such, except where this could be seen as a restriction on trade.

For example, excise duties are to be brought broadly into line, as is VALUE ADDED TAX. The movement of goods will, for example, be controlled by a single common document and no border checks will be carried out between member states. In the future (after 1991), common standards are more likely to be applied on price and content labelling, trade marks, electronic payments systems and advertising.

The impact on retailing is likely to be concerned with cross-border co-operation, which will be physically easier but paradoxically will be governed by a more active competition policy; managing cross-border relationships; more complex supply chain management; ultimately, cross-border competition.

single-line store A retail outlet which sells a comprehensive range of goods within one merchandise category (e.g. hi-fi store).

single sourcing Locating and selecting one particular organization to supply goods and/or services.

site A piece of land on which a (retail) building or other development is, or is intended to be, located.

situation analysis See SWOT ANALYSIS.

situation audit See SWOT ANALYSIS.

size lining The selection of a limited number of predetermined physical measurements to govern the range of garments, shoes etc. to be offered for sale in order to meet typical anticipated demands.

skimming The action of a supplier to a market in seeking to attract only those segments within the market (who may be numerically small in number), willing to pay high prices for new items of merchandise or specifically designed services etc.

slogan The words or phrase, which by repetition in ADVERTISING, SALES PROMOTION etc. become associated with a product (e.g. 'A Mars a day helps you work, rest and play'); hook, catchline, strapline.

social class The rank or degree in society into which an individual is admitted or born by virtue of the acquisition of the appropriate qualifying characteristics (e.g. title of nobility, or degree). See also SOCIO-ECONOMIC CLASSIFICATION.

social forecasting The prediction of the likely future interdependent, interpersonal behaviour of existing and potential members of a particular culture, group etc. QUALITATIVE RESEARCH methods may be applied, for example, to anticipate changes in aesthetics and fashion with regard to clothing style and colours for the following season.

social responsibility Aspects of attitudes and behaviour of organizations and individuals in so far as they are affected by the standards, opinions etc. held by significant others. Such responsibility arises from a belief that actions should address themselves to the needs of society and take into account the interest of all the STAKE-HOLDERS involved.

socio-economic   classification A categorization of members of a society, especially for market segmentation purposes, using income and occupation as the defining variables. The best known system for this is the JICNARS group, which employs the categories A, B, C1, C2, D, E.

A Persons included in this category are those in the most senior managerial and professional occupations. They comprise approximately 3 per cent of the population in the UK (e.g. university professors, directors of major public companies, partners in larger professional practices).

B Persons included in this category are those in the senior to middle managerial occupations, professional employees and owners of small businesses. They comprise approximately 14 per cent of the UK population (e.g. lecturers, store managers).

C1 Persons included in this category are those in junior managerial and supervisory occupations, most recently qualified professionals (not in   partnership)   and   comprises approximately 27 per cent of the UK population.

C2 Includes skilled manual workers and comprises approximately 26 per cent of the UK population.

D Includes semi-skilled and un-skilled manual workers, comprising approximately 21 per cent of the UK population.

E Includes those at the lowest level of subsistence, and in the least well paid unskilled occupations. It comprises 9 per cent of the UK population.

socio-economic   group *See* SOCIO-ECONOMIC CLASSIFICATION.

soft furnishings That category of consumer goods encompassing household textiles, bedlinens etc.

soft good Any item of merchandise made from textiles (soft furnishings, clothes, carpets etc.); a loose term often used within mixed merchandise retailers to describe such goods, and other items such as books etc. that do not fit neatly into any other category.

soft sell A technique employed by representatives whereby customers are encouraged to make a purchase on the basis of deliberation on the merits of a product offered with little or no overt persuasive intervention from the representative. Such techniques may suit hesitant or reluctant customers who need time to consider a purchase and who may dislike the intervention of salespersons. *Compare* HARD SELL.

soft technology The application of designed systems of interaction, such as management systems or reward systems, to the purposes of an organization. This is in contrast to HARD TECHNOLOGY, whose principal manifestation is in the form of machinery.

software An ordered set of instructions (program) for a computer, written for a specific purpose, which

	Types of finance		Sources of finance
Long-term	Equity	personal funds ordinary shares, preference shares	Stock Exchange, USM, Third Tier, Over-the-counter, BES, venture capitalists
	Debt debentures, bank loans, commercial paper	Merchant banks, commercial paper market, venture capitalists	
	Hybrid various convertibles	Venture capitalists	
Short-term	Internally generated		Cash from sales
	Externally sourced		Trade credit, bank overdraft

guide the machine in the execution of the tasks required by the user (e.g. Spaceman software system for SPACE ALLOCATION).

sole distributor The only retailer, wholesaler, agent etc. in a defined area, territory, trade etc. who is allowed to sell a certain product. For example, an electrical retail chain may be the sole distributor of Bang & Olufsen equipment in a region of the UK.

sole trader Individual who engages in a business on his/her own account with unlimited liability.

source In marketing communication, the transmitter of the message. The transmitter may be the ostensible source (e.g. a well known personality appearing in a COMMERCIAL), or source characteristics may be attributed to the medium in which the communication arises (e.g. television or a source with different effects from magazine advertising). The principal determinants of audience reaction to a source are that transmitter's visibility, credibility, attractiveness to, and power over, the audience.

source of finance Any person, institution or mechanism available to a business as a provider of cash or other forms of near-cash to be used as capital in the continued operation of the business.

Finance can be provided by the owners of the business (*see* EQUITY), the business itself by way of profits, or by outside lenders (in which case it is called DEBT finance). In addition, hybrid forms of finance have assumed some importance in recent years; also known as 'convertibles', these are instruments which start off as loan finance with the option to convert to equity at a specified date and conversion rate. Options for UK businesses are briefly listed on p.139.

source of supply For a retailer, those

places or persons from where and/or whom merchandise is obtained. This may include manufacturers, wholesalers, primary producers, importing agents and members of the public (for secondhand and charity shops etc.). The exact mix depends on the nature of the retail business. Choosing sources of supply can be one of the most fundamental decisions in retailing.

sourcing The process of locating and selecting appropriate organizations or individuals who are able to supply required goods and services. In total the process may involve the identification of, contact with, evaluation of and, finally, negotiation with the selected sources.

space allocation Within store format retailing, the methods by which an organization decides upon the physical extent to which merchandise is to occupy available store footage. The process can involve not only gross allocation, but, at a more detailed level, the 'rationing' of the available FIXTURES.

Analogous processes are used in determining the number of pages etc. to be devoted to particular ranges, lines, items of merchandise in mail order CATALOGUES.

There are a number of methods of allocating space to products in a store which are commonly used. One is to give space to products with the largest share of sales in a particular market. Another method is to allocate space to products on the basis of their DIRECT PRODUCT PROFITABILITY, after taking into account the direct costs attributable to each product.

space planning See SPACE ALLOCATION.

span of control The number of subordinates who report directly to a given manager or supervisor.

special A product line, item of merchandise, specifically purchased for promotional purposes (e.g. low-priced washing machines being offered in a promotion, or sale, of WHITE GOODS).

speciality good An item of merchandise which, through its limited application or particular features which limit its appeal, has particular benefits for only a narrow MARKET SEGMENT (e.g. a fishing rod, fine wine, or a sports car).

speciality store A retail OUTLET which either (a) sells SPECIALITY GOODS or (b) retails a merchandise ASSORTMENT of great depth but limited width (e.g. a health food store or delicatessen).

speciality wholesaler A CHANNEL intermediary who sells a narrow range of merchandise but one that is usually stocked in great depth.

specialty good See SPECIALITY GOOD.

specialty store See SPECIALITY STORE.

specialty wholesaler See SPECIALITY WHOLESALER.

spend 1. To disburse money in exchange for a purchase.
2. Loosely, the total volume of expenditure on a particular item or activity (e.g. 'The total advertising spend was £4m.').

split shipment An occasion where the supplier cannot send all the ordered goods at the same time. The goods not shipped initially are back-ordered for later shipment.

sponsor 1. Individual or organization who provides funds to enable an event to take place, or individual etc. to pursue an activity, which would otherwise not take place or occur only in reduced scale, content etc.

2. In corporate finance, the issuing house that carries out the activities associated with the issue of additional shares for an existing company or a wholly new venture.

sponsorship The activity of providing funding for events, individuals etc., in which the provider is not directly involved, for a range of potential motives. The motives for sponsorship range from the altruistic (e.g. sponsoring a marathon runner for charitable purposes) to effectively the purchase of the publicity accruing to a major sporting event, television series etc. (e.g. Virginia Slimms tennis tournament, ITV weather sponsored by Powergen).

spot check A systematic examination, carried out at indeterminate intervals, of work (often where cash handling is concerned) to ensure that standards are being maintained.

spot sale A transaction which requires immediate cash payment, and/ or immediate delivery.

spreadsheet A form of computer SOFTWARE which facilitates the manipulation of varying data sets which share a common underlying structure (e.g. sales figures per weekly period).

A spreadsheet consists of an arrangement of rows and columns in the form of a grid of cells (intersec-tions between a row and column), into which the user can enter text (e.g. column headings), numbers (e.g. specific sales figures) or instructions to carry out arithmetic processes (e.g. add all values of cells in a particular row or column to give total weekly sales).

Spreadsheets have been employed by retailers, for example, for calculations of gross profits by products, evaluations of promotions, stock control and for all routine accounting procedures. They are particularly valued where a large number of routine calculations are required on a frequent and regular basis (e.g. a monthly sales analysis by product). They are also the basis for more sophisticated models of analysis (e.g. DIRECT PRODUCT PROFITABILITY).

staff 1. Individuals employed in a unit, company or organization.

2. Those involved in support activities necessary to maintain, or improve, a company's operations, especially in distinction to line managers.

staff scheduling Management activity in determining the times to be worked by individual members of an organization, in order to ensure that the organization is able to meet customer demand etc. In retailing, in particular, staff scheduling at the unit level is problematical because of the large numbers of part-time staff employed and the extended trading hours of many retailers.

stakeholder A group or individual who has a significant interest in a business by virtue of some formal or informal relationship with it (e.g. employees, management, customers, shareholders, government, interest groups within society).

stand Within an exhibition or a selling area, the items of furniture used as a framework or basis for a display, especially when incorporating a dais or platform to raise the displayed items above the floor level.

standard A policy, rule, procedure or target, defined in measurable ways, which is established by a company, government, or regulatory authority to guide the actions of others in producing goods and services that conform to the established pattern or requirement.

standardization The determination of STANDARDS for basic PRODUCT measures or limits and the process of ensuring that weights or measures conform to standards.

standing order 1. A regular requirement, placed with a supplier by a retailer, for certain specific quantities of a GOOD each week or month.
    2. (UK) An instruction by a depositor to a bank or building society to pay regular (monthly) payments out of the depositor's account to another named account. The payments will continue until further instructions are given by the depositor.

staple merchandise Those goods, the sale of which constitutes the greatest proportion, or most important part, of a retailer's, wholesaler's takings (e.g. 'basic' white blouses in women's outerwear).

staple stock plan A method of determining the level of inventory and desired re-order pattern for those items of merchandise central to a retailer's offer in such a way as to ensure a minimum of stockouts consistent with an economic ordering pattern.

statement *See* FINANCIAL STATEMENT.

stationery A class of goods, and type of retail OUTLET, concerned with paper-based communication, including such items as papers, pens, inks, files etc.

statistic A summary measure, obtained by calculation, which represents an indication of a characteristic of the full data set (e.g. mean, COEFFICIENT OF CORRELATION), or can be used as a test of the extent to which (SAMPLE) data fits some theoretical, mathematical MODEL (e.g. chi-square statistic).

statistical analysis The evaluation and interpretation of numerical data that has previously been collected, reduced, collated and/or coded. Such analysis attempts to describe the data, explore relationships that exist within them and test if the data are consistent with (prior) hypotheses and theories.
    Although statistical analysis has its roots in the medical and physical sciences, parallels can be drawn, for example, between a medical experiment to evaluate responses to a new drug (compared to a control), and a retail MAIL ORDER experiment to evaluate responses to a new DIRECT MAIL pack (compared to the traditional pack).

statistical measure *See* STATISTIC.

statistical techniques and tests Methods employed in STATISTICAL ANALYSIS, FORECASTING and hypothesis rejection or acceptance which normally have a theoretical base in probability and sampling theory. Examples of the many statistical techniques include non-parametric tests, LINEAR REGRESSION and multi-dimensional scaling, the last of which has been successfully used in the analysis of retail IMAGE within several retail sectors.

Also if, for example, a retail organization wished to evaluate the effect of the level of formal education of employees on managerial capability, a statistical test (in this case, a chi-square test) can be made of the hypothesis that managerial capability is unaffected by the level of formal education. Should this hypothesis be rejected, on the basis of data collected on a random sample of the employees, then further research would be suggested to explore the relationship between managerial capability and level of formal education.

stock 1. Physical inventory: the total amount of merchandise items held by a member of a CHANNEL OF DISTRIBUTION for resale.

2. The merchandise displayed, and available for sale, in a STORE.

3. Shares, or other documents, warrants etc. which represent a capital holding in a company or share in bonds issued by governments etc. as a means of debt financing.

4. To maintain an inventory in a particular line of merchandise.

5. To place inventory ready for sale on FIXTURES etc.

stock code An alphanumeric cypher which identifies an item of inventory.

stock control *See* INVENTORY CONTROL.

stock cover A ratio of the average weekly sale for an item of merchandise to the current inventory of that item. This ratio is used in conjunction with knowledge of delivery time scales as part of inventory control.

stock-in-trade Goods which are held by a company for resale to customers at a given point in time, or those goods generally sold by a particular (type) of retailer (e.g. meats are the stock-in-trade of butchers).

stock-keeping unit (SKU) That physical item of merchandise in an INVENTORY which represents the smallest amount in which the retailer values such inventory, which may be larger than the quantity in which he/she is prepared to sell (e.g. the stock-keeping unit for apples may be a case even though they are sold per lb).

stock rotation The practice of storing and displaying older merchandise items in front of newer items of the same merchandise. Such patterns of usage and display serve to assist in ensuring that items are sold before their SELL-BY DATE, or before the introduction of the new SEASON's colours etc.

stock shortage The situation where insufficient merchandise is available to satisfy the current level of demand.

stock-to-sales method A technique of planning opening stock requirements on the basis of a sales forecast for the period, using the value (number of items) of goods held for resale as a ratio to the expected sales value (volume) for a period, compared to historical ratios, as a basis for decision as to merchandise requirements.

stock turnover The number of times during a specified period (usually one year) that the average INVENTORY is sold. The measurement of inventory and sales needs to be expressed on a similar basis; units, selling PRICE or cost price values. It gives an indication of the firm's selling efficiency and space utilization.

The speed of stock turnover depends on, among other things, the nature of the goods sold. A large supermarket might be expected to have a stock turnover of 15 to 20, while for furniture, the rate of stock turnover is likely to be lower (i.e. 3 to 5 per year).

stock valuation The method used to determine the monetary worth of items of merchandise held for resale. Selected methods need to reflect the trading conditions of the company and the standard allowable accounting procedures (e.g. LIFO, FIFO etc.) in a particular jurisdiction. Problems in stock valuation include obsolescence of stock, selecting the appropriate valuation method and (possibly) the treatment of production overheads. Changes in these treatments can affect reported profit.

stockist A retail outlet selling any particular range, item, brand etc. of merchandise.

stockout The situation that arises when insufficient INVENTORY is available to meet current demand, especially when this leads to empty retail FIXTURES.

stockpile Physical inventory of an undifferentiated kind held in heaps for subsequent use or sale (e.g. coal, grain). More generally, any reserve inventory held against unforeseen demand, or any particularly large/high levels of inventory.

stockroom An area of retail business premises reserved for storage of inventory, and to which (usually) customers are not admitted.

stocktake The physical counting and valuation of an inventory, usually undertaken by retailers at periodic intervals, to obtain control and accounting data.

stocktaking The process of counting and valuing inventory held by a company at a given point in time. Because of the diversity and complexity of the stocks held by some retailers, this can be a large-scale and time-consuming activity. In some trades and situations the task is subcontracted to specialist firms, or a system of PERPETUAL INVENTORY is instituted.

stockturn *See* STOCK TURNOVER.

storage 1. The holding or carrying of goods for the time that elapses between manufacture and final sale. Storage costs will be incurred by manufacturers, wholesalers and retailers, based on the capital 'tied-up' in stored goods and the costs of providing adequate storage conditions, security etc.

2. A space for storing goods.

store 1. A SHOP, especially a large one.

2. To hold goods in stock.

3. *See* STOCKROOM.

store atmospherics The perceptual and psychological climate of a retail outlet as experienced by customers (and potentially as designed by the operator). The chief determinants of atmosphere are visual design (style, fashion, lighting, colours etc.), levels of activity, spatial characteristics (aisle width, customer density) other customers, merchandise, prices, other sensory inputs (smells, music, touch). *See also* ATMOSPHERICS.

store audit *See* RETAIL AUDIT.

store card *See* CREDIT CARD.

store design The conception and execution of the controllable elements in the physical appearance of a retail outlet, especially the FASCIA and windows, FIXTURES, flooring, merchandising system, LAYOUT etc. The considerable psychological impact of the various elements of design (*see* STORE ATMOSPHERICS) mean that many retailers retain specialist consultancies, or have in-house departments concerned with store design, and are engaged in a continuing programme of updating and change, in an effort to maintain and/or enhance IMAGE and differentiation.

store detective An employee of a retailer (or specialist agency) used in an outlet to prevent stock losses etc., however occurring (e.g. paperwork, delivery, staff, shoplifters). The store detective is usually responsible to a chief of security rather than to a department manager. Day-to-day duties include floor patrol, suspect identification and surveillance, investigation of any losses, identification of security problem.

store image The persisting, psychological picture of a retailer held in the minds of customers and others. The picture may have visual components, based on STORE DESIGN, but these are usually enriched by 'personality' elements derived from STORE ATMOSPHERICS, ADVERTISING and other communications and a view of the MARKET SEGMENT targeted by, or attracted to, the store.

store layout The manner in which merchandise is grouped, and space allocated, within an outlet. There is evidence to suggest that the particular chosen pattern of layout should reflect the nature of the merchandise and the buying behaviour associated with it (e.g. GRID PATTERN layout in supermarkets).

store manager An individual with day-to-day responsibility for planning, directing and controlling a single retail outlet. The store manager is often responsible to an area controller or sometimes directly to head office or the board of directors. His or her normal responsibilities include sales, security, personnel and training, safety and hygiene, costs.

store operations In a divisionally organized firm, that department responsible for the manner of the day-to-day conduct of business activities in the retail branches, in distinction to HEAD OFFICE functions such as BUYING, MARKETING etc.

store traffic The volume of pedestrian flow, consisting of customers and other store visitors, passing through a particular retail outlet, or in front of a particular outlet. Data on this type of pedestrian flow is used both in the investigation and management of STORE OPERATIONS and in defining rental for a particular site.

straight rebuy A situation where the goods that are purchased are similar in almost all respects to items purchased on at least one previous occasion. The term is typically used of a re-order of a regularly purchased product. The buying decision process in such situations is often thought to be truncated or habituated.

strategic business unit (SBU) Any subdivision or part of a commercial organization, the trading performance of which is significant in terms of the overall performance of the business, and which could meaningfully be treated as a separate entity.

strategic goal A desired state or outcome for a business which is of importance in determining that ability of that business to survive and prosper. The precise nature of the degree of specification required for a goal (or objective, target etc.) is unresolved; similarly, the particular meaning to be attached to 'strategic' varies from author to author.

strategic objective *See* STRATEGIC GOAL.

strategic target *See* STRATEGIC GOAL.

strategy The means by which the corporate objectives of an enterprise are to be achieved; the 'great work' of an organization. *See also* CORPORATE STRATEGY.

stratified sample *See* SAMPLING METHODS.

street vendor One who sells by retail in a public location, especially roadways etc., normally not from a SHOP.

string street (USA) A group of stores selling compatible PRODUCT LINES located side by side along a road or a number of consecutive blocks.

structural change A shift in the relative importance of different sectors in an economy, which occurs over time and is difficult to reverse (e.g. the change in the proportion of the GDP contributed by the manufacturing and service sectors in developed economies). In retailing, structural changes occur between the food and non-food sectors, where, as countries develop, a greater proportion of the retail activity comes to be associated with the non-food sector. Organizational structural changes also occur in retailing, within a particular country, between the proportion of INDEPENDENT RETAILERS to MULTIPLE RETAILERS.

structure A description of the underlying relationships between the component parts of a system or the output of interaction between such components. For example, a price structure provides a rationale for pricing a range of goods according to size and quantity; a career structure demonstrates the manner by which career moves and rewards are determined.

structure plan (UK) The basic statutory document required by the Town and Country Planning Act 1968, which sets out the desired land use pattern under the control of local government. Such structure plans are prepared by county councils and provide the general guidelines along which development should be allowed to take place. Plans cover a range of themes, including housing, industry, transportation, recreation and waste disposal as well as retailing.

style 1. The characteristic mode or fashion prevailing at a particular time, or arising from a set of particular influences, that serves to identify or categorize manufactured, artistic, presentational etc. artefacts (e.g. in the French style).
   2. The qualities of elegance, distinctiveness etc. exhibited in a way likely to impress observers favourably.
   3. To design or fashion, especially with regard to the major characteristics, any object, entity etc. in a way that serves to differentiate it from other similar things.

subsidiary An identifiable (often legally separate) trading organization or STRATEGIC BUSINESS UNIT which is owned or controlled by another organization.

substitute *See* SUBSTITUTE GOOD.

substitute good A GOOD which may be bought in place of another (e.g. pork in place of beef).

succession planning Establishing those individuals who are considered capable of replacing management and staff who are liable to be promoted, transferred or leave in the period under review.

suggestion selling *See* SOFT SELL.

supermarket A retail outlet of between 2,500 and 25,000 square feet, devoted to the sale of food plus associated non-food items, normally encompassing a considerable degree of SELF-SELECTION and service, where

payment is normally accepted utilizing a CHECKOUT operation.

superstore A large retail outlet with a selling area in excess of 25,000 square feet (2,500 square metres), located on an freestanding SITE with associated car parking and a selling area (principally) on one level. The term is used particularly of grocery stores and other 'out-of-town' outlets.

supplier An organization or individual who makes available goods and services to other organizations and individuals, in the form required by them (e.g. a manufacturing company, agricultural concern, wholesaler, or member of the public).

supply chain Those successive institutions involved in the process by which goods are moved from the point of production to the point of sale. It may include factories, depots (supplier, wholesaler or retailer) and transport facilities (operated by suppliers, wholesalers or retailers).
   Supply chain management involves forecasting, purchasing, distributing, inventory handling, ordering and in-store systems, and is greatly facilitated by an efficient information handling system. Most retailers can benefit from adopting a 'systems approach', in which the activities of all the parts of the supply chain are co-ordinated, in those circumstances where the co-operation of participants can be secured.

Supply of Goods and Services Act 1982 (UK) A piece of legislation which extends similar rights to the buyer and seller of services as the SALE OF GOODS ACT 1979. Goods being supplied as part of a service (e.g.

pipes when plumbing in a washer), must be of merchantable quality, fit for the purpose and correspond with the description given. The service itself must be carried out with reasonable care and skill in order that the goods fulfil the purpose for which they were purchased.

surcharge A levy applied in excess of normal payment, in circumstances where a supplier etc. has acted in ways beyond the conditions of contract.

surplus 1. Stock which is extra to requirements. This is sometimes sold in a special SALE of surplus stock.
   2. Capacity in a WAREHOUSE or other STORAGE unit, which is not currently in use.

switch selling The practice, through personal representation, of persuading a potential customer to purchase a product in preference to, or replacement of, that which they initially intended. The situation requiring this may arise through a number of circumstances, but the technique may be deliberately employed in questionable circumstances when the product that is used to initiate consumer interest may, in fact, never have been available.

SWOT analysis An acronym for Strengths, Weaknesses, Opportunities and Threats – descriptive of the headings under which a situational audit is carried out as part of a systematic business planning approach.
   Strengths and weaknesses are those things the company does particularly well or badly, its special abilities or disabilities which may be used to build advantages or produce

disadvantages compared with its competitors. Another term, broadly synonymous with 'strengths' is 'distinctive competencies' – abilities or characteristics of the company which make it stand out from its competitors. All the operational areas of the business may be scrutinized – STORE OPERATIONS, BUYING, MARKETING, PERSONNEL etc.
   Whereas strengths and weaknesses are features of the company itself, opportunities (with one exception) and threats are features of the trading environment, external to the company. Most of these will be in the future, although some may have already occurred. Because they are external to the company they may be less obvious, more far-reaching and more difficult to identify and appraise. They may include, for example, political and legal changes, the local or global economy, technological changes and social changes.
   The one exception to the statement that opportunities are external to the firm is the opportunity to improve performance by better utilizing strengths and eliminating weaknesses (e.g. consolidation and productivity improvements).
   Having identified strengths, weaknesses, opportunities and threats, the task becomes one of building on strengths, improving upon weaknesses, taking advantage of opportunities and countering threats.

symbol group An organization of independent retailers, trading under the same FASCIA, who obtain some of the benefits enjoyed by CHAINS through their co-operative actions, especially with respect to MARKETING and BUYING. In several cases, symbol groups are organized and/or supported by particular wholesalers serving independent retailers (e.g. SPAR). *See also* VOLUNTARY GROUP.

synergy That characteristic of a system which distinguishes system outputs from the potential or actual outputs of any component or subsystem. Business synergy may arise through the creation of additional substantial benefits after the combination of two previously separate STRATEGIC BUSINESS UNITS or the addition of RANGE extensions, or through, for example, a reduction in HEAD OFFICE overhead to be allocated across an enlarged number of stores, or the carry-over of customer goodwill from one BRAND to its use in a new product area.

system Any identifiable organization, or existing set of relationships between interacting components, that can be seen to produce outputs that are directed towards the achievement of some objective or desired state.

systematic sample *See* SAMPLING METHODS.

T

T-account The particular stage of the layout of monetary amounts when subdivided into a debit and a credit side. Such accounts are commonly used as part of a manual DOUBLE-ENTRY BOOKKEEPING system.

tactic The stratagem, ploy or device to be used by an organization, manager etc. in response to a particular set of circumstances, especially when the circumstances involve competitive activity.

tag A usually removable LABEL attached to an item of merchandise giving pertinent information (e.g. size, price, quantity, washing instructions); a security tag is a device, in the form of a label etc. that is attached to merchandise prior to sale, and removed at the POINT OF SALE. If the tag is not removed, taking the merchandise out of the store causes the tag to activate an alarm system.

tamper-evident packaging Wrapping which provides a measure of security, in that entry to the contents causes obvious damage to the enclosing material. Such packaging is especially used for foodstuffs, pharmaceuticals etc.

tare The weight equivalent to that of the container and any associated PACKAGING, which, when deducted from the gross weight of the package, gives the exact (nett) weight of the contents.

target audience The group of individuals to whom ADVERTISING, DIRECT MAIL etc. is specifically aimed, which may be determined by gender, age, location, SOCIO-ECONOMIC CLASSIFICATION, or any other relevant MARKET SEGMENTATION variable.

target customer An individual possessing the characteristics – age, gender, LIFESTYLE etc. – which are believed, by a seller, to make that individual a potential purchaser of the seller's products.

Target Group Index A proprietary system of market intelligence based on an annual survey which categorizes light, medium and heavy users of various products with age, gender, SOCIO-ECONOMIC CLASSIFICATION and readership patterns etc.

target market That group of individuals or organizations for whom a firm creates and maintains its products, and whose needs, wants, preferences and desires are specifically acknowledged and addressed by the firm. Retailers, particularly clothing or fashion, may identify several target MARKET SEGMENTS for their merchandise and use different TRADING NAMES to present the specific range of merchandise believed to meet the needs, wants etc. of a particular group of potential customers.

tariff A tax placed upon imported goods or services, as a means of raising government revenue and/or controlling entry for such IMPORTS into a particular domestic market.

technical selling The disposing or transferring of complex mechanical, electrical, electronic etc. products, to a purchaser, in a situation which requires expert knowledge of some or all involved in such disposal or transferal. Such a process may require long customer–seller involvement, and the salesperson, or other member of the selling organization, will often give technical support for a considerable period after delivery. Examples would be the sales (to retailers) of large mainframe computers.

technology The application of any skill, art, craft or knowledge to the processes, machines and devices used by humans in their pursuit of objectives.

telephone selling The attempt to dispose of, or transfer, products to purchasers by speaking to such potential purchasers from a distance, using appropriate apparatus for transmitting and receiving such (sound) messages. The telephone is the only channel of communication used in such a process, which can be seen as a proactive method, as opposed to TELESALES which is a mainly reactive system.

Telephone selling is used for LEAD GENERATION for many high-cost items that require detailed specification at a later stage (e.g. double glazing, time-share holidays). The principal advantage is that it can be cost-effective in terms of time and distance covered.

telesales The use of the telephone as a medium for interactions relating to the disposal or transfer of products to a purchaser, particularly where used for taking routine customer orders and servicing customer needs. It is often used for regular repeat orders, and computer-based systems now enable orders to be processed directly from a keyboard input made by a telesales operator. Such systems are used extensively by local and national newspapers for classified advertising and in particular by MAIL ORDER retailers, whose clients may find it convenient to place orders by telephone.

teleshopping A form of retailing of goods and/or services, based on a VIEWDATA system which (ideally) allows for the provision of information about products for sale (price, availability etc.), and the associated ordering and payment methods to be completed remotely. Although the technology has been available since the late 1970s, progress with teleshopping has been very limited in the UK (and elsewhere). Further development may be expected in two main ways: the incorporation of the technology into existing mail/telephone ordering operations; and, longer-term, for routine grocery and household shopping, the establishment of niche suppliers in areas where there are concentrations of high income people who place a high value on their personal time. *See also* HOME SHOPPING.

teletext Information or promotional material in the form of 'pages' of printed words, transmitted to the home via the medium of television to viewers who have sets capable of receiving the appropriate signals. The viewer can summon the pages but cannot otherwise interact directly with the system. The two systems currently available in the UK are Ceefax, provided by the BBC, and Oracle, provided by ITV. *See also* VIDEOTEX.

terms of contract Those particular items within a legal agreement that govern, dictate, indicate etc. the manner in which the parties to the agreement are to discharge their particular obligations.

tertiary The service sector of the economy; in distinction to the primary (agriculture and extractive industries) and secondary (manufacturing) sectors.

test market *See* MARKET TEST.

textile The department(s) within a retailer who offer merchandise made from fabric or material other than clothing (e.g. household linens, carpets, piece goods). The term is sometimes used to designate the non-grocery offer of a supermarket, particularly where it involves selling clothes.

theme display An interior or window arrangement of different products which are associated with a particular unifying idea (e.g. a display based on the theme of skiing holidays, French

wines etc.). *See also* CROSS-MERCHANDISING.

third party 1. Persons or organizations other than the principals involved in a (business) relationship. For example, retailers and manufacturers may employ a third party (a specialist distribution company) to operate the vehicles and warehouses on their behalf.
  2. In insurance, a contract taken out by an individual or organization which provides protection (cover) to the individual or organization against liability caused by accidental injury or death to others. Retailers, for example, are required to have third party insurance for injury to visitors or customers to their premises.

third-party distribution The use, by retailers and manufacturers of outside organizations for transporting and warehousing of goods. (*Compare* OWN ACCOUNT.) Such distribution companies may be engaged to operate a transport fleet, or a network of depots or both, on behalf of the client company. The exact nature of the service depends on the detailed contract drawn up by the parties which may well specify performance criteria such as delivery frequencies, delivery times, quantities, costs etc.
  The main advantages of using third party distribution rather than own account are: (i) the retailer avoids the need to invest in equipment and facilities, and hence improves cash flow; (ii) use can be made of the specialist expertise of the distribution companies possibly resulting in lower costs, or a better service, or both; (iii) inventory levels are normally reduced; (iv) the retailer faces fewer personnel problems since distribution

staff are employed by the third party; (v) changes to the distribution network may be made more smoothly and results in more flexibility to cope with unforeseen changes in the marketplace.

Many retailers have their own distribution facilities and also use third parties at peak periods, hence avoiding excess distribution capacity during the slack trading times of the year.

third-party plan A CREDIT CARD or other facility offered to customers on behalf of a retailer (and often bearing the retailer's name) by a separate financial institution.

threshold 1. A minimum amount, or number, which must be attained before a process, activity etc. is triggered.

2. The minimum number of people in a CATCHMENT AREA required to ensure the profitable supply of a good or service. Those requiring a large number of people may be referred to as *high-order* goods or services; and conversely, those able to exist with a small number are called *low-order*.

tied house (UK) A retail outlet for the sale of beers, wines and spirits which is owned by a brewer, or in a contractual relationship with a brewer, such that the outlet is able to sell only that brewer's products.

till At its simplest, a compartmentalized drawer into which a retailer places CASH received from customers. Mechanical, electro-mechanical and electronic devices now exist which incorporate such a drawer, and additionally allow for the total of a purchase transaction, and change due

in any transaction, to be calculated and automatic records to be generated of items, departmental and other types of sales data. In their most developed current form, tills are linked into EPOS, EFTPOS and EDI systems.

time series analysis The use of statistical techniques to collate, reduce, evaluate and interpret data which is recorded at regular periodic intervals (daily, weekly, monthly, quarterly, annually). For retailers the main interest in this subject lies in the relatively simple time series MODELS which provide measures of TRENDS and SEASONAL VARIATIONS in sales or cost data.

If the causes (e.g. seasonal effects) of historical variations of sales or cost figures are identified, extrapolation into the future can act as a forecasting aid to BUDGETING. Additionally, long-term trends and seasonally adjusted figures can be studied within an overall planning process.

time utility That property of goods and services whereby benefits and satisfaction are derived by users through possession at a particular moment (e.g. the time utility of an aircraft seat). *See also* UTILITY.

tip The extra payment given, in excess of the standard charge, for service rendered or expected (e.g. to a waiter or taxi driver).

token 1. A (gift) voucher of a specified value which can be exchanged for goods such as books or records.

2. A metal, or plastic, disc which is used as a substitute for a coin in a slot machine (e.g. carwash, fruit machine).

token charge A nominal payment, usually for an essential service, which does not cover the full cost of the service (e.g. a token charge for using a room for a meeting).

token order A request for supplies of products made in anticipation of much larger required quantities at a future date, usually placed to show good faith on the part of the purchaser.

token payment 1. A sum of money, offered in partial recompense for expenditure incurred by another where the payee does not acknowledge a contractual liability for any, or full, payment.
 2. A sum of money, offered as partial discharge for a debt, by a debtor on occasions where he or she is unable to meet a contractually acknowledged amount in full at a given time.

tort A legal term describing a civil wrong or injury arising out of an act or failure to act, independently of any contract and which can give rise to an action for damages (e.g. trespass, libel).

Total Distribution Cost (TDC) Analysis The calculation, evaluation and interpretation of all the prices paid when physically moving goods (transport, packaging, warehousing, loss and damage, labour) and the balancing of such prices against the perceived benefits of better CUSTOMER SERVICE. For example, a manufacturer might decide to use air freight rather than surface freight to deliver an expensive product to a retailer in order to reduce stockholding costs and response times. The calculation of the total cost of transportation is

relatively easily achieved for alternative methods of delivery. What is more difficult to calculate is the commercial benefit of better service.
 In car retailing, for example, a vehicle retailer might have to guarantee the availability of spare parts within a certain time to achieve an order from a fleet buyer. High availability can be achieved by holding high stocks locally or by the manufacturers or retailers holding stock centrally and using a fast distribution system to deliver a part to a garage once the vehicle requires it.

town centre management A defined and co-ordinated set of policies, actions and activities undertaken to establish, maintain and enhance appropriate (successful) shopping environments in densely populated urban concentrations. Critical elements in town centre management might include land use control, leasing, environmental quality, public safety, marketing, occupational mix and the co-ordination of services. Ideally such management requires close planning, working and financial co-operation between local authorities, developers, managing agents and the retail and commercial community.

TRADACOMS (UK) The standard common language for ELECTRONIC DATA INTERCHANGE of trading messages between manufacturers, retailers and carriers. *Compare* EDIFACT.

TRADANET (UK) A VALUE-ADDED NETWORK operated by the ANA (*see* ARTICLE NUMBERING ASSOCIATION, Appendix 2) for use by companies wishing to employ TRADACOMS for ELECTRONIC DATA INTERCHANGE of trading messages. For members of the network, trading messages are sent to a central point, from which they are transmitted to the trading partner. Use of the network avoids the need for individual communication lines between each set of partners and ensures speedy telecommunications exchanges.

trade 1. An act, or instance, of buying and selling PRODUCTS.
2. The exchange of commodities for money or other commodities.
3. People, and practices, of a particular type of business, industry etc. (e.g. the retail trade).

trade area analysis Collection, collation, reduction, evaluation and interpretation of data relating to the geographical distribution, travel patterns, levels of income, expenditure etc. of potential customers of a STORE, SHOPPING CENTRE etc. located at a particular SITE.

trade association A group having as its members the participants in any particular sector of the economy, or activities associated with any particular type of manufacturing process or line of merchandise.

trade counter A facility made available at a retail outlet for those whose professional or other occupation requires the use of items typically sold in such an outlet to purchase such goods, usually at a discount, located in a customer service area separate from the general retail sales area (e.g. in hardware or decorating stores).

Trade Descriptions Act 1972 (UK) Consumer protection legislation designed to ensure that products, prices etc. are described truthfully.

trade directory A book listing all those engaged in the provision of particular types of manufacture, services etc., especially those associated with a particular class of products, or useful in connection with a particular line of merchandise etc.

trade discount *See* DISCOUNT.

trade fair An exhibition devoted to the particular lines of merchandise, class of goods etc., which is attended by buyers and sellers of such items, often drawn from a wide geographical area.

trade-in An older model of a CONSUMER DURABLE whose value is allowed for as part of the payment for a newer version or model of a similar good (e.g. a customer's current car can be traded in to obtain a discount on the purchase of a new car from the retailer).

trade marketing Within consumer goods sales, those activities of a manufacturer etc. in pursuing mutually beneficial exchange relationships with retailers, or other CHANNEL intermediaries, prior to full consumer purchase.

It is the area of the marketing mix which is devoted to the support of the channel. It involves decisions about the offer in terms of assortment, pricing and margins, DIRECT PRODUCT PROFITABILITY contribution, point of sale and merchandising, and special sales promotions. The effort ranges from providing a standardized package to smaller independent retailers, to the complex negotiation with a large key account where a specific single company presentation of the benefits and potential earnings from stocking a brand or range of brands will be made. In addition, trade marketing includes support systems for handling and crediting returns or damaged goods as agreed in the account negotiation.

The freeing of EC trade restrictions, as a result of the Single European Act 1992, has caused some UK manufacturers to consider the economies of scale of pan-European brands. Thus trade marketing to a retailer has to be planned across all EC markets which are of interest. Some UK manufacturers are seeing it as a way of escaping from UK retailers' buying concentrations and regaining some initiative for negotiation.

trade marketing mix *See* TRADE MARKETING, MARKETING MIX.

trade name The title or mark given to an item of merchandise, especially where the item is a particular manufacturer's version of a generic product (e.g. pharmaceuticals); the identification of the products, outlets etc., of a business organization where that organization's actual legal title is different from the trading style adopted.

trade-off The acceptance of particular disbenefits associated with a particular course of action in order to obtain the specific advantages of that course of action, especially where the choice of the selected action is made at the expense of other options available at the time. (E.g. Retailers may choose to increase the number of depots which will increase depot

costs, in order to save transport costs and reduce the risk of out-of-stock situations; buyers may purchase large quantities of particular items of merchandise in order to benefit from quantity DISCOUNTS, in the knowledge that such an action will increase the amount of capital tied up in STOCK.)

trade press Publications, containing information and advertisements, which are aimed at specific industries or sectors.

trade price The (lower) unit cost of items of merchandise which is offered by (especially) wholesalers to purchasers whose livelihood depends on the use, or resale, of such items. Such purchasers pay lower prices than a normal retail customer would upon presentation of proof (e.g. a letterhead) of being a business buyer. Some cash-and-carry wholesalers (e.g. MAKRO) have deliberately developed a policy of only selling items at trade prices to business customers.

trade show *See* TRADE FAIR.

trade union An organization of workers whose principal purposes include the regulation of relations between workers and employers, particularly with respect to the negotiation of conditions of employment. For UK statutory purposes a trade union is 'recognized' if it participates in collective bargaining, and it is 'independent' if it is free from control or interference by an employer. Generally, the level of unionization in retailing is low. In the UK fewer than a fifth of employees are trade union members, and they are concentrated in a relatively small number of firms.

trade-up 1. To encourage a customer to purchase a higher-grade and more expensive PRODUCT than was originally intended.

2. To provide, and offer for sale, more expensive PRODUCTS in order to emphasize the reputation of a retail organization, particularly when accompanied by an updating and/or improvement in the design of the outlet, facilities provided etc.

trademark The name, design, style associated with a particular product or manufacturers's offering, used in the marketplace to distinguish it from other similar products. In many jurisdictions it is possible to obtain protection for trademarks, and to engage in actions for PASSING OFF and infringement against those who seek to defraud the public by presenting other products as those of the trademark owner.

trader One who engages in the buying, selling or exchanging of goods, services or commodities.

trading account *See* INCOME STATEMENT.

trading area A geographically delineated region from which a retail outlet, or other business, attracts its customers. It is assumed that for customers within a trading area there is a non-zero probability of their making a purchase from the selling organization.

trading down The practice of offering for sale lower-priced (lower-standard) products to satisfy the demands of customers who may not be willing or able to afford similar products at a higher market price.

trading impact The estimated effect, on volume sales of existing retail outlets, of the opening of a new store, shopping centre etc. in a trade area.

trading name The style or title under which business is conducted, particularly where this is different from the legal designation of the organization (e.g. Aldi for Albrecht Discount).

trading pattern The 'regular' variations in TURNOVER of an organization which are observed to occur at specific times of the day, week, month, year etc. Trading patterns by hour of the day and/or by day of the week may be of primary interest with regard to STAFF SCHEDULING, whereas monthly, quarterly or annual trading patterns may affect BUYING and INVENTORY CONTROL decisions. Long-term planning may require an examination of trading patterns over several years to identify any cyclical variations in trade.

trading profit *See* PROFIT.

trading stamp A single piece of gummed paper, of specified value, given by a retailer to customers which can be subsequently redeemed for cash or goods. Each individual stamp is of low value, and customers will normally need to collect books of trading stamps in order to obtain a worthwhile redemption.

Trading Standards Service (UK) A local authority provision established to enforce the legislation which exists to promote, and protect, fair and safe buying and selling practices. The service may (loosely) be called Trading Standards, Consumer Protection, Consumer Services, Public Protection or the old name of Weights and Measures.

Trading Standards Officers employed by the Service inspect shops and markets, take samples for analysis, scrutinize advertisements and labels comparing them with products, investigate complaints, give advice to traders and verify and stamp weighing and measuring equipment for trade use.

traffic 1. *See* STORE TRAFFIC.

2. The vehicles moving on a road system, or passing particular points within the system over a period of time.

traffic count The enumeration of vehicles passing a particular point on a road system over a given period.

traffic management The planning, control and supervision of the purchase and maintenance of vehicles, and the scheduling of vehicle movements, associated with the transportation of goods by a vendor or purchaser. Also used to denote the process of planning for, and controlling of, the circulation of vehicles within the street system of an urban area.

training 1. Practical instruction by means of exercises and experiences.

2. That section or department of a retail organization concerned with human resource development.

3. Education, particularly of a vocational nature (e.g. the training of engineers).

transaction Any unitary interchange between parties to a commercial relationship, undertaken to provide mutual benefit.

transfer of title The passing of the legal right to possession of property, goods etc. from one person, organization etc. to another. The transfer of title of goods in the UK is subject to the SALE OF GOODS ACT 1979.

transfer pricing The process of assigning a monetary value to goods which are passed from one cost centre to another within an organization. In theory, PROFIT is maximized when a MARGINAL COST approach to transfer pricing is used.

transnational retailing A term often used to mean the process of selling goods/services directly to consumers for their personal use or on behalf of others, where such consumers reside in a country different from the home country of the seller's organization. In this sense it is used as an alternative to the term 'international retailing', whereas etymologically, it means 'retailing across a single nation'.

transport model An abstract representation of a system for carrying goods, people etc. which is usually (but not necessarily) computerized, and which enables the user to test, change, analyse etc. the representation and thereby assess the effects of changes to the real system.

travel agent Retail business which provides a SERVICE for customers making journeys for recreational or business purposes. Travel agents may sell the products of tour operators and airlines, or put together travel itineraries and packages for individual customer needs.

tray A flat, shallow-sided container

used for the storage and display of items of merchandise or their handling whilst in transit.

tray pack An outer, consisting of a shallow, flat receptacle into which taller items are placed, and which is then completely enclosed in SHRINK WRAPPING or some other outer cover.

trend 1. In MARKETS, the gradual changes taking place (e.g. there is a trend towards the consumption of READY MEALS).
2. The general underlying movement and direction of time series data (*see* TIME SERIES ANALYSIS) over a medium to long period of time. The trend of historical data can be measured, and an extrapolation of the trend may provide an aid to FORECASTING.

trial balance A two-column list of CREDIT and debit entries, being the amount shown as the residue of accounts, which is made to allow a check that the totals of each column agree and to ensure that the rules of DOUBLE-ENTRY BOOKKEEPING are being observed.

trial offer 1. An introductory incentive to buy a new product at a low price which aims to attract customers.

2. An agreement which allows a customer time to try out a product before purchasing or returning it. It is a technique often used in MAIL ORDER, where the customer has not had a previous opportunity to see or handle the merchandise for sale.

trial size An item of merchandise sold, or given away, in a smaller portion than usual, in order to attract

potential customers by encouraging them to sample the merchandise (e.g. breakfast cereals, soap powders, gloss paint).

trickle down The social process believed to occur whereby innovations, developments in style, fashion etc. are first adopted by those SOCIAL CLASSES having the highest prestige and are then in turn adopted by classes of lesser prestige.

trim Decorative strip, edging, ornamentation etc., applied to FIXTURES, items of merchandise etc.

trolley A small wheeled vehicle, pushed by the customer, into which are placed merchandise items selected in SELF-SERVICE outlets.

turn round To make a loss-making company or retail outlet into one which makes a profit.

turnaround In PHYSICAL DISTRIBUTION, the time taken for a ship or other vehicle to unload from one trip and reload for the next.

turnover The total SALES REVENUE of an organization in a given period, before any deductions; or the sales revenue accruing in a period of trade (gross takings) of a particular retail outlet etc.

turnover rent A method of determining the annual sum to be paid by a hirer of property such as a retail outlet to the owner of the property, based on an agreed percentage of annual gross takings of the outlet but subject, normally, to a minimum basic annual figure. For example, rent may be 10 per cent of turnover with a minimum basic rent of £20,000 per year. If the retailer has a turnover of £300,000 per annum, then the year's rent will be 10 per cent of £300,000 = £30,000. If, however, the retailer has a turnover of £150,000 per annum, the year's rent will be the minimum basic figure of £20,000 (and not 10 per cent of £150,000). This system is more widely used in the USA than in the UK. *See also* ZONE A RENTAL.

turnround *See* TURNAROUND.

twig An informal term for a STORE which is smaller than a BRANCH in that the merchandise offered is restricted. It is likely to be located in a NEIGHBOURHOOD SHOPPING CENTRE, where a full branch cannot be justified.

twin pack Two similar items, normally sold individually, which are displayed and offered for sale in a single carton, container, banded together etc.

tying contract A formal agreement which specifies that the buyer (or lessee) must purchase additional goods or services in order to obtain the intended goods e.g. shop FIXTURES with the purchase of the lease of premises.

typology Taxonomy; a consistent set of means for classifying items of interest into particular categories, usually on the basis of some expressed set of underlying variables.

U

undercharge To sell products, either deliberately or accidentally, for less than the authorized price pertaining to them at the time.

undercut To charge lower prices for an item than those charged by competitors.

underline A short caption placed beneath an illustration.

underpayment The act of offering in discharge of contract insufficient monies to make for full discharge.

underpricing Charging a lower monetary amount for goods or services than is justified by the level of demand for such goods or services. If done deliberately by a retail organization it may be part of a strategy to increase its MARKET SHARE for a product (group).

undersell To offer items for purchase at a lower price than than those charged by a competitor.

underweight The act, often considered either a breach of contract or a criminal act, of selling goods smaller or less than the indicated mass.

unique selling proposition (USP)

That exclusive benefit(s) of a product which differentiates it from competitive offerings, and which can, if desired, be used as a key theme in advertising the product.

unit pack A carton, container, box etc. containing only a single item of merchandise (e.g. an electric plug, a single pair of socks).

unit pricing A method of labelling whereby the packaging of merchandise (or the SHELF EDGE LABEL) is marked with the item cost, as well as the charge per unit of measurement (e.g. cost per ounce or per litre). Such information facilitates the value-for-money comparison of single and multipacks of competing brands. Unit pricing is often used to highlight the economies obtainable from bulk purchases, and, in theory, unit pricing should result in fairer competition, and greater consumer awareness.

unitization The use of a standard container (or PALLET) to move merchandise within the transport and distribution system, in order that unloading and loading is made easier because the container (or pallet), rather than individual boxes of goods, is moved. Large containers of 20 or 40 feet in length are commonly used to move manufactured goods by ship, train and lorry. Goods are often bought and sold in 'container loads' to facilitate their transportation. When the transportation 'unit' is the pallet then, as with containers, there are agreed international standards for pallet sizes. The main value of moving goods on pallets is (as for containers) the ease of handling. For example, the manufacturer may pack merchandise on a full, or 'half', pallet that is small enough to be delivered into a retail store, so that the pallet forms the base of the display within the store. In fashion retailing, manufacturers may place garments directly onto hanging rails that are carried into a store to go directly on display.

Universal Product Code (UPC) (USA) An industry-wide cypher of merchandise identification, whereby each manufacturer of merchandise is assigned a unique six-digit number by the Uniform Code Council. Manufacturers etc. then add a further five digits to identify the particular product, and a check digit. When translated into a BARCODE, the universal product code can be read by a scanner and the product information transmitted to the computer. Such a system requires the manufacturers to pre-mark the goods or packaging with the barcode and number.

unsecured credit That sum accruing, in respect of monies advanced or goods delivered against future payment etc., which is not backed by an agreement on the part of the debtor to surrender assets to discharge the debt, should it not be met in the course of ordinary business.

up front Payment or part-payment made in advance of the receipt of a GOOD or SERVICE (e.g. for a package holiday, or for a book ordered through a bookseller).

up-market Describing a product which appeals to, or has been designed to appeal to, wealthier customers, or to those believed to be more discerning. *Compare* DOWN-MARKET.

upstream Literally, in the direction against the current. The term is used in the context of the CHAIN OF DISTRIBUTION to indicate the direction of the source of the raw materials and components that make up a product.

usage rate (USA) Average sales per day measured in units of merchandise, as opposed to dollars.

use-by date The day displayed on a perishable good beyond which it should not be consumed, or utilized. Use-by dates are being substituted for SELL-BY DATES and BEST-BEFORE DATES in several jurisdictions, on the basis that a retailer has no right to sell a product beyond its use-by date, and anyone that consumes or uses such a product after such a date, does so at their own risk.

user A consumer that benefits from a product which cannot be possessed directly, especially a service, or one who enjoys benefits associated with a purchase made by another.

user-friendly In computing, the characteristic of SOFTWARE which can be relatively easily learnt and applied by a non-computer expert and which is achieved by the provision of self-explanatory screen menus, structured input instructions, 'help' facilities etc. The term is gradually attaining a wider usage as a positive selling point for other pieces of equipment etc. (e.g. 'user-friendly cash machine').

utility The mechanisms by which value is added to a product. *Form utility* is added during manufacture; *time, place and possession utilities* are provided by the CHANNEL OF DISTRIBUTION. The utility added by possession of an additional unit etc. of a product is seen to be diminishing. This diminishing marginal utility underpins the classic demand curve.

V

VALS Values and Life-Styles. A method of MARKET SEGMENTATION created by SRI International, based on psychological and sociological theories of purchase behaviour of consumers. The VALs segments, with a breakdown of relative proportions in the USA population, are as follows:

Segment	Characteristics	% of US population
Actualisers	successful, sophisticated	8
Fulfillers	principle-orientated, well-off	11
Believers	traditional, middle-income	16
Achievers	status-orientated, well-off	13
Strivers	status-orientated, award-seeking	13
Experiencers	action-orientated, well-off	12
Makers	action-orientated, practical	13
Strugglers	low-income, low-skills	14

value added That extra complement of worth that is produced by the work, actions etc. undertaken by a manufacturer or CHANNEL intermediary in moving a good or service closer to the point of final consumption. The added value is usually regarded as the additional profit, and those costs incurred, at each stage of the distribution process.

value-added network (VAN) A paid-for communication arrangement for facilitating the transmission and reception of messages by ELECTRONIC DATA INTERCHANGE users (manufacturers, suppliers, wholesalers, retailers etc.), which acts as a central electronic 'mailbox' and 'posting' system for the subscribers, thereby avoiding the need for separate communication links between each pair of users. With such a service, a retailer can transmit orders etc. through the network to several suppliers, a supplier can transmit invoices etc. to several retailers, each day.

value added tax (VAT) A charge, levied by the government, on the difference between the cost of inputs and the monetary worth of outputs of any organization involved in manufacture and the CHANNEL OF DISTRIBUTION. Thus, it follows that the tax is ultimately borne by the final consumer, who does not charge for his or her final output. At all other stages in the distribution channel intermediaries act as collectors of the tax which has become due at that stage. Retailers charge the full amount on the sales value of a given item based on the rate in force in that jurisdiction at a given time.

values Those beliefs, percepts, attitudes etc. held by members of a society, organization, group etc. which determine the rating or evaluation of any psychological object in terms of its intrinsic worth, or in terms of the intrinsically held evaluatory scale of the observer.

variable cost A charge which changes directly and proportionately with alterations in the level of output (e.g. cost of ingredients in preparing processed food).

variance analysis The systematic procedure for identifying and examining the underlying causes for differences that arise between actual out-turns and BUDGET expectations (e.g. analysis gives rise to cost variances, volume variances etc.).

variety store A retail outlet offering a wide (and deep) ASSORTMENT of non-food household goods, usually on a mass merchandise basis (*see* MASS MERCHANDISER).

vending The process of distributing, and/or selling by retail, items of merchandise or services through the customer operation of machines, rather than the use of conventional stores or mail order approaches. Vending constitutes a small but significant sector of total retail sales in many developed markets, especially for items such as food and drink for consumption at the time, confectionery, personal items etc.

vending machine A device for the sale or distribution of small items direct to the user or customer through a mechanism for the insertion of coins, tokens, jetons etc., and the delivery at that time of the required item to the user (e.g. for the sale of tea and coffee, postage stamps).

vendor One who sells, especially in a contractual situation for the sale of major capital items, or one who sells in the ordinary course of continuing business.

venture capital Finance made available for a commercial undertaking characterized by risk of loss as well as the opportunity for high returns, particularly when provided to a new enterprise by financial institutions specializing in such lending.

vertical blocking Merchandising of stock from top to bottom of a FIXTURE. *Compare* HORIZONTAL BLOCKING.

vertical integration The action of any business organization in seeking to acquire, merge, develop etc. other CHANNEL intermediaries occupying positions in the chain prior, or subsequent, to its own position (e.g. a wholesaler buying a retail chain, or a manufacturer acquiring distributors in the same line of trade).

vicarious liability Responsibility, in a legal sense, which may accrue to an individual or organization through the action of others either acting or failing to act on the principal's behalf.

videotex An information distribution system based on local display of information from a remote computer. There are two principal types: *viewdata*, in which the information is broadcast to the receiver using telephone lines or cables (e.g. Prestel, Minitel), and TELETEXT, in which the information signal is broadcast over the air as a supplementary part of the normal television signal from the transmitter.

viewdata *See* VIDEOTEX.

Visa One of the two principal international CREDIT CARD systems, to which individual card issuers may belong. The existence of the international system provides for mutual recognition of other issuers cards, centralized clearing facilities and other merchant benefits. From the consumer's point of view, the system's existence provides greater flexibility in patronage and card usage.

visual display unit (VDU) A monitor or screen, attached to a computer, on which stored information is made visible at the command of the computer user.

visual merchandising *See* IN-STORE MERCHANDISING.

volume A quantity of items. For example, sales volume is the number of items sold, in contrast to sales revenue, which is the money received from sales.

volume discount *See* DISCOUNT.

voluntary chain *See* VOLUNTARY GROUP.

voluntary group In retailing, an association of companies or individuals working together to gain mutual benefits, such as quantity DISCOUNTS, through joint buying from suppliers, particularly when associated with the adoption of common FASCIAS, BRANDS etc.

W

want Any non-essential physical or mental requirement of an individual, the failure to satisfy which may deprive that individual of anticipated pleasure but not threaten his or her survival. The distinction drawn between NEEDS, wants and desires is an arbitrary and controversial one.

want slip A small PRO FORMA on which a store employee will record requested merchandise which is not currently in stock.

warehouse 1. A building (or part of a building) which is used to store merchandise prior to sale, distribution or use.
 2. A commercial wholesale establishment.

warehouse location The siting of buildings used to store merchandise prior to its sale, distribution or use, normally in positions which are accessible to the main arterial routes. In the UK, warehouses were formerly often located near the railway and canal systems, but now road access, particularly through the motorway system, is of prime importance.

warehouse store (USA) A large, hangar-scale outlet offering a 'no-frills' merchandise display, limited customer service and value-for-money goods.

warranty *See* GUARANTEE.

waybill A document attached to goods on conveyance by air which specifies their class, source and destination, together with details of the route to be taken and the transit charge.

Weights and Measures Acts 1963/1979 (UK) An area of law concerned with ensuring that goods are sold in proper calibrations of heaviness, size, dimension etc. The legislation is enforced by the Trading Standards Officers (*see* TRADING STANDARDS SERVICE) and breach of the legal requirements can render the (retail) organization liable to prosecution and a fine or imprisonment for committing a criminal offence.

welfare provision The creation and implementation of procedures to benefit management and staff working for a company, group or unit in such areas as health, safety and pensions.

wheel of retailing A theory which suggests that institutions which sell products directly to the final consumer for personal consumption will commence as cut-price, low-cost, low-margin, low-status operations and will then subsequently TRADE UP, thereby increasing operating costs (improvements in display, more prestigious locations and premises, more costly marketing strategy etc.), which in turn makes such institutions vulnerable to new, low-cost, entrants to the market.

white good A domestic appliance, especially the larger type such as a cooker, refrigerator etc., so named from the early tendency for such products to be presented in white enamel. The term is used in distinction to BROWN GOODS in electrical retailing.

wholesaler An organization which buys goods and resells them either to retailers, who will sell them on to the public, or to companies, who will use the goods for the production of other goods and services.

width That characteristic of ASSORTMENT that refers to the number of different (though possibly related) lines of merchandise carried by a retailer. *Compare* DEPTH.

window display The presentation (often involving the use of MANNEQUINS, colour co-ordination etc.) of examples of a retail store's merchandise, in positions highly visible to persons passing the store FRONTAGE, in such a way as to attract interest in the merchandise and invite entry into the store. Window displays are often designed and arranged by specially trained personnel.

window dressing 1. *See* WINDOW DISPLAY.

2. The act of creating a WINDOW DISPLAY.

window shopping The act of looking at products displayed by a retail outlet without entering the outlet at the time. Often employed by potential customers engaged in COMPARISON SHOPPING.

word processing A computerized office system that is used for preparing, amending and filing documents, such as letters, reports and memoranda, which is a feature in the administrative sections of most retail organizations because of its advantage in efficiency over manual systems and the relatively inexpensive installation costs.

Word processing SOFTWARE packages can be purchased for use on a MICROCOMPUTER. The text, which is entered via the keyboard, is displayed on the VISUAL DISPLAY UNIT (VDU). Documents created using the system may be stored on hard or FLOPPY DISKS for future use. A printer is attached for the production of HARD COPIES of the documents.

With a conventional typewriter, the correction of a small error can be awkward, while a major revision of a report could entail hours of retyping. With word processing, such changes are generally easy and fast to perform. Word processing can provide the means to, for example, correct mistakes and change wording, move text around in a document, use bold type or italics, align text in blocks, undo unwanted changes, check spelling, use different print size, style and quality, and incorporate mailing lists to standard letters.

work pattern 1. The details of the

allocation and scheduling of staff (full-time and part-time) which have been prepared to meet the needs of an organization's (trading) commitments.

2. The description of the jobs and tasks an employee undertakes in terms of the proportion of time spent on each job or task.

working capital That money which is not tied up in fixed assets, but which is used to keep the day-to-day operations of the business going. Working capital is needed to purchase stocks for sale and supplies for use by any retail business, and includes any petty cash balances held by the business. The basic working capital holding can be extended by bank overdraft facilities, but is usually not financed solely by bank borrowing. Trade credit also acts, in effect, as part of the working capital of the retail business.

wrapper The packing, normally of paper, Cellophane, polythene, aluminium foil etc., or a combination of these, which encloses an item.

wrapping The outer packaging on merchandise (or the act of enclosing merchandise in such packaging) which protects the enclosed merchandise, decorates it and/or makes easier it for conveyance.

Y

yellow good A consumer product that involves high measurement on four of Aspinwall's selected parameters; gross margin, adjustment, time of consumption and search time. The replacement rate of these goods is low. Yellow goods are broadly related to what are more commonly referred to as 'shopping goods'. *Compare* RED GOOD.

Yellow Pages A set of directories, which are clearly identifiable by their colour, of local commercial telephone numbers and DISPLAY ADVER-TISING, appropriate versions of which are delivered to telephone subscribers in that local (business) area. Advertising revenue helps recoup the cost of making the directories freely available. The particular format of using, literally, yellow pages for such directories is adopted by telephone companies in a number of countries, often publishing under licence.

yuppie 'Young upwardly mobile professional person', indicating a certain type of LIFESTYLE of a group of consumers.

Z

zero-rated (UK) A term for items, such as food and children's clothing, which are subject to a nil rate of VALUE ADDED TAX, at a particular point in time.

zip code (USA) An acronym for Zoning Improvement Plan code. The system of postal cyphers (based originally on five figures, but now extended to nine), which identifies a mailing address for easier sorting and dispatching. It is a very important classification for those organizations using DIRECT MARKETING techniques which assume that purchase patterns are (partly) determined by where consumers live. *Compare* POSTCODE; *see also* ACORN.

Zone A rental The annual amount to be paid by a retail tenant, in £ per square foot for the first 20 feet back from the shop front (Zone A), which is agreed by the retailer and landlord. The next 20 feet is Zone B (where rental per square foot is half that for Zone A), and the next 20 feet again is Zone C (where rental per square foot is a quarter that for Zone A).

Thus, for a shop whose front is 30 feet wide, and which goes back 50 feet, where the agreed Zone A rental is £40 per square foot, the following calculation gives the annual rental.

Zone A:
  30 × 20 = 600 square feet
  at £40 per square foot = £24,000
Zone B:
  30 × 20 = 600 square feet
  at £20 per square foot = £12,000
Zone C:
  30 × 10 = 300 square feet
  at £10 per square foot = £3,000

Total rental = £39,000 per annum

zone pricing A method of charging for deliveries made up of a factory payment plus a freight rate dependent on the preclassified region to which the goods are to be delivered.

Appendices

Appendix 1 Abbreviations and acronyms

ABTA Association of British Travel Agents (*see* Appendix 2).
ACORN A Classification of Residential Neighbourhoods (*see* ACORN).
AGB Audits of Great Britain (*see* Appendix 2).
ANA Article Numbering Association (*see* Appendix 2).
ASA Advertising Standards Authority (*see* Appendix 2).
ATM AUTOMATIC TELLER MACHINE.
BCAP BRITISH CODE OF ADVERTISING PRACTICE.
BCSC British Council of Shopping Centres (*see* Appendix 2).
BFA British Franchise Association (*see* Appendix 2).
BOM Beginning of month.
BRAD British Rate and Data Ltd.
CBD CENTRAL BUSINESS DISTRICT.
CCTV CLOSED CIRCUIT TELEVISION.
CIF COST INSURANCE FREIGHT.
CKD COMPLETELY KNOCKED DOWN.
COD Cash on delivery.
COGS COST OF GOODS SOLD.
COI CENTRAL OFFICE OF INFORMATION.
CRS Co-operative Retail Services (*see* Appendix 3).
CV CURRICULUM VITAE.
CWS Co-operative Wholesale Society (*see* Appendix 3).
DBMS DATABASE MANAGEMENT SYSTEM.
DITT Distributive Industries Training Trust (*see* Appendix 2).
DIY Do it yourself.
DMU DECISION-MAKING UNIT.
DPC Direct product costing.
DPP DIRECT PRODUCT PROFITABILITY.
DR Publication formerly known as *Drapers Record* (*see* Appendix 4).
EAN European Article Numbering Association (*see* Appendix 2).
EBQ ECONOMIC BATCH QUANTITY.
EC European Community.
EDI ELECTRONIC DATA INTERCHANGE.
EDIFACT *See* EDIFACT.
EDP ELECTRONIC DATA PROCESSING.
EFT Electronic Funds Transfer.
EFTPOS Electronic Funds Transfer at the Point of Sale (*see* EFTPOS).
EOC Equal Opportunities Commission (*see* Appendix 2).
EOM End of month.
EOQ ECONOMIC ORDER QUANTITY.
EPOS Electronic Point of Sale (*see* EPOS).
FIET Fédération Internationale des Employés Techniques (*see* Appendix 2).

FIFO First in first out (*see* FIFO).
FMCG Fast-moving consumer goods (*see* FMCG).
FOB FREE ON BOARD TERMS OF SALE.
GDP GROSS DOMESTIC PRODUCT.
GNP GROSS NATIONAL PRODUCT.
IGD Institute of Grocery Distribution (*see* Appendix 2).
IT INFORMATION TECHNOLOGY.
JICNARS Joint Industry Committee for National Readership Research.
JIT JUST IN TIME.
KD KNOCKED DOWN.
KVI KNOWN-VALUE ITEM.
LIFO Last in first out (*see* LIFO).
MEAL Media Expenditure Analysis Ltd (*see* Appendix 2).
MIS MANAGEMENT INFORMATION SYSTEM; sometimes marketing information system.
MkIS Marketing information system.
MOPS MAIL ORDER PROTECTION SCHEME.
MRP Manufacturer's recommended price.
MSA METROPOLITAN STATISTICAL AREA.
NAB National Association of Broadcasters (*see* Appendix 2).
NARB National Advertising Review Board (*see* Appendix 2).
NBC National Broadcasting Company.
NCTA National Cable Television Association (*see* Appendix 2).
NCVQ National Council for Vocational Qualifications (*see* Appendix 2).
NPD NEW PRODUCT DEVELOPMENT.
NPV Net present value.
NRTC National Retail Training Council (*see* Appendix 2).
NSOS Nielsen Store Observation Service.
OFT OFFICE OF FAIR TRADING.
OR OPERATIONAL RESEARCH.
OSCAR Outdoor Site Classification and Audience Research (*see* OSCAR).
P&L Profit and loss account (*see* INCOME STATEMENT).
PDCU Portable data capture unit.
PLOF PRICE LIST ORDER FORM.
PR PRESS RELEASE; PUBLIC RELATIONS.
QRS QUICK RESPONSE SYSTEM.
ROCE Return on capital employed (*see* RATIO ANALYSIS).
ROI Return on investment (*see* RATIO ANALYSIS).
RPI Retail Price Index.
RPM Retail Price Maintenance (*see* PRICE MAINTENANCE).
RRP RECOMMENDED RETAIL PRICE.
RTE Radio Telefis Eirann, the Irish state broadcasting organization, Dublin.
RTE Ready to eat.
SBU STRATEGIC BUSINESS UNIT.
SEG Socio-economic group (*see* SOCIO-ECONOMIC CLASSIFICATION).
SKU STOCK-KEEPING UNIT.
SWOT Strengths, Weaknesses, Opportunities, Threats (*see* SWOT ANALYSIS).
TDC TOTAL DISTRIBUTION COST 'ANALYSIS'.
TGWU Transport and General Workers' Union.
TVEI Technical and Vocational Education Initiative.
UPC UNIVERSAL PRODUCT CODE.
URPI Unit for Retail Planning Information (*see* Appendix 2).

USP UNIQUE SELLING PROPOSITION.
VALS Values and Life-Styles (*see* VALS).
VAN VALUE-ADDED NETWORK.
VAT VALUE ADDED TAX.
VDU VISUAL DISPLAY UNIT.
ZIP Zoning Improvement Plan (*see* ZIP CODE).

Appendix 2 Retail-related associations and major data suppliers

Advertising Standards Authority (UK) An independent limited company established by the advertising industry to provide a system of self-regulation for non-broadcast advertising, based on the proposition that advertising should be 'legal, decent, honest and truthful'.
Address: 15/17 Rigmount Street, London, WC1E 7AW
Telephone: 071-580 0801

Article Numbering Association An organization formed by the UK's leading manufacturers, wholesalers and retailers to establish, develop and administer article numbering and barcode scanning in the UK. By 1990 over 5,000 firms were members. The Association also publishes manuals, guidelines and standards to implement the system of article numbering and provides educational material to help explain the system to member companies and other interested parties.
Address: 6 Catherine Street, London, WC2 5JJ
Telephone: 071-836 2460

Association of British Travel Agents An organization that looks after the interest of travel agents and tour operators in Great Britain and Ireland. It has a code of conduct and runs a public protection scheme in the event of financial failure of a member company.
Address: 55–57 Newman Street, London, W1P 4AH
Telephone: 071-637 2444

Audits of Great Britain Ltd A large market research company which operates throughout the world, specializing in providing continuous research data. It is particularly associated with the Television Consumer Audit (a consumer panel), AGB Market Track (which provides information on retail performance and consumer behaviour in over 250 markets) and AGB Television (which measures television audiences on behalf of the UK Broadcasters' Audience Research Board).
Address: The Research Centre, West Gate, London, W5 1UA
Telephone: 071-991 2020

British Council of Shopping Centres An organization managed by a board representing shopping centre owners, developers and managers, retailers and consultants. In addition to publishing the journal *Shopping Centre Horizons* and encouraging research and further education, the BCSC organizes meetings, an annual conference and shopping centre awards.
Address: College of Estate Management, Whiteknights, Reading, RG6 2AW
Telephone: (0734) 861101

British Franchise Association An organization formed in 1977 by British and international companies involved in the distribution of goods and services through independent outlets under franchising and licensing agreements. Its aims include that of establishing ethical franchising standards; members have to conform to a Code of Business Practice and are rigorously investigated prior to acceptance as full members.

The BFA provides a forum for the interchange of information and franchising expertise amongst members of the public and the wider business community. It publishes information to assist potential franchisees making business judgements and investment decisions. It runs education programmes, arbitration procedures, seminars, regular members' meetings and public relations activities. It is also the representative of British franchising in negotiations with government and international bodies.

Address: Franchise Chambers, Thames View, Newtown Road, Henley-on-Thames, Oxfordshire, RG9 1H
Telephone: (0491) 578049

British Retailers' Association An association which represents the interests of the multiple retailers and department stores in Britain. It has approximately 240 corporate members operating about 32,000 stores and employing 750,000 people. *See also* RETAIL CONSORTIUM *below*.

Address: Commonwealth House, 1–19 New Oxford Street, London, WC1A 1PA
Telephone: 071-404 0955

British Standards Institution A quasi-governmental organization in the UK which sets down procedures and minimum standards for the production of goods and services. The Kite Mark logo on products is an indication that they meet the appropriate specification.

Address: 2 Park Street, London, W1A 2BS
Telephone: 071-629 9000

CACI A company which provides demographic and marketing databases containing census and other data. It markets the widely used ACORN system of residential classification.

Address: 59–62 High Holborn, London, WC1V 6DX
Telephone 081-404 0834

CCN Systems A company owned by Great Universal Stores (*see* Appendix 3). It developed the geodemographic classification system MOSAIC, based on UK census and housing data and financial information obtained from the Lord Chancellor's Office.

Address: Talbot House, Talbot Street, Nottingham, NG1 5HF
Telephone: (0602) 410888

Consumers Association A UK organization (the trading subsidiary of the Association for Consumer Research) established to protect consumers' interests in trading situations. Acting as an independent body, the association regularly publishes, through *Which?* and sister magazines, reports on the nature and standards of specific goods and services, and on investigations of trading malpractice.

Address: 14 Buckingham Street, London, WC2N 6DS
Telephone: 071-839 1222

Co-operative Union Ltd The national federation of Britain's over 100 retail co-operative societies and associated organizations such as the Co-operative Wholesale Society Ltd (*see* Appendix 3) and the Co-operative Insurance Society Ltd. It is not a

trading body but is responsible for representation, advice, information and education for the Co-operative Movement. *See also* RETAIL CONSORTIUM *below*.
    Address: Holyoake House, Hanover Street, Manchester, M60 0AS
    Telephone: 061-832 4300

Distributive Industries Training Trust A trust fund established in 1984 to encourage and finance training for employees in the UK distributive industries. The Trust's funds were the residual monies left after the ending of the Distribution Training Board. The Trust is due to liquidate itself by 1994. In awarding grants the Trust are guided by six policy items. These imply a particular focus on pump-priming new ventures, giving priority to smaller firms, on distance learning projects and research.
    Address: 56 Russell Square, London, WC1B 4HP
    Telephone: 071-636 9811

Edeka The Edeka Zentrale AG is a German federation of regional buying groups. The headquarters of the group is in Hamburg. Membership consists of 32 wholesalers and 13,500 independent retailers, with a total selling area of 2,800,000 square metres.
    There are eight regional groups, each supplying between 500 and 1,000 retailers. Activities include the operation of superstores, discount stores, an involvement in DIY and leisure centres and the supply of the food departments of large chain stores.

EFTPOS UK A UK company, created in December 1986 with representatives from retail and financial institutions, to co-ordinate and supervise the establishment of a nationwide EFTPOS network. In the event their work was overtaken by individual banks who introduced their own parallel systems, and the organization was disbanded in April 1990. The main reasons for the lack of success of EFTPOS UK Ltd were seen to be unnecessarily sophisticated terminals and the costs involved to retailers.

Equal Opportunities Commission A UK public body established by Parliament in 1975. Its main aim is to prevent people being treated unfairly because of their gender, and, in the area of employment, to prevent discrimination against married people. Although the Commission is able to use persuasion to influence a case of discrimination, it has the option of taking legal action. The Commission publishes a wide range of leaflets, booklets and posters dealing with many aspects of the sex equality legislation.
    Address: Overseas House, Quay Street, Manchester, M3 3HN
    Telephone: 061-833 9244.

European Article Numbering Association The International Article Numbering Association – the body founded in 1977 responsible for administering article numbering internationally, outside North America. It was originally called the European Article Number Association and all member countries use the 13-digit article number.
    Address: Rue Des Colonies 54 Kolonienstraat 1000 Brussels, Belgium
    Telephone: 02 218 7674.

Fédération Internationale des Employés Techniques An EC advisory body that conducts research into the design of improved working conditions for employees that would enhance their productivity and reduce stress and fatigue. Some notable research areas in the retail sectors are ergonomically designed checkouts and improved visual display unit presentations intended to reduce eye strain and observer error.

Goad A company founded by Chas E. Goad which specializes in the provision of shopping centre plans (maps), in conjunction with the Ordnance Survey. In addition, for each shopping centre, information is given on the name and trade of each retailer, pedestrian areas, car parks, early closing and market days and details of new developments. In 1990 over 1,000 plans were available in the UK, 91 in the Netherlands, 34 in France, 15 in Belgium and 5 in Eire.

Address: 8–12 Salisbury Square, Old Hatfield, Hertfordshire, AL9 5BJ
Telephone: (0707) 271171

Institute of Grocery Distribution (IGD) A non-profit- making organization with registered charity status whose membership is made up of manufacturers, wholesalers and retailers. The institute exists to make a contribution towards the development, commercial operation and standing of the grocery trade; its principal objectives are (i) the collection, analysis and dissemination of information pertaining to the industry; (ii) the encouragement of development leading to more efficient operations; (iii) the provision of assistance to improve the manpower resource of the industry; (iv) the encouragement of discussion and mutual understanding with the industry; (v) the improvement in general awareness and understanding of the industry. The Institute's policy is controlled by a 60-member council drawn from the IGD regional branches.

Address: Grange Lane, Letchmore Heath, Watford, WD2 8DQ
Telephone: (0923) 857141

Intercontinental Group of Department Stores An association covering 22 countries, with members in Europe, Australia, Asia, Africa and South America, whose objectives are to stimulate mutual co-operation, information exchange and the development of general approaches amongst department stores. The association has its headquarters in Switzerland.

International Association of Department Stores A society with members from the UK, France, Netherlands, Spain, Belgium, Denmark, Switzerland, Sweden, Norway and Germany, whose objectives are to promote and exchange information and research in the management of large-scale retailing.

Address: 72 Boulevard Hausmann, F-75008, Paris, France

'Keep Sunday Special' Campaign A pressure group formed to try to retain some restrictions on Sunday trading in Britain. The Group consists of representatives of the National Chamber of Trade, the Co-operative Union, USDAW, the Shopworkers Union, and all the major church denominations. The campaign's supporters are in favour of an updated law based on exempt outlets (rather than exempt goods, which the Shops Act 1950 favours). The choice of outlets is based on the R.E.S.T. principles: outlets important for recreation, emergency goods and services, social gatherings and travel.

Address: The Jubilee Centre, Jubilee House, 3 Hooper Street, Cambridge, CB1 2N2

Mail Order Traders' Association An association of leading general catalogue mail order companies in the UK. The association, in agreement with the Office of Fair Trading, has produced a code of practice statement which members display in their catalogues. *See also* RETAIL CONSORTIUM *below*.

Address: 25 Castle Street, Liverpool, L2 4TD
Telephone: 051-227 4181

Media Expenditure Analysis A UK monthly publication providing a digest of television, radio and press expenditure for brands and advertisers. Its main purpose is to provide a continuous and accurate monitor of advertising activity which can be used by marketing management, advertising agencies and media owners. The monitoring is achieved by a comprehensive examination of the display advertising in all local and national press and television together with a selection of radio contractors. Overall, MEAL monitors over 350,000 advertisements covering 20,000 brands on a monthly basis.

    Address: 63 St Martin's Lane, London, WC2N 4JT
    Telephone: 071-240 1903

Mintel Publications Ltd A UK research and publishing organization which issues regular reports on consumer markets and trade sectors. Included in their portfolio are: *Mintel Daily Digest* – business news; *Mintel Market Intelligence* (monthly) – market studies with consumer research; *Mintel Retail Intelligence* (bi-monthly) – retail trade sector analysis.

    Address: 18–19 Long Lane, London, EC1A 9HE
    Telephone: 071-606 4533/6000

National Advertising Review Board A US self-regulatory organization which considers complaints about the nature of advertisements.

National Association of Broadcasters A US association, representing radio and TV stations, which promotes radio and television broadcasting and assists members in legal and censorship disputes.

National Cable Television Association A US association, representing parties with an interest in the cable TV industry, which supports the industry through research and publications and assists members in legal matters.

National Council for Vocational Qualifications Set up by the UK government to achieve a coherent national framework for vocational qualifications in England and Wales.

National Federation of Retail Newsagents An organization established in 1919 by Alexander McLaren to represent and protect the interests of retail newsagents throughout the British Isles. The organization allocates its resources to improve the conditions and status of newsagents within the retail trade. This includes maintaining minimum wage rates and influencing legislation generally within the sector, and providing insurance and other forms of pecuniary assistance to members. It has approximately 32,000 members.

    Address: 2 Bridewell Place, London, EC4V 6AR
    Telephone: 071-353 6816

National Retail Training Council Formed in the UK in 1983, funded by the RETAIL CONSORTIUM (*see below*) and the DISTRIBUTIVE INDUSTRY TRAINING TRUST (*see above*) with 'one overriding objective – to improve training standards in the retail industry'. It consists of representations from trade associations, trade unions and educationalists and has a small full time management team. The NRTC provides a number of services on behalf of the retail industry (for example, it provides the focus for a number of retailing training initiations, including the development of the National Vocational Qualification for the retail trade).

    Address: Bedford House, 69–79 Fulham High Street, London, SW6 3JW
    Telephone: 071-371 5021

New Consumer An independent, not-for-profit research and publishing organization whose aim is to mobilize consumer power for economic, social and environmental change by providing information on companies' involvement in various political, trading and ethical activities such as third-world sourcing, environmental responsibility and animal and human rights.
Address: 52 Elswick Road, Newcastle upon Tyne, NE4 6JH
Telephone: 091-272 1148

Nielsen A division of the Dun & Bradstreet Corporation. The world's largest marketing research organization, operating in 27 countries. Since the 1930s Nielsen have been best known for their retail audit services, but their new generation of services spans continuous marketing information, ad hoc quantitative and qualitative research, media research, market modelling, merchandising and coupon clearing. The Scantrack service uses retailers' EPOS data to analyse sales, prices and promotional activity in grocery outlets. The organization publishes an annual *Retail Pocket Book*.
Address: (UK) Nielsen House, London Road, Headington, Oxford, OX3 9RX
Telephone: (0865) 742742

Retail Consortium A body representing the majority of British retailers at local, national and European level, which is made up of six constituent members – BRITISH RETAILERS ASSOCIATION, CO-OPERATIVE UNION LTD, MAIL ORDER TRADERS' ASSOCIATION (*see above*), National Chamber of Trade, Specialist Retailers' Group and Voluntary Group Association – and is affiliated to the European Confederation for Retailing.
Address: 1–19 New Oxford Street, London, WC1A 1PA
Telephone: 071-404 4622

Shopping Hours Reform Council A UK pressure group formed in November 1988 to try to persuade the Home Office to introduce legislation to reform the Shops Act 1950. In its present form, the Act prohibits the majority of retailers in England and Wales from trading on Sunday. The Council has the support of a wide variety of retailers, manufacturers and consumer representatives. It proposes three main changes to the law: (i) all shops should be free to open for limited hours on a Sunday; (ii) smaller community retailers should be allowed to open on Sundays without restrictions; (iii) there should be protection for shop workers against discrimination for refusing to work on Sundays.
Address: 36 Broadway, London, SW1A 0BH
Telephone: 071-233 0366

Unit for Retail Planning Information The URPI Group for the UK provides a retail planning information and advice service. Services include the provision of demographics, expenditure estimates and market analyses; retailer, store, shopping centre and other data in report form or as computer data sets; advice and help on data, data sources, retail planning methods and site assessments; market research; and computer software.
Address: 7 Southern Court, South Street, Reading, RG1 4QS
Telephone: (0734) 588181

Verdict Research An organization which publishes various annuals on the performance of the UK retail trade under the *Verdict on ...* series name.
Address: 112 High Holborn, London, WC1V 6JS
Telephone: 071-404 5042

Appendix 3 Major European and North American retail enterprises

Ahold (Netherlands)
Turnover £2.17bn (1989)
Units 873
Employees 23,900 (Netherlands), 25,600 (USA)
Sector Food
Trading names Albert Hejin, Etos, Alberto, Gall & Gall
Head office Zaandam, Netherlands
Turnover ranking in sector 1st in Holland; 31st in EC
Recent history and activities Nearly 92 per cent of turnover comes from the Albert Hejin franchising arm of the company from 452 outlets and which accounts for 25 per cent of the Dutch grocery market. It has a majority holding in a voluntary group and has expanded into the USA, Germany and Belgium. It is involved in food production and packaging, and is developing interests in wines and spirits, pharmacy and teleshopping. It helped develop a pan-European buying group with Argyll (UK), Casino (France) and Asko (Germany).

Albertsons Inc. (USA)
Turnover $7.42bn (1989)
Number of outlets 465
Employees 37,000
Sector Food retailing
Head office Boise, Ohio
Turnover ranking in sector 7th in USA
Recent history and activities Albertsons operates a range of outlets from supermarkets to warehouse stores in states throughout the South and West.

Aldi Einkauf (Albrecht KG) (Germany)
Turnover £6.00bn+ estimated (1990)
Units 2,100
Sector Food
Trading names Aldi, Hofer
Head office Mulheim-Ruhr, Germany
Turnover ranking in sector 1st in Germany; 2nd in EC
Recent history and activities Aldi is split into Aldi Nord and Aldi Sud, which are run as independent organizations with close operating links. They are privately owned companies controlled by the Albrecht Foundation, which has a policy of disclosing the minimum amount of information. Aldi operates a chain of limited range discount food shops with outlets selling about 480 lines. Exclusive label sales account for up to 90 per cent in some stores. The organization is represented as Aldi in Holland, Belgium, Denmark, France, the UK and the USA, and as Hofer in Austria.

American Stores Company (USA)
Turnover $22.00bn (1989)
Number of outlets 1,460
Employees 170,400
Sector Food retailing
Trading names Acme, Super Saver, Jewel-Osco, Skaggs, Alpha Beta
Head office Irvine, California
Turnover ranking in sector 1st in USA
Recent history and activities The company trades in over 26 states, primarily in self-service supermarkets, but it also has interests in drug stores and food processing.

Argyll Plc (UK)
Turnover £4.1bn (1989)
Units 838
Employees 63,000
Sector Food
Trading names Safeway, Presto, Lo-Cost
Head office Hayes, Middlesex, England
Turnover ranking in sector 4th in UK; 15th in EC
Recent history and activities The company bought the UK Safeway chains for £680m in 1987. Trading is to be concentrated under the Safeway fascia, which has own label sales of 40 per cent. Argyll has joined Casino (France), Asko (Germany) and Ahold (Netherlands) to form the European Retailing Alliance.

Asda Plc (UK)
Turnover £3.55bn (1989)
Units 190
Employees 62,722
Sector Food
Trading names Asda
Head office Leeds, England
Turnover ranking in sector 7th in UK; 23rd in EC
Recent history and activities Largely based in the north of England, Asda bought 61 of the Gateway stores from Isosceles in 1989. It was an instigator of the creation of edge-of-town superstores in the UK. There was an abortive merger with MFI in 1985. In 1990 entered into an arrangement with the former moving spirit of Next (a retailer of targeted, limited range fashion goods), George Davies, to sell clothing in Asda outlets.

Asko Deutsche Kaufhaus-Asko Schaper (Germany)
Turnover £3.09bn (1988)
Units 354
Employees 28,100
Sector Food, DIY, clothing, photography
Trading names Realkauf, Continent, Divi, Esbella
Head office Saarbrucken, Germany
Turnover ranking in sector 9th in Germany; 19th in EC
Recent history and activities In 1987 Asko bought 80 per cent of Adolf Schaper, a major retail and wholesale food operator, as well as acquiring most of Schaper's retail subsidiary, Realkauf. Asko operates 90 self-service department stores, 89 DIY mar-

kets, 33 discount clothing centres and 7 cash and carry stores. It also controls a chain of over 2,000 photographic shops and kiosks. It has interests in the USA and has entered into joint ventures with two Dutch companies – HDB and Merison.

Auchan (France)
Turnover £2.78bn (1988)
Units 288
Employees 32,000
Sector Food, clothing, DIY, electrical, sports
Trading names Auchan, Alcampo, Leroy-Merlin, Decatholon, Kiabi
Head office Croix, France
Turnover ranking in sector 6th in France; 21st in EC
Recent history and activities Auchan is a family- owned company with over 60 per cent of turnover from food sales. Its core business is 39 hypermarkets throughout France. It is building up a presence in the catering sector with its Flunch cafeterias, and was an innovative force in the introduction of discount self-service petrol outlets. The parent company (Mulliez) also controls Phildar Wool and Knitting retail company. There are associate companies in Spain, the USA and Italy.

Au Printemps (France)
Turnover £3,78bn (1988)
Units 2,000
Employees 20,000
Sector Department stores, food, mail order
Trading names Printemps, Prisunic, La Redoute
Head office Paris, France
Turnover ranking in sector 3rd in France; 11th in EC
Recent history and activities Large parts of the company operate on a franchised or affiliated basis. Out of 2,000 outlets, the company owns only 477. It has recently acquired the country's largest mail order company, La Redoute, and owns over 40 per cent of Euromarche, a major hypermarket operation. It is represented in the Caribbean, West Africa, the Middle East and Portugal.

The Boots Company Plc (UK)
Turnover £3.38bn (1989)
Units 2,380
Employees 78,600
Sector Variety, chemists, opticians, children's, DIY, motor accessories
Trading names Boots, Children's World, Fads, Do it All, Halfords
Head office Nottingham, England
Turnover ranking in sector 8th in UK; 24th in EC
Recent history and activities Boots has a dominant position in the UK toiletries and cosmetics markets, with a 40 per cent share of sun preparations and 35 per cent of cosmetics, and is the second largest optician in the UK. It has its own pharmaceutical manufacturing division which accounted for £0.5bn of turnover in 1989. Up to 50,000 lines, including audio products, electricals and household goods, are carried in the larger Boots stores. Boots acquired the DIY and car repair and accessories of Payless and Halfords in 1989 when taking over the Ward White group. The Payless DIY operations were merged with W. H. Smith's Do It All in 1991.

The Burton Group Plc (UK)
Turnover £1.818bn (1989)
Units 1,865
Employees 37,000
Sector Men's and women's clothing, department stores
Trading names Burton, Top Man, Top Shop, Principles, Evans, Dorothy Perkins, Debenhams, Harvey Nicholls, Champion Sport
Head office London, England
Turnover ranking in sector 12th in UK; 37th in EC
Recent history and activities The strategy of the Burton Group has been to target markets through a series of acquisitions and product development. Burton used to trade as a concession within Debenhams before buying the company, which has been a significant factor in increased profits. The charismatic Chairman and Chief Executive Ralph Halpern was replaced in 1990 and was awarded one of the largest-ever severance packages.

C&A Brenninkmeyer (Germany)
Turnover £2.37bn (1988)
Units 158
Sector Clothing
Trading names C&A Brenninkmeyer, Foxy Fashion
Head office Dusseldorf, Germany
Turnover ranking in sector 10th in Germany; 27th in EC
Recent history and activities The largest retailing subsidiary of the privately owned C&A fashion giant. Traditional stores trade between 3,000 to 12,000 square metres, carrying clothing for the whole age range. 30 outlets trade as Foxy Fashion aimed at the younger market. The C&A group trades world-wide but Germany is one of the few countries where figures are released owing to legal requirements. Estimated sales for the UK are £0.56bn from 110 stores; and for the Netherlands 0.70bn from 75 stores. The company discloses the minimum amount of information.

Campeau Corporation (Canada)
Turnover $3.26bn (1987)
Number of outlets 487
Sector Department and food stores
Trading names Allied Stores, Federated Stores, Jordan Marsh, Stern's
Turnover ranking in sector Largest department store group in Canada
Recent history and activities Campeau acquired two subsidiaries in 1988 – Allied Stores Corporation and Federated Department Stores Inc. It also has interests in supermarkets. Retailing accounts for about 10 per cent of the corporation's business interests. The current trading conditions in North America, coupled with high interest rates, have adversely affected the company's financial situation.

Carrefour (France)
Turnover £6.00bn (1988)
Units 195
Employees 42,900
Sector Food, household goods, textiles
Trading names Carrefour, Comptoirs Modernes, Carfuel, Castorama
Head office Evry, France

Turnover ranking in sector 1st in EC
Recent history and activities One of the first hypermarket operators in France, Carrefour also trades in Spain, Argentina and Brazil. In the USA it has a share in the Cosco Wholesale Corporation, and has holdings in France in Comptoirs Modernes (a chain of 900 local stores and 180 supermarkets), an insurance broking company, petrol stations, manufacturing and property developers and the leading French DIY company, Castorama.

Carter Hawley Hale Stores Inc. (USA)
Turnover $2.78bn (1989)
Number of outlets 112
Employees 24,500
Sector Department stores
Trading names The Broadway, Weinstock's
Head office Los Angeles, California
Turnover ranking in sector 5th in USA
Recent history and activities The company is known for pioneering developments in the use of expert systems for management training and operations.

Casino (France)
Turnover £3.29bn (1988)
Units 3,300
Employees 31,470
Sector Food, restaurants
Trading names Casino, Cedis, Mammouth, Paridoc
Head office St. Etienne, France
Turnover ranking in sector 5th in France; 17th in EC
Recent history and activities Almost 70 per cent of Casino's sales derive from food retailing. Most of its 3,000 stores in France are under 400 square metres selling area. It is developing a pan-European food buying operation with Argyll (UK), Asko (Germany) and Ahold (Netherlands). In October 1989 its 65 per cent share in Obi (DIY) was sold to Castorama.

The Circle K Corporation (USA)
Turnover $3.49bn (1989)
Number of outlets 3,507
Employees 27,264
Sector Food retailing
Trading names Circle K
Head office Phoenix, Arizona
Turnover ranking in sector 11th in USA
Recent history and activities Circle K operates in 25 states mainly in the West and South. It has 104 stores in the UK as well as joint venture and licence agreements in five other countries.

Co-op AG (Germany)
Turnover £3.44bn (1988)
Units 2,000
Sector Food and general stores
Trading names Co-op Plaza, Bienefeld, Richter

Head office Frankfurt, Germany
Turnover ranking in sector 7th in Germany; 16th in EC
Recent history and activities The group is owned by four foreign banks. A series of foreign acquisitions in the 1980s caused problems for the group, which reported a loss in 1988.

Co-op Italia (Italy)
Turnover £2.43bn (1988)
Units 1,300
Employees 19,000
Sector Food
Head office Milan, Italy
Turnover ranking in sector 1st in Italy; 25th in EC
Recent history and activities 1,300 member outlets belong to over 450 member co-operatives. Co-op Italia experienced rapid expansion in the 1980s by increasing the size of stores and the number of employees. 70 per cent of sales are from food.

Co-operative Retail Services (CRS) (UK)
Turnover £1.05bn (1987)
Units 520
Employees 23,800
Sector Food, non-food, funerals
Trading names Leos, Living, Stop and Shop, Pioneer
Head office Manchester, UK
Turnover ranking in sector 18th in UK
Recent history and activities The largest retail consumer co-operative society in the UK. Created in 1934 as a wing of the Co-operative Wholesale Society, its original function was to develop trade in new areas, but its growth has been due mainly to its ability to absorb smaller societies, many of which were in financial difficulties, into its operations. 70 per cent of its turnover is in food.

Co-operative Wholesale Society (CWS) (UK)
Turnover £2.678bn (1990)
Units 442 (retail)
Employees 27,500
Sector Food, non-food, funerals, banking, insurance, farming
Trading names Co-op, Concepts
Head office Manchester, UK
Recent history and activities The national manufacturing and wholesaling arm of the UK retail co-operative movement, CWS operates its own retail outlets in Scotland, Northern Ireland and north-eastern and south-eastern England, which account for a quarter of turnover. It also owns the Co-operative Bank and Co-operative Insurance Society and has interests in travel, opticians, farming and funerals.

Cora/Bouriez (France)
Turnover £3.61bn (1988)
Units 789
Sector Food
Trading names Cora, Soc Eur de Supermarches, Gro, Gro-Est
Head office Croissy Beauborg, France

Turnover ranking in sector 4th in France; 14th in EC
Recent history and activities The Cora Retail operation is owned by the Bouriez Group. It operates nearly 700 small neighbourhood stores; the remainder of its operation being of either a hypermarket or supermarket format. It is also becoming involved in home shopping.

El Cortes Ingles (Spain)
Turnover £2.28bn (1988)
Units 26
Employees 31,000
Sector Department stores, food
Trading names El Corte, Hipercor
Head office Madrid, Spain
Turnover ranking in sector 1st in Spain; 30th in EC
Recent history and activities El Cortes has 19 city centre department stores and 7 hypermarkets. Growth is financed by the group's own resources. El Corte has a strategy of having the largest possible outlets carrying the widest range of goods. It maintain a high public profile by advertising heavily.

Dayton Hudson Corporation (USA)
Turnover $13.64bn (1989)
Number of outlets 578
Employees 140,000
Sector Department and speciality stores
Trading names Hudson's, Drayton's, Target, Lechmere, Mervyn's
Head office Minneapolis, Minnesota
Turnover ranking in sector Largest department store group in USA
Recent history and activities The corporation operates in 36 states, mainly in department stores, and also has interests in discount stores.

Dillard Department Stores Inc. (USA)
Turnover $3.05bn (1989)
Number of outlets 135
Employees 37,000
Sector Department stores
Trading names Dillard
Head office Little Rock, Arkansas
Turnover ranking in sector 5th in USA

Docks de France (France)
Turnover £2.14bn (1988)
Units 2,200
Employees 21,244
Sector Food, catering
Trading names Mammouth, Doc Service
Head office Tours, France
Turnover ranking in sector 8th in France; 33rd in EC
Recent history and activities Numerous subsidiary companies in France cover different geographic areas of the country. The company's operations vary between small stores, supermarkets and hypermarkets, and it was an instigator of the central buying group, Paridoc. It is also represented in Spain and the USA.

FDB (Co-op) Group (Denmark)
Turnover £2.38bn (1988)
Units 1,588
Employees 22,500
Sector Food, variety stores
Trading names FDB, OBS!, Irma, Kvickly, Fakta
Head office Alberslund, Denmark
Turnover ranking in sector Largest retailer in Denmark; 26th in EC
Recent history and activities FDB accounts for between 22 and 24 per cent of the national market in food. It operates not only as a food retailer but also as a producer of dairy and other products. FDB is a wholesaler and a central purchasing organization for affiliated co-operative societies.

Federated Department Stores Inc. (USA)
Turnover $4.86bn (1989)
Number of outlets 675
Employees 60,300
Sector Department and speciality stores
Trading names Bloomingdales, Burdines, Goldsmith's, Rich's
Head office Cincinnati, Ohio
Turnover ranking in sector 4th in USA
Recent history and activities The company was acquired by the Campeau Corporation in May 1988, which has resulted in major restructuring of its retail activities. It has sold off its children's stores and a number of its department stores to May's.

Food Lion Stores Inc. (USA)
Turnover $4.71bn (1989)
Number of outlets 475
Employees 40,736
Sector Food retailing
Trading names Food Lion
Head office Salisbury, North Carolina
Turnover ranking in sector 9th in USA
Recent history and activities Food Lion operates in supermarkets in North and South Carolina, Georgia, Maryland, Delaware and Florida.

Galaries Lafayette (France)
Turnover £2.31bn (1988)
Units 137
Employees 17,750
Sector Food, department stores
Trading names Galaries Lafayette, Monoprix, Super-M, Inno, Di-Fra
Head office Paris, France
Turnover ranking in sector 7th in France; 29th in EC
Recent history and activities The company has affiliated department stores in Singapore, Bangkok and Luxembourg. It has recently set up a chain of specialist womenswear outlets and operates a home shopping service.

Gateway Corporation Plc (UK)
Turnover £4.517bn (1989)
Units 500
Employees 73,600

Sector Food
Trading names Gateway, Somerfield
Head office London, England
Turnover ranking in sector 5th in UK; 20th in EC
Recent history and activities Gateway is controlled by Isosceles, which took over in 1989. It sold 61 superstores to Asda and will concentrate on stores up to 2,000 square metres under the Somerfield fascia and a 430 chain of Gateway stores of up to 1,000 square metres.

Giant Food Inc. (USA)
Turnover $2.98bn (1989)
Number of outlets 145
Employees 24,500
Sector Food retailing
Trading names Giant Food
Head office Landover, Maryland
Turnover ranking in sector 12th in USA
Recent history and activities Giant Food operates supermarkets in Washington DC, North Virginia and Maryland.

GIB Group (Belgium)
Turnover £3.67bn (1988)
Units 1,200
Employees 31,800
Sector Food, department stores, catering, DIY
Trading names Maxi, Nopri, Unic, Brico-GB, Sarma
Head office Brussels, Belgium
Turnover ranking in sector Largest retailer in Belgium; 13th in EC
Recent history and activities Almost £3.06bn of GIB's sales comes from the Belgian retail network. The group is moving into franchising food, DIY, perfume, car care and catering. Until late 1989 GIB had a 50 per cent stake in IKEA. It has formed links with Vendex (Netherlands) and Rewe-Liebbrand (Germany) to form Eurogroups. GIB has a 25 per cent stake in Sainsbury's (UK) Homebase.

The Grand Union Company (USA)
Turnover $2.71bn (1989)
Number of outlets 369
Employees 23,000
Sector Food retailing
Head office Wayne, New Jersey
Turnover ranking in sector 13th in USA
Recent history and activities The company operates four different store types – food centres, food markets, community stores and supermarkets.

The Great Atlantic & Pacific Tea Company (USA)
Turnover $10.07bn (1989)
Number of outlets 1,200
Employees 92,000
Sector Food retailing
Trading names Super Fresh, Kohl's, Pantry Pride, Future Stores, A&P, Waldbaum's, Farmer Jack, Food Emporium

Head office Montvale, New Jersey
Turnover ranking in sector 4th in USA
Recent history and activities The company operates in 25 states and in Canada, but mainly in the New York and Connecticut areas. 52.4 per cent of the company is owned by Tengelmann of Germany.

Great Universal Stores Plc (UK)
Turnover £2.625bn (1989)
Units 13
Employees 32,156
Sector Mail order
Trading names Various Catalogues, Burberry's, The Scotch House
Head office Manchester, England
Turnover ranking in sector 9th in UK; 28th in EC
Recent history and activities GUS operates home shopping catalogues with the use of over 2 million agents. The largest mail order company in the UK, it operates at least seven different catalogues. It has divested itself of most of its store-based operations, including the Times Furnishing, Home Charm and Lennards footwear chains.

Hertie-Waren (Germany)
Turnover £1.90bn (1988)
Units 300
Employees 25,000
Sector Department stores, variety shops
Trading names Hertie, Nug Optimus
Head office Frankfurt, Germany
Turnover ranking in sector 11th in Germany; 34th in EC
Recent history and activities The company sold many of its variety stores in the late 1980s and also withdrew from hypermarkets. Recent acquisitions include a textile chain and diverse areas such as consumer electrical and entertainment products, toys, books and restaurants. The 72 department stores account for £1.67bn of turnover.

The Home Depot Inc. (USA)
Turnover $2.77bn (1989)
Number of outlets 75
Employees 17,500
Sector DIY
Head office Atlanta, Georgia
Turnover ranking in sector Largest in USA
Recent history and activities The company operates a chain of retail warehouse stores in eight southern states.

Imasco Limited (Canada)
Turnover $5.62bn (1987)
Number of outlets 1,900
Sector Drug stores, restaurants
Trading names Shoppers Drug Mart, People Drug Stores, Hardee's
Head office Montreal, Quebec
Turnover ranking in sector Largest drug store retailer in Canada
Recent history and activities Inasco has over 500 franchised and owned pharmacies in Canada, and licenses over 2,500 restaurants under the Hardee trading name.

Karstadt/Neckermann (Germany)
Turnover £4.52bn (1988)
Units 220
Employees 67,000
Sector Department and variety stores, mail order, sports
Trading names Karstadt, Neckermann, Runners Point
Head office Karstadt-Essen; Neckermann, Frankfurt, Germany
Turnover ranking in sector 4th in Germany; 8th in EC
Recent history and activities Karstadt is Germany's largest department store operation, with 152 stores. Neckermann is third in mail order. An agreement was signed in 1988 with Aldi to open new food halls in the Karstadt department stores. The Neckermann part of the group also has interest in a travel business.

Kaufhof (Germany)
Turnover £3.69bn (1988)
Units 472
Employees 42,600
Sector Department and variety stores
Trading names Kaufhof, Kaufhalle, Mode und Sport, Reno
Head office Cologne, Germany
Turnover ranking in sector 6th in Germany; 12th in EC
Recent history and activities The Kaufhalle outlets focus on cheap goods in the clothing, footwear and textile sectors. The group has recently expanded into speciality non-food chains such as sports and fashion, footwear and audio/video, and has banking and travel subsidiaries. In January 1990 the group announced that it was floating 25 per cent of the shares in Kaufhalle to raise £70m to expand the chain.

Kingfisher Plc (UK)
Turnover £2.910bn (1989)
Units 1,800
Employees 58,800
Sector Variety stores, DIY, electrical, consumer durables, car care, toiletries
Trading names Woolworth, B&Q, Comet, Superdrug, Charlie Brown
Head office London, England
Turnover ranking in sector 6th in UK; 22nd in EC
Recent history and activities In the mid-1980s the group underwent a major restructuring programme. The Woolworth stores concentrate on six areas of merchandise – children's clothing, toys and books, stationery and confectionery, records and entertainment, home and garden, kitchens, and 'looks' (cosmetics). The B&Q DIY and Comet electrical chains are dominant in their sectors, with B&Q providing over one-third of group profits. The group is developing standalone units from the Woolworth product mix (e.g. Kidstore and Woolworth Entertainments).

K Mart (USA)
Turnover $29.55bn (1989)
Number of outlets 3,934
Employees 365,000
Sector Mass merchandising
Trading names K Mart, Waldensbrooks, Pay Less Drugstores
Head office Troy, Michigan

Turnover ranking in sector 2nd in North America and USA
Recent history and activities 2,300 K Mart discount stores are operated in the USA and Canada. The company is also involved in book retailing, drug stores and warehouse home centres.

The Kroger Co. (USA) (1989)
Turnover $19.08bn
Number of outlets 1,300
Employees 170,000
Sector Food retailing
Trading names Dillon, Price Savers, Loaf 'n' Jug
Head office Cincinnati, Ohio
Turnover ranking in sector 2nd in USA
Recent history and activities The company operates a chain of supermarkets in 29 states, primarily in the South, Southwest and Midwest and also has a chain of convenience stores in 11 states. It is also involved in food processing. The food stores account for almost 95 per cent of company turnover.

Kwik Save Group Plc (UK)
Turnover £1.181bn (1988)
Units 643
Employees 10,059
Sector Food
Trading names Kwik Save
Head office Prestatyn, North Wales
Turnover ranking in sector 14th in UK; 39th in EC
Recent history and activities The group operates discount food stores with minimal attention paid to store ambience. Branded goods are sold at discounted prices. It is particularly strong in the north of England and Wales, but has been expanding from these geographical areas recently.

John Lewis, Partnership Plc (UK)
Turnover £2.046bn (1989)
Units 111
Employees 37,700
Sector Department stores, food
Trading names John Lewis, Waitrose
Head office London, England
Turnover ranking in sector 11th in UK; 36th in EC
Recent history and activities The distinctive feature of the John Lewis group is that all employees are partners in the organization and share in the profits. The food chain, Waitrose, has over 80 supermarkets, and there are 23 John Lewis department stores in the largest cities. The partnership operates a price pledge under the slogan 'Never knowingly undersold'. It also has wholesaling, manufacturing, export and agricultural interests.

The Limited Inc. (USA)
Turnover $4.64bn (1989)
Number of outlets 3,100
Employees 63,000

Sector Fashion
Trading names Limited Stores, Lane Bryant, Werner Warren
Head office Columbus, Ohio
Turnover ranking in sector 2nd largest speciality chain in USA
Recent history and activities The group caters mainly for women aged 15 to 40. It has its own manufacturing company and a mail order company.

Littlewoods Organisation Plc (UK)
Turnover £1.63bn (1989)
Units 120
Employees 23,197
Sector Mail order, chain stores
Trading names Littlewoods, Inside Story, Index
Head office Liverpool, England
Turnover ranking in sector 13th in UK; 38th in EC
Recent history and activities The largest private company in the UK, and the second largest mail order group, Littlewoods is involved in home shopping, catalogue stores (through Index) and football pools.

Loblaw Companies Limited (Canada)
Turnover $8.63bn (1987)
Number of outlets 360
Sector Food retailing
Trading names Loblaws Supermarkets, Ziggys, Zehr's, Gordon
Head office Ontario, Canada
Turnover ranking in sector 2nd in Canada
Recent history and activities Loblaw has interests in food retailing and wholesaling in both Canada and the USA, and has an 85 per cent stake in a manufacturing company.

Marks & Spencer Plc (UK)
Turnover £5.6bn (1990)
Units 679
Employees 75,100
Sector Food, clothing, housewares, financial services
Trading names Marks & Spencer, Brook Brothers, Kings Supermarket, D'Allaird's
Head office London, England
Turnover ranking in sector 3rd in UK; 7th in EC
Recent history and activities The UK accounts for over 80 per cent of the company's profit; it has operations in Canada, the USA, and mainland Europe. All M&S sales are of their exclusive 'St Michael' label, with food accounting for over 35 per cent of total retail business. The company has introduced its own in-store charge card and financial services business authorized to sell unit trusts. In 1988 it acquired the USA companies of Brook Brothers and Kings supermarkets, and has entered into joint ventures with both Asda and Tesco. The company does very little advertising, preferring to invest in community involvement and sponsorship.

The May Department Stores Co. (USA)
Turnover $12.04bn (1989)
Number of outlets 3,000
Employees 115,000

Sector Department, footwear and discount stores
Trading names Venture, Caldos, Volume Shores, Loehmann's
Head office St. Louis, Missouri
Turnover ranking in sector 2nd largest department store group in USA
Recent history and activities The company has retailing interests in over 40 states, with nearly 2,500 footwear stores. It has additional activity in shopping centres and a trading stamp company.

Melville Corporation (USA)
Turnover $7.55bn (1989)
Number of outlets 3,900
Employees 100,541
Sector Footwear
Trading names Thom McAn, Meldisco, CVS, Marshall's, Chess King
Head office Harrison, New York
Turnover ranking in sector Largest speciality chain in USA
Recent history and activities The corporation has over 2,000 leased shoe departments mainly in K Mart stores in addition to its own retailing interests. It is also represented in the menswear, health and beauty, hosiery and household furnishings sectors.

Nordstrom Inc. (USA)
Turnover $2.67bn (1989)
Number of outlets 67
Employees 28,000
Sector Speciality stores
Head office Seattle, Washington
Turnover ranking in sector 3rd largest speciality chain in USA
Recent history and activities Nordstrom operates 46 speciality stores and 10 stores in six states. It has 11 leased shoe departments in Hawaii.

The Oshawa Group Limited (Canada)
Turnover $3.80bn (1988)
Number of outlets 1,900
Sector Food retailing
Trading names IGA Markets, Food City Markets, Dutch Boy Food Markets
Head office Ontario, Canada
Turnover ranking in sector 4th in Canada
Recent history and activities The group is involved in food wholesaling, franchising and supply. It also has interests in department stores, drug stores and a property subsidiary.

Otto Versand (Germany)
Turnover £4.19bn (1988)
Units 17
Employees 30,000
Sector Mail order, sports goods, fashion
Trading names Otto Versand, Schwabversand, Heinrich Heine
Head office Hamburg, Germany
Turnover ranking in sector Leading mail order business in world; 10th largest retailer in EC
Recent history and activities The company is represented throughout Europe, the USA

and Japan. It has set up a joint venture in a cash-and-carry food operations with Rewe-Liebbrand. In 1986 it acquired a 50 per cent stake in Together from Freemans (UK). The company has plans to develop Rainbow Home Shopping, in which it has a 60 per cent stake. Half its sales are outside Germany.

J. C. Penney Company Inc. (USA)
Turnover $16.40bn (1989)
Number of outlets 3,650
Employees 198,000
Sector Mass merchandising
Trading names J.C.Penney, Thrift Drug, The Treasury Drug Centre
Head office New York
Turnover ranking in sector 3rd in USA
Recent history and activities The company operates a nationwide chain of 600 department stores and over 1,000 Thrift drug stores, as well as a TV home shopping operation. It sells a wide range of merchandise from apparel to automotive products.

Promodes (France)
Turnover £4.28bn (1988)
Units 2,200
Employees 30,000
Sector Food
Trading names Continent, Shopi, Champion, Red Food, Prairie, Dia
Head office Mondeville, France
Turnover ranking in sector 2nd in France; 9th in EC
Recent history and activities Promodes has extensive interests abroad with its hypermarket operation, Continent, being particularly strong in Spain and Portugal. It is also represented in Germany, Italy, the USA, Japan and French- speaking African countries. Apart from food retailing, Promodes is involved in wholesaling and supplying the food trade and claims to serve up to 34,000 'associates'. Over a third of turnover is from outside France.

Rewe-Liebbrand (Germany)
Turnover £5.20bn (1988)
Units 2,800
Employees 46,350
Sector Food
Trading names HL Supermarkets, Penny, Minimal, Euromarket, Toom
Head office Bad Homburg, Germany
Turnover ranking in sector 2nd in Germany; 3rd in EC
Recent history and activities The company is controlled by Rewe-Zentral AG. It also operates a wholesale division supplying about 1,000 retailers. It is a member of a pan-European buying group with GIB (Belgium) and Vendex (Netherlands).

Rite Aid Corporation (USA)
Turnover $2.86bn (1989)
Number of outlets 2,200
Employees 29,900
Sector Drug stores
Trading names Rite Aid, Drug Balance, Super PX, Ad Inc

Head office Shinremanstown, Pennsylvania
Turnover ranking in sector 3rd in USA
Recent history and activities The company, which is represented in 22 states, is involved in grocery wholesaling and retailing in addition to its main interests of drug stores. It is also involved in discount books and specialized blood banking.

Safeway Stores Inc (USA)
Turnover $14.32bn (1989)
Number of outlets 1,118
Employees 110,000
Sector Food retailing
Trading names Safeway, Busy Baker, Truly Fine, White Magic
Head office Oakland, California
Turnover ranking in sector 3rd in USA
Recent history and activities Safeway has nearly 900 stores in the western USA and over 200 in Canada. The company went private in 1986, and from 1987 onwards has been involved in the disposal of many interests, including the UK chain.

J. Sainsbury Plc (UK)
Turnover £7.257bn (1989)
Units 390
Employees 88,000
Sector Food, DIY
Trading names J. Sainsbury, Homebase, Shaws, Savacentre
Head office London, England
Turnover ranking in sector Largest in UK; 4th in EC
Recent history and activities The largest UK food retailer, Sainsbury also owns Savacentre (a hypermarket operation) and the US grocery chain Shaw's. It has a 75 per cent controlling interest in Homebase DIY (the Belgian group GIB owns the other 25 per cent share) and a 50 per cent shareholding in Haverhill Meat Products and Breckland Farms. Own label accounts for over 50 per cent of sales.

Schickedanz Quelle (Germany)
Turnover £3.17bn (1988)
Employees 40,000
Sector Mail order, department stores, photographic
Trading names Quelle Versand, Sinn, Foto-Quelle
Head office Furth, Germany
Turnover ranking in sector 8th in Germany; 18th in EC
Recent history and activities Mail order sales concentrate on textiles and most of this is generated in Germany. The majority of the store-based retailing turnover comes from the 21 Quelle department stores, which account for 20 per cent of the group annual turnover. The group is represented in Austria and France, and there are small mail order and showroom operations in Hungary, Bulgaria, Poland and Yugoslavia.

Sears Plc (UK)
Turnover £2.091bn (1989)
Units 2,935
Employees 52,306
Sector Clothing, footwear, mail order, jewellery, sports and leisure

Trading names include Selfridges, British Shoe Corporation (includes Saxone, Freeman Hardy & Willis, Dolcis, Trueform, Lilley & Skinner, Curtess), Miss Selfridge, Fosters, Hornes, Olympus, Millets, Freemans, Mappin & Webb
Head office London, England
Turnover ranking in sector 10th in UK; 35th in EC
Recent history and activities Over 2,000 of Sears' outlets are footwear-based, with a 25 per cent share of the UK market. It operates over 1,000 concessions.

Sears Roebuck & Co. (USA)
Turnover $53.91bn (1989)
Number of outlets 1,400
Employees 500,000
Sector Mass merchandising
Trading name Sears
Head office Chicago, Illinois
Turnover ranking in sector Largest in the world
Recent history and activities The company operates a variety of stores, ranging from general merchandise to surplus and business systems centres. It has a 60 per cent interest in Sears, Canada.

W. H. Smith Group Plc (UK)
Turnover £1.298bn (1989)
Units 1,700
Employees 28,300
Sector Books, stationery, recorded entertainment, DIY, travel agents
Trading names W H Smith, Sherratt & Hughes, Waterstones, Our Price, Do It All
Head office London, England
Turnover ranking in sector 15th in UK; 40th in EC
Recent history and activities The company operates its own distribution network which also serves other newsagents. The DIY and record chains are fairly recent additions (1979 onwards) and acquisitions have included sites from Virgin to expand the Our Price arm, and Waterstones the booksellers. The company has over 300 stores in both the USA and Canada. The Do It All DIY stores were merged with Boots' Payless in 1991.

The Southland Corporation (USA)
Turnover $8.42bn (1989)
Number of outlets 8,700
Employees 48,114
Sector Food retailing
Trading name 7-Eleven
Head office Dallas, Texas
Turnover ranking in sector 6th in USA
Recent history and activities The company operates and franchises self-service convenience stores. It is generally recognized as the instigator of extended shopping hours for convenience stores. It was recently acquired by Japan's operator of 7-Eleven stores.

Steinberg Inc. (Canada)
Turnover $4.49bn (1987)
Number of outlets 450
Sector Food retailing

Trading names M.Stores, Valdi Stores, Smithy's Super Valu
Turnover ranking in sector 3rd in Canada
Recent history and activities The company operates food stores in Quebec and Ontario, and has subsidiary interests in department stores, franchising convenience stores and shopping centre development.

The Stop & Shop Companies Inc. (USA)
Turnover $4.63bn (1989)
Number of outlets 274
Employees 42,000
Sector Food retailing
Trading names Bradlees Discount, Stop and Shop
Head office Boston, Massachusetts
Turnover ranking in sector 10th in USA
Recent history and activities The group is also involved in department stores and has a diverse manufacturing division.

Storehouse Plc (UK)
Turnover £1.310bn (1989)
Units 731
Employees 30,352
Sector Variety stores, home furnishing, speciality
Trading names BHS, Mothercare, Habitat, Richards, Blazer, Heals
Head office London, England
Turnover ranking in sector 16th in UK; 41st in EC
Recent history and activities The group was formed out of the current separate trading names under the influence of Sir Terence Conran. It operates in the USA and Europe. It underwent a major rationalization in 1990, with large-scale redundancies. The Conran shop was sold back to its founder and four Heals stores were closed. Mothercare is the market leader in products for the 0–2-year age range.

Supermarkets General Holdings Corporation (USA)
Turnover $6.29bn (1989)
Number of outlets 418
Employees 51,000
Sector Food retailing
Trading names Patmark, Purity Supreme, Heartland, Angelo's
Head office Woodbridge, New Jersey
Turnover ranking in sector 7th in USA
Recent history and activities The company operates over 200 supermarkets and 150 drug stores. It is also involved in the retailing of garden and household products.

Tengelmann (Germany)
Turnover £4.61bn (1988)
Units 4,290
Employees 56,400
Sector Food, DIY, discount stores
Trading names Plus, Super Plus, Basis, Grosso, Kaiser, A&P, Lowa, OBI, Alois Bronner, L. Gottlieb, Price, Prima
Head office Mulheim-Ruhr, Germany

Turnover ranking in sector 3rd in Germany; 6th in EC
Recent history and activities The group operates supermarkets, hypermarkets, drug stores and off-licences, with interests in DIY stores and Pizza Hut fast food units. It has interests in North America (the A&P food chain and Dominion Stores), the Netherlands and Austria. Over half the turnover comes from the A&P subsidiary.

Tesco Plc (UK)
Turnover £5.003bn (1989)
Units 374
Employees 75,658
Sector Food
Trading names Tesco
Head office Hertfordshire, England
Turnover ranking in sector 2nd in UK; 5th in EC
Recent history and activities Currently concentrating on the development of superstores, which accounts for over half of the company's sales area, Tesco acquired the Yorkshire-based Hillards chain in 1987. It has undertaken various joint venture schemes with Marks & Spencer. Tesco was a leader in introducing nutrition labelling. Own- label products account for about 50 per cent of sales.

Toys R Us Inc. (USA)
Turnover $4.78bn (1989)
Number of outlets 600
Employees 32,700
Sector Toy retailing
Trading names Toys 'R' Us, Kids 'R' Us
Head office Paramus, New Jersey
Turnover ranking in sector Largest in the world
Recent history and activities The company has over 400 toy stores in the USA and nearly 100 overseas. It is also involved in children's wear retailing, and has a joint venture with fast food operator McDonalds aimed at the Japanese market. At Christmas season the company increases its staffing by 20,000.

Vendex International (Netherlands)
Turnover £2.16bn (1988)
Units 1,565
Employees 85,200
Sector Department stores, food, mail order, DIY, books, consumer durables
Trading names Vroom, Dressman, EDI, Toro, Konmar, Edah
Head office Amsterdam, Netherlands
Turnover ranking in sector 2nd in Holland; 32nd in EC
Recent history and activities The majority of retailing interests are in the home market. Vendex is also represented in Belgium, Luxembourg, Germany, the USA, Brazil and Japan. In 1989 the company joined the new Eurogroup (a pan-European buying group) including GIB (Belgium) and Rewe-Liebbrand (Germany).

The Vons Companies Inc. (USA)
Turnover $5.22bn (1989)
Number of outlets 193
Employees 35,000

Sector Food retailing
Trading names Vons Supermarkets, Vons Food & Drug Combination Stores
Head office El Monte, California
Turnover ranking in sector 8th in USA
Recent history and activities Apart from its retailing interests, the company is also involved in food processing, dairy products and baking.

Walgreen Co. (USA)
Turnover $5.39bn (1989)
Number of outlets 1,400
Employees 46,600
Sector Drug stores, restaurants
Trading names Walgreen Drug Stores
Head office Deerfield, Illinois
Turnover ranking in sector Largest drug store chain in USA
Recent history and activities The company has manufacturing facilities for the production of health, beauty and household products.

Wal-Mart Stores Inc. (USA)
Turnover $25.92bn (1989)
Number of outlets 1,215
Employees 365,000
Sector Discount stores
Trading names Wal-Mart, Sam's Wholesale Clubs, Dot Discount Drug Stores
Head office Bentonville, Arkansas
Turnover ranking in sector Largest in USA
Recent history and activities The Wal-Mart retail stores are represented in 23 states in the South, Southwest and Midwest. The company also has two hypermarkets.

George Weston Limited (Canada)
Turnover $11.03bn (1988)
Sector Food retailing
Head office Ontario, Canada
Turnover ranking in sector Largest in Canada
Recent history and activities The company is involved in supermarket retailing and wholesaling food in both Canada and the USA. Its food manufacturing interests range from fisheries to chocolate and dairy goods.

Winn-Dixie Stores Inc. (USA)
Turnover $9.15bn (1989)
Number of outlets 1,270
Employees 94,000
Sector Food retailing
Trading names Winn-Dixie
Head office Jacksonville, Florida
Turnover ranking in sector 5th in USA
Recent history and activities The food store operation is limited to 13 southern states.

F. W. Woolworth Co. (USA)
Turnover $8.82bn (1989)
Number of outlets 11,150
Employees 132,000

Sector Mass merchandising
Trading names Woolworth, Woolco, Kinney, Foot Locker, Kids Mart, Susies
Head office New York
Turnover ranking in sector 4th in USA
Recent history and activities The company operates its general merchandise stores throughout the USA, Canada, Mexico and West Germany. It sold its UK operations in 1982.

Appendix 4 Retail academic and trade journals and periodicals

Cabinet Maker and Retail Furnisher (Benn Retail Publications Ltd, weekly) A periodical aimed at retailers, wholesalers and manufacturers of furniture, carpets and soft furnishings in the UK.
Address Sovereign Way, Tonbridge, Kent, TN9 1YZ
Telephone (0732) 364422

Carpet and Floor Coverings Review (Benn Retail Publications Ltd, fortnightly) A magazine for UK carpet and floor coverings, retailers and wholesalers. It has regular news articles on carpet products and companies, people, and financial indicators, together with short feature articles on new developments and topical issues.
Address Sovereign Way, Tonbridge, Kent, TN9 1RW
Telephone (0732) 364422

Cash and Carry Wholesaler (Whitehall Press Ltd, monthly) News, product and market reports for UK wholesaler distributors of grocery and allied products.
Address Earl House, Earl Street, Maidstone, Kent, ME14 1PE
Telephone (0622) 59841

Checkout (Blakebeck Ltd, monthly) News and features on the UK food retailing scene.

Address 11 Napier Place, London, W14 8LG
Telephone 071-603 4655

Chemist and Druggist (Benn Retail Publications Ltd, weekly) A magazine for UK wholesalers and retailers in pharmacy, cosmetics and toiletries. It has regular articles on business news, people and coming events, and features articles on new developments and topical issues.
Address Sovereign Way, Tonbridge, Kent, TN9 1UX
Telephone (0732) 364422

Clothing World (EPR Ltd, monthly) News, business information and special feature articles for the UK clothing industry. The feature articles are on general issues such as forecasting growth areas or marketing, as well as on specific issues such as barcode labelling or contracts of employment.
Address 80 Richardshaw Lane, Pudsey, Leeds, LS28 6BN
Telephone (0532) 393355

Convenience Store (William Reed Ltd, fortnightly) A magazine for 'neighbourhood retailing'. It is a controlled-circulation publication which is distributed to more than 50,000 readers in the UK, and contains articles on market surveys, book reviews, and new equipment and methods.
Address Broadfield Park, Crawley, West Sussex, RH11 9RJ
Telephone (0293) 613400

Co-op Retail Review (CWS Library and Information Unit, monthly) A periodical covering all aspects of retailing in the UK. It is designed to give Co-op Retail Societies' senior officials and directors a succinct account of the significant news items in retailing which have recently appeared.
Address CWS Ltd, Library and Information Unit, New Century House, Manchester, M60 4ES
Telephone 061-834 1212

Co-operative News (Co-operative Press Ltd, weekly) The newspaper of the UK Co-operative Movement. It contains regular news on co-operative issues including the Movement's trading activities, political campaigns, membership activities and features on manufacturers, products, brands and market trends.
Address Co-operative Press Limited, Progress House, 418 Chester Road, Manchester, M16 9HP
Telephone 061-872 2991

Directory of European Retailers (Newman Books Ltd, annually) Country-by-country listings of major retailers in Western Europe, although including Hungary and Turkey as well. Information provided includes addresses and telephone numbers of head offices, lines of business, numbers of employees and outlets, and the names of key personnel. There are also sections which list buying agents both in Europe and elsewhere in the world, overseas commercial representatives, and retail journals and periodicals. *See also* RETAIL DIRECTORY *below*.
Address 48 Poland Street, London, W1V 4PP
Telephone 071-439 3321

Discount Merchandiser (Schwartz Publications, monthly) News and trends in US retailing with the major emphasis on discount retailing of all types and all product fields. Schwartz Publications is a division of Macfadden Holdings.
Address 233 Park Avenue South, New York, NY 10003, USA
Fax 212 684-2048

DIY Superstore (monthly) A controlled-circulation trade publication for store managers, regional controllers, head office personnel (buyers, directors) employed by DIY superstores, grocery superstores with DIY interests and national DIY wholesalers within the UK.
Address Streatfield House, Carterton, Oxford, OX8 3XZ
Telephone (0993) 840240

DIY Week (Benn Publications Ltd, weekly) A publication aimed at manufacturers and retailers of home improvement, gardening and housewares merchandise and covering news and features related to those markets.
Address Sovereign Way, Tonbridge, Kent, TN9 1RW
Telephone (0732) 364422

DR – The Fashion Business (International Thomson Business Publishing Ltd, weekly) Formerly known as *Drapers Record*, a periodical directed at retailers and wholesalers in clothing fashion, textiles and hosiery. It contains topical news and financial items, product news, and feature articles on UK manufacturing and retailing opportunities.
  Address Greater London House, Hampstead Road, London, NW1 7QZ
  Telephone 071-387 6611

Electrical Retailing (IBTM Ltd, monthly) News and features for retailers, wholesalers and manufacturers of consumer electronics and domestic electrical appliances.
  Address Queensway House, 2 Queensway, Redhill, Surrey, RH1 1QS
  Telephone (0737) 768611

ERT (Electrical and Radio Trading) (Reed Business Publishing Ltd, weekly) A magazine aimed at UK retailers of brown goods, covering retail news and trends together with product and manufacturer information.
  Address Quadrant House, The Quadrant, Sutton, Surrey, SM2 5AS
  Telephone 081-661 3500

European Directory of Retailers and Wholesalers First published by Euromonitor in 1988, this directory contains listings of over 3,000 European wholesalers and retailers in 17 countries, providing information on addresses, turnover, outlets and employees. These are supplemented by overviews of the European retail scene, and sections which provide details of information sources, and statistical summaries of the distributive trades in each country.
  Address 87–88 Turnbull Street, London, EC1M 5QU
  Telephone 071-251 8024

Extel Cards A card index listing over 5,000 publicly quoted companies. The index includes financial data for the last five years and qualitative information extracted from the company's annual report.
  Address Fitzroy House, 13–17 Epworth Street, London, EC2A 4DL
  Telephone 071-251 3333

Fashion Weekly (International Thomson Business Publishing Ltd, weekly) News items, personality interviews, general information and a buyer's guide for clothing retailers.
  Address Greater London House, Hampstead Road, London, NW1 7QZ
  Telephone 071-387 6611

The Grocer (William Read Ltd, weekly) Comprehensive information on the grocery industry.
  Address 5–7 Southwark Street, London, SE1 1RQ
  Telephone 081-407 6981

Harpers Sports and Leisure (Harpers Publishing) A magazine published in the UK every third Tuesday. It includes news and features on manufacturers and retailers involved in sports goods of all types.
  Address 47a High Street, Bushey, Watford, Herts, WD2 1BD
  Telephone 081-950 9522

The Independent Grocer (Reed Business Publishing, fortnightly) A magazine for independent, convenience store and licensed grocers in the UK.
  Address Quadrant House, The Quadrant, Sutton, Surrey, SM2 5AS
  Telephone 081-661 3500

International Journal of Retail and Distribution Management (MCB University Press Ltd, bi-monthly) A journal aiming to encourage communication between retail managers, researchers and educators on practical matters. It incorporates *Retail and Distribution Management* and the *International Journal of Retailing.*
   Address 62 Toller Lane, Bradford, BD8 9BY
   Telephone (0274) 499821

International Review of Retail, Distribution and Consumer Research (Routledge, quarterly) A journal which reports on research into retailing undertaken by academic, government and commercial institutions with an emphasis on theoretical, conceptual, empirical and managerial issues.
   Address 11 New Fetter Lane, London, EC4P 4EE
   Telephone 071-583 9855

Journal of Retailing (New York University, quarterly) A medium for new and significant contributions to the theoretical and practical understanding of retailing. The executive and editorial boards consist entirely of representatives from US academic institutions, and the content is generally directed at retailing in the USA.
   Address PO Box 465, Hanover, PA 17331, USA
   Telephone (717) 632 8448

Key Note Publications offering a range of approximately 200 overview reports covering different market sectors, and form a useful source of secondary data on both consumer and industrial markets. The reports bring together statistical data plus informed opinion on the market sector analysed by (i) industry structure, (ii) market sizes and trends, (iii) recent developments, (iv) future prospects. In addition, profiles of the major players operating in the market are given reports which are updated on an approximately three-year cycle.
   Address 28/42 Banner Street, London, EC1Y 8QE
   Telephone 071-253 3006

Menswear (International Thomson Business Publishing Ltd, weekly) A magazine covering news and issues relating to the design, manufacture and retailing of mens' clothing in the UK.
   Address Swiss Cottage, 100 Avenue Road, London, NW3 3TP
   Telephone 071-935 6611

Mintel *See* MINTEL PUBLICATIONS LTD in Appendix 2.

Nurseryman and Garden Centre (N&GC) (Benn Business Magazines Ltd on behalf of the Horticultural Trades Association, twice monthly) News and features on the garden trade and related do-it-yourself merchandise.
   Address Heath Road, Boughton Monchelsea, Maidstone, Kent, ME17 4JD
   Telephone (0622) 747740

Research Index (fortnightly) An index of articles published in about 100 newspapers and periodicals; titles are classified by subject and company.

Retail (Capel-Cure Myers, quarterly) Short articles on new developments, innovations and acquisitions in retailing, and a comprehensive retail databank covering general economic indicators and specific retail company ratings, profits, earnings and dividends.

Address 65 Holborn Viaduct, London, EC1A 2EU
Telephone 071-236 5080

Retail and Distribution Management *See* INTERNATIONAL JOURNAL OF RETAIL AND DISTRIBUTION MANAGEMENT *above.*

Retail Attraction (AGB Business Publications Ltd, six issues a year) A magazine directed at senior retail management, display managers, designers, shopfitters, architects and interior designers world-wide.
Address Editorial and Advertising Offices, Audit House, Field End Road, Eastcote, Middlesex, HA4 9LT
Telephone 081-868 4499

Retail Business (Economist Publications Ltd, monthly) Covers UK consumer goods markets.
Address 40 Duke Street, London, W1A 1DW
Telephone 071-493 6711

Retail Confectioner Tobacconist (CTN Enterprises Ltd, monthly) Covers products and services for the CTN trade.
Address 53 Christchurch Avenue, North Finchley, London, N12 0DH
Telephone 081-445 6344

Retail Control (National Retail Federation of the United States of America) A publication aimed at the Retail Financial Executive, covering all aspects of management in retailing.
Address Financial Executives Division, National Retail Federation, Retail Services Division, 100 West 31st St., New York, NY 10001, USA.
Telephone 212 244-8780

Retail Directory (Newman Books Ltd, annually) Listings of UK and Irish retailers and retail organizations, with head office addresses and telephone numbers, lines of business, and numbers of outlets. For many companies the names of key personnel are also included. The heading in the directory are: Trade Associations; Department Stores and Principal Shops; Department Store Groups; Large Retail Groups; Multiple Shops; Co-operative Societies; Out-of-Town Shopping; Cash and Carry; Voluntary Associations and Buying Groups; Mail Order Firms; Concessions and, Credit Traders. In addition there are listings of shopping centres and precincts, and shopping street surveys of over 400 towns and cities in the UK and Eire. *See also* DIRECTORY OF EUROPEAN RETAILERS in Appendix 4.
Address 48 Poland Street, London, W1V 4PP
Telephone 071-439 3321

Retail Jeweller (International Thomson Business Publishing Ltd, fortnightly) A periodical for the jewellery trade.
Address Swiss Cottage, 100 Avenue Road, London, NW3 3TP
Telephone 071-935 6611

Retail Marketing and Management (CWS, monthly) A magazine aimed at senior officials and directors in the Co-operative Movement. It includes features on management and marketing issues, co-operative news and trends and products, brands and manufacturers.
Address Progress House, 418 Chester Road, Manchester, M16 9HP
Telephone 061-872 2991

Retail Monitor (Euromonitor, monthly) Covers a wide range of topics, including company and sector reports, retail trends and statistics.
Address 87–88 Turnbull Street, London, EC1M 5QU
Telephone 071-251 8024

Retail Price Index (monthly) The General Index of Retail Prices measures the changes in retail prices of goods and services purchased by UK households (excluding 'pensioner' and 'high income' groups). Regular sources of the index include *Employment Gazette, Monthly Digest of Statistics* and *Economic Trends*. The 'all items' index is a weighted mean of price index numbers measured for the following goods and services: Food, catering, alcoholic drink, tobacco, housing, fuel and light, household goods, household services, clothing and footwear, personal goods and services, motoring expenditure, fares and other travel costs, leisure goods, leisure services. It is often used as a measure of UK price inflation, while components of the index can be used similarly, or as a means of 'index linking'. For example, the amount insured under a household contents insurance policy may be linked to the household goods component of the index.

Retail Technology (Remus Publishing Ltd, monthly) Latest news features on retail technology products and applications, and more general articles on, for example, the use of technology for staff control, security, EPOS, needs of fashion retailing, etc.
Address 19 Grange Mills, Weir Road, London, SW12 0NE
Telephone 081-675 9133

Retail Update (British Retailers Association, monthly) A newssheet published for the UK Retail Consortium (*see* Appendix 2) covering economic issues and statistics, retail news in the UK and the rest of Europe, book reviews and a calendar of forthcoming conferences and events.
Address Bedford House, 69/79 Fulham High Street, London, SW6 3JW

Retail Week (MBC Retail Publications, weekly) Covers all aspects and all sectors of UK retailing.
Address Warwick House, Swanley, Kent, BR8 8JF
Telephone (0322) 669411

Service Industries Journal (Frank Cass & Co. Ltd, quarterly) A journal covering a wide range of issues related to service industries.
Address Gainsborough House, Gainsborough Road, London, E11 1RS
Telephone 081-530 4226

Shoe and Leather News (International Thomson Business Publishing Ltd, weekly) A magazine for retailers and wholesalers in the shoe and leather industry.
Address Greater London House, Hampstead Road, London, NW1 7QZ
Telephone 071-387 6611

Shopping Center World (Communication Channels Inc., monthly) A magazine covering news and issues relating to shopping centre design, construction and management in the USA.
Address 6255 Barfield Road, Atlanta, GA 30321, USA

Super Marketing (Reed Business Publishing Group, weekly) A newspaper covering news about and features on UK food retailing.
Address Quadrant House, The Quadrant, Sutton, Surrey, SM2 5AS
Telephone 081-661 3500

Superstore Management (Faversham House Group Ltd, monthly) News, management reports and feature articles. The focus is predominantly on UK superstores and department stores, but there are special reports on international or 'Euroretailing' issues.
Address Faversham House Group Limited, 111 St James Road, Croydon, Surrey, CR9 2TH
Telephone 081-684 4082

Which? (Consumer's Association, monthly) A magazine which shows the results of independent tests on competing consumer goods and services. The results of tests often receive national media coverage (e.g. 1 in 20 people have been given the wrong amount of money – or none at all – from an automatic teller machine), and special issues are often devoted to particular consumer interests (e.g. *Holiday Which?*, *Motoring Which?*, *Money Which?*).
Address 14 Buckingham Street, London, WC2N 6DS
Telephone 071-839 1222